Woman of Letters: A Life of Virginia Woolf

Parallel Lives: Five Victorian Marriages

Writing of Women: Essays in a Renaissance

Jazz Cleopatra: Josephine Baker in Her Time

JAZZ
CLEOPATRA

JAZZ
CLEOPATRA

JOSEPHINE BAKER
IN HER TIME

BY
PHYLLIS ROSE

DOUBLEDAY

NEW YORK   LONDON   TORONTO

SYDNEY   AUCKLAND

BY DOUBLEDAY

day Dell Publishing Group, Inc.
York, New York 10103

al of an anchor with a dolphin
ks of Doubleday,
a division of Bantam Doubleday Dell Publishing Group, Inc.

Library of Congress Cataloging-in-Publication Data
Rose, Phyllis.
Jazz Cleopatra : Josephine Baker in her time / by Phyllis Rose. —
1st ed.
p.   cm.
Bibliography: p.
Includes index.
ISBN 0-385-24892-X
1. Baker, Josephine, 1906–1975.   2. Dancers—France—Biography.
I. Title.
GV1785.B3R66   1989
793.3'2'0924—dc19
[B]   88-35585
CIP
ISBN 0-385-24891-1

Excerpt from lyrics of "Harlem on My Mind" by Irving Berlin on page 170:
Copyright © 1933 Irving Berlin. Copyright © renewed 1960 Irving Berlin.
Reprinted by permission of Irving Berlin Music Corporation.

Drawings for chapter headings: *Josephine Baker vue par la presse francaise*, Beinecke
Rare Book and Manuscript Library, Yale University.

Cover and frontispiece photographs by Hoyningen-Huene/*Vanity Fair.* Copyright © 1930 (renewed
1958) by the Condé Nast Publications Inc. Front cover and frontispiece photograph by courtesy of the
Harvard Theatre Collection, Harvard College Library, Harvard University. Back cover photograph by
courtesy of the Beinecke Rare Book and Manuscript Library, Yale University.

Emil Ascher, Inc. Excerpt from "La Petite Tonkinoise."
Used by permission. All rights reserved.

TO
L. D.

CONTENTS

PREFACE

When I was in Paris in the early 1980s, an Air France poster campaign encouraged people to fly to the great cities of the world. Giant posters presented a characteristic and usually banal image of one of the city's inhabitants: for Bombay, a snake charmer. For New York, the poster depicted an enormous black man on roller skates holding a huge portable stereo cassette player on one shoulder. I thought that only in France would this image be a come-on. Furthermore, there was an error. The man was black, but he was not American. His features were too unblended, too West African, to be those of a roller skater in Central Park. With his Senegalese looks, his big grin, and his "New-Yorkais" gym gear and electronics, he was a French fantasy of American negritude.

Somewhere between my registering with a certain pleasure the French infatuation with black America and my realizing how much fantasy there was in the infatuation, this book was conceived. I was in Paris that summer doing preliminary work on a book about Hemingway. Under the pressure of that poster, plus my own desire to pay tribute to American culture more generously defined, Hemingway turned into what seemed to me the richer figure of Josephine Baker.

Specifically, she entered my mind because a friend of mine was writing an article about Georges Simenon, who had an affair with Baker in the twenties. When the piece ran, it had a picture of Simenon with Baker, dressed in a beaded chiffon dress, crossing her eyes. The picture claimed me in a way I could not explain. In part, I was delighted by her ability to mock her own beauty and glamour. She seemed to be saying, "What am I doing in this dress? in this body?" I have thought a lot since then about the face she made in the photograph. I did not know at the time how it connected with a black comic tradition, nor did I understand all the ways—if I understand them now—in which it functioned in Baker's psychic life, but it intrigued me and seemed to lead me to interesting matters. Although there were others, photographs of her cross-eyed grins became for me important "texts."

As I worked on this book, people would ask me why I was interested in

Josephine Baker. What had drawn me to her? How had I come to the idea? Because I could not answer it simply, the question became a torment for me. From sincerity I was driven to subterfuge in my reply. In Paris, I said I had decided to write about Josephine Baker because it gave me an excuse to come to Paris. This was considered a graceful and stylish response. In America, I hid behind psychologizing and said that the answer to that question was what gave me the impetus to write the book and so I could not answer before the book was written for fear of dissipating my motivation.

The truth was, my choice was made as instinctively as it is when you fall in love. You do not compose a list of qualities and accomplishments you admire and look for a person to embody them. You see someone. You light up inside. If the choice is a deep one, the lists, reasons, and rationalizations come later, along with new interests and a larger frame of reference for life. For the commitment to a different person—whether imaginative, as in the case of biography, or physical, as in the case of love—is often renewing.

When I started this book, I wanted something from Josephine Baker: a certain spontaneity, fearlessness, energy, joy. At the same time, I was soon writing about the way in which European audiences of the 1920s, seeking a renewal that was decidedly racial, focused their fantasies of finding joy, freedom, and energy all the more easily on Baker because she was black. It did not take me long to sense that I might be participating in the very phenomenon I was trying to describe, and the thought was so disturbing that I could only continue my work through sheer discipline and control, which were the very qualities from which I had been seeking relief.

As I continued to live imaginatively with Josephine Baker and got to know her better, however, she began to detach herself from the fantasy. Although she certainly had a lot of energy, courage, and optimism, I saw that a great deal of her spontaneity was, as it is for any performer, an illusion produced by hard work, an illusion that required more and more work to sustain the longer she lived. Her bravado was real enough—this was no wilting flower—but it also concealed insecurities and fears. Someone whom I had liked for her jubilant promiscuity turned out to be someone who gave herself superficially with great ease but in a meaningful way with the greatest possible difficulty, someone who distrusted men and tried to deflect—the eye-crossing was important here too—their erotic intensity, someone who deployed lightheartedness as a kind of self-protection.

By the time I finished the book, revising all the time to catch up with my own changing sense of Baker, I was taken aback to realize that after five years I had come to see her in a number of ways as not all that different from myself. It made me wonder if I had not imposed on her some of my own sensibility, and perhaps I have. But I would prefer to take that risk rather than imagine her as someone so different from myself that she borders on being another species.

At its least benign, the question "What brought you to Josephine Baker?" noted an incongruity in this endeavor that came out in one man's coarse rhetorical question: "What is a white intellectual doing writing about a black nymphomaniac?" The opposition of "white intellectual" and "black nymphomaniac" seemed nasty to me then and still does. Besides, that word "nymphomaniac," used in the fifties to designate any woman who was more active sexually than the speaker thought she should be, what excuse does anyone have for trotting it out these days? But the quick answer I would now give to that question is: "You'd be surprised how much we have in common."

If I did not have my say about Josephine Baker, people might not credit the degree to which, in our fantasies at least, we cross, the degree to which she wanted to be remembered for her ideas or the degree to which in my dreams I am onstage in fox and feathers with an audience madly applauding. To consider us so different that we could have nothing to say about each other flattens us both and minimizes our common cultural heritage, not to say our humanity.

This book is divided into three sections whose chronological range is radically different. My focus lingers longest on Baker's first year in Paris, 1925–26, and in the first section I also explore the racial mythologies that conditioned her success as well as the career in the American theater that preceded it. The second section covers the rest of the period between the wars and traces her transformation into a European star, while the third section, covering the years from 1939 to her death in 1975, focuses on her war work, her civil rights activism, and the children she adopted and called her Rainbow Tribe.

A biography is a way of perpetuating someone's life and the meaning he or she believed it contained. I would hope in some way to help perpetuate Josephine Baker's courage, vitality, and idealism.

Middletown, Connecticut
November 1988

PART I
LETTING GO

1925-26

The ragamuffin look, 1927.

Roger-Viollet, Paris.

CHAPTER 1
SAVAGE DANCE

In 1925, at a pretty Parisian theater which was losing money because the high postwar cost of living discouraged theatergoing, a desperate effort was made by the management to draw a new audience. Banking on the recent popularity in Paris of things African, they turned their stage over to a black song-and-dance show organized by an American woman based in Paris, Caroline Dudley. She had gone to New York in the summer of 1925 and hired the black songwriter Spencer Williams to produce some music and Miguel Covarrubias, the Mexican artist famous for his sketches of Harlem nightlife, to design the sets. Dudley also recruited a blues singer, Maud de Forest, and got the pianist Claude Hopkins to put together a band. To dance she hired Josephine Baker, already well known on Broadway for her ability to make her body do almost anything and to keep her eyes crossed at the same time. Baker had made a sensation in Sissle and Blake's show *Shuffle Along* and was working that summer at the Plantation Club in Times Square, doing comic dance routines and occasionally going on for Ethel Waters, the show's star. On September 15, 1925, two dozen black musicians, singers, and dancers, including clarinetist Sidney Bechet, sailed for France with Dudley on the SS *Berengaria* and arrived in Paris seven days later.

Rehearsals began immediately. It was hot in the theater, so to practice routines and pose for publicity stills they went up onto the roof. People in nearby buildings who heard the music and leaned out windows to watch were treated to the sight of coffee-skinned Josephine Baker in tank top and shorts, dancing in the sun like nothing they'd ever seen.

The grinning, wide-eyed young woman exploded into energy just barely contained by skin and a human form. Every part of her seemed to go in a different direction, flung from some central volcano of spirit. She made faces and flailed about. She shook her rear end, then drew it in and strutted in place. The radiance of her personality and her joy in life seemed to express themselves in her body.

She was nineteen and felt on top of the world. Performing like this, she felt plugged into a vast source of energy, more alive than usual. Under the pressure of attention, which makes some people fold up, Josephine opened, flowered, and spewed effervescence. When she stopped dancing and the camera swung her way, catching the Eiffel Tower behind her, she turned in her knees and crossed her eyes. She did that when she was scared, to ward off anxiety, and sometimes she also did it when she was happy, to express her happiness. She had grimaced her way to fame on Broadway, crossing her eyes to such good effect in *Shuffle Along* that she was fifth principal in Sissle and Blake's next show, *The Chocolate Dandies*. On the roof of the Théâtre des Champs-Élysées, she crossed her eyes from sheer joy of being in Paris, of being so far from her native St. Louis, of being on the verge—she could feel it—of new conquests.

. . .

At first, the managers of the Théâtre des Champs-Élysées, Rolf de Maré and André Daven, were not entirely happy with the Revue Nègre. They feared it was noisy, with too much tap dancing and too little erotic appeal. Maud de Forest's blues sounded to them like "spirituals," and they found them depressing. To their eyes, the costumes were ridiculous. In the first scene, the women wore high-buttoned green shoes with red laces and flower- and fruit-covered hats. In despair, they contacted their friend Jacques Charles, a producer at the Moulin Rouge, and asked him, as a special favor, to see what he could do to improve the Revue Nègre.

Jacques Charles later claimed that he totally revamped the Revue Nègre, which was hopeless when he saw it in rehearsal. He also claimed that the leading lady was a fat horror who sang gospel songs and that he replaced her with an unknown girl he had the good taste to pick out of the chorus. In fairness to Maud de Forest, it should be said that she was, if somewhat rounder than Baker, not fat, that she had a lovely voice and an elegance of her own, and that she would be remembered by many people as the star of the Revue Nègre. In fairness to Josephine Baker and Caroline Dudley, it should be said that the dancer had been hired to dazzle. This was no unknown chorus girl plucked from anonymity by the inspired hand of Gallic sophistication.

What Jacques Charles did was shift the balance of attention so that it was directed more than ever at Baker. There was relatively little else he could do. The opening was in ten days; the sets had come with the show; the music had to be left to the jazz musicians. The full-company acts had to be kept more or less intact, but Charles agreed that the show needed something. It was noisy and inelegant, and worst of all, it wasn't black enough.

The chorus line, which was typical of black revues in Harlem nightclubs and on the Broadway stage, did not seem authentic to the Frenchman. Precision dancing, he thought, might be appropriate for German or English girls, but not for blacks, who, as everyone knew, were instinctive dancers, incapable of discipline. The Revue Nègre's line of dancers who all kicked at the same time therefore seemed to him a misguided effort to put on airs for the French, and the effect was merely pretentious.

A more authentic black dance was needed, and to fill the need, Jacques Charles, the director of music-hall spectacles, expert in the fantasy life of Parisian males, invented what he called the "Danse Sauvage," giving it a prominent place at the end of the program. For this piece of authenticity Josephine Baker and her male partner were dressed in Charles's notion of African costume—bare skin and feathers.

Josephine Baker at first refused to dance bare-breasted in the Danse Sauvage, threatening to leave the show and go home. She was not a striptease dancer, and as an American, she was unaccustomed to the French acceptance of female nudity above the waist. One doesn't have to attribute an exaggerated modesty to her to understand why she was appalled by the suggestion that she make her Paris debut semi-naked. Yet it is true that once she got used to the idea it took her a long time to put her clothes back on.

There was another man watching the rehearsals who agreed with Jacques Charles about Josephine Baker. This was Paul Colin, a young artist who, because he happened to know André Daven, had been given the job of creating posters for the shows at the Théâtre des Champs-Élysées. He was a painter with no experience designing posters, but he needed work and was determined to succeed. He sat for three hours at the rehearsals trying to get a sense of what American blacks were like, as opposed to the West African blacks he was more used to seeing in France.

Poor Maud de Forest, ostensibly the star of the show, interested him no more than she had the other Frenchmen. She had a good enough face, but a face could be created with makeup. Legs and breasts were what counted. The extraordinary body he was looking for he found in Josephine Baker, and he decided to feature her in his poster. Because he was a thorough researcher, Colin felt he had to get to know her body better before he went to work.

After dinner on that first day of rehearsals, she came to his studio and posed. He wanted her nude, but she was embarrassed. "In spite of her magnificent body, she was extremely modest," said Colin. He tried to convince her it was necessary, a task made all the more difficult because he spoke no English and she spoke no French. He drew sketches to explain what he wanted and she used her body to say no.

All day long people had been badgering her to take off her clothes. Monsieur de Maré had said there was no such thing as modesty among artists, and she was getting used to the idea of appearing semi-naked onstage, before an audience of two thousand who seemed no more than a dark blur. But to take off her clothes in front of one man was different. Because she had suspected beforehand that he would want her nude, she had put on a bra so she would have more to take off —the wisdom of the strip-poker player. But she absolutely refused to take off more than that.

Posing in underpants, she stood arms akimbo while he sketched her. To her amazement, he did nothing but sketch her. As the minutes went by, she got to like the strange situation in which a man looked at her hard and did not try to make love to her. By the next night she felt comfortable and posed for him completely naked.

Colin had the effect on Baker of making her, for the first time in her life, feel beautiful. He could not stop looking at her and his eyes lit up with what he saw. She had hardly ever seen that in the eyes of a man, certainly not in the eyes of a white man. She already knew she could get men to like her if she laughed and clowned, but to be liked for what she was in repose was a new sensation.

In the poster Paul Colin designed for the Revue Nègre, Josephine Baker appears arms akimbo, with a great deal of her vivacity captured in her pose. But her face, with its exaggerated lips, barely rises above the stereotypes of Sambo art for all Colin's "research," and the two black male faces balancing her are such grotesque stereotypes that it's hard now to look at this poster with any pleasure, however technically well designed it is. Nevertheless, it did its job. Posted all over Paris, Colin's graphic helped make both artist and model famous.

Four days after the troupe's arrival, a week before the opening night, Daven and de Maré arranged a preview performance of the Revue Nègre for journalists and celebrities. Their purpose was to get the town talking about the show before it even opened, and to that end they invited tastemakers and trendsetters, including Mistinguett, the greatest star of the music-hall stage, the artists Van Dongen and

Léger, Paul Guillaume, the art dealer and enthusiast of African art, the actress Cécile Sorel, the cabaret performer Jane Renouardt, the historian Robert Chantemesse, and people of fashion like the Princess Murat and Baron Biedermann, in addition to dozens of writers.

The preview began at midnight, when the curtain went down on the show then reaching the end of its run at the Music-Hall des Champs-Élysées. The main attraction of that show was the fakir, Tara Bey, who allowed his body to be tortured onstage and seemed to feel nothing. He stood stock-still, dressed in white robes, hands lifted to heaven, while hatpins were stuck in his cheeks and daggers through his throat. The blood from the neck wound would flow or not flow, depending on the desire of the audience. When his show was over and the house had cleared, the fakir took his place in the audience with the fifty or so other invited guests.

The cast presented two of the nine scenes they would do the following week, and the audience was ecstatic. In one ravished sentence, a journalist sounded the keynotes of Parisian response to the Revue Nègre: "We don't understand their language, we can't find a way to tie the scenes together, but everything we've ever read flashes across our enchanted minds: adventure novels, glimpses of enormous steamboats swallowing up clusters of Negroes who carry rich burdens, a caterwauling woman in an unknown port, . . . stories of missionaries and travelers, Stanley, the Tharaud brothers, Batouala, sacred dances, the Sudan, . . . plantation landscapes, the melancholy songs of Creole nurses, the Negro soul with its animal energy, its childish joys, the sad bygone time of slavery, we had all that listening to the singer with the jungle voice, admiring Louis Douglas's hectic skill, the frenetic virtuosity of that dancer with rubber legs, and the pretty coffee-colored ragamuffin who is the star of the troupe, Josephine Baker." Another journalist, more coherently, predicted: "Paris, which loves life, grace, color, good taste, and real talent, will love and applaud them."

In the audience at large, the response was enthusiastic.

"Bravo!" said Léger, who had done African-inspired sets and costumes for the ballet *The Creation of the World.*

"It's stupefying!" said Cécile Sorel.

"It's Cubist!" said Jane Renouardt.

"Still, it won't make us forget the Parthenon friezes," said a cynical holdout who understood the gravity of what would turn out to be at stake—nothing less, as some French intellectuals saw it, than the fate of the Western tradition of art. Was Greece to bow before Africa?

After the preview, there was a dazzling supper party at the theater, arranged by de Maré. Baker entered on the arm of Paul Colin. Last seen onstage wearing almost nothing, she was now clothed in a dress by Paul Poiret, one of the most fashionable designers of the moment. The contrast was lost on no one and underlined a message Parisians were ready to hear: put a pretty savage in a Paul Poiret dress and she could be a princess.

The cast mingled with the audience and drank champagne. Until then (although the dancer and choreographer Louis Douglas had managed to sneak Josephine Baker one glass of anisette) the cast had been strenuously kept from liquor, on the grounds that they were unaccustomed to it because of Prohibition. But that night the champagne flowed and fueled the hilarity. The American dancers got on the tables and did encores. Mistinguett, a bit jealous of the attention they were getting, joined them on the tables and showed her own beautiful legs. She shook her head and rolled her eyes in imitation of them.

"I got so into the dance," she said, "that for a moment there I really thought I was black myself."

"That's because you've drunk too much champagne," the fakir told her.

The publicity so brilliantly generated by this preview gave people time to realize that the opening of the Revue Nègre was likely to be another of those Events so beloved by Parisians—when cultural history was made, when the closely watched trajectory of French culture hit some piece of historical reality and bounced off in another direction. The opening of Alfred Jarry's play *Ubu Roi* in 1896 had been such an event, the 1905 show of works by Matisse, Derain, and Vlaminck had been another, the first performance of Stravinsky's *The Rite of Spring* in 1913 another, and the 1917 debut of *Parade*, the all-star collaboration of Picasso, Satie, Cocteau, and Massine, the most recent. In the week between the preview and the opening night, journalists honed their phrases for animal energy, jungle rhythms, and the dark gods of Africa.

It was time for the French to define themselves again—this time by appropriating what they needed of what they imagined the black soul to be.

Josephine Baker's soul had been formed by poverty and rejection.

She was born in 1906 in St. Louis, a city the French sometimes locate in a mythical "Louisiana" and imagine as a moss-hung, warm-aired place. But even in 1906 St. Louis was a big midwestern city with cold winters and a black section across the Mississippi River in East St. Louis that was one of America's worst slums—not the plantation land of French fantasies.

Josephine Baker was the daughter of Carrie McDonald, who had come to the city two years before with her mother and her aunt Elvara from South Carolina, where their ancestors, both black and Indian, had been slaves. They were part of the mass migration of blacks from the rural South to the cities of the North in the first two decades of this century which, in the Bible-rich imagery of the black historical imagination, is often referred to as "The Flight out of Egypt."

From her mother Josephine inherited her extraordinary body and her tenacity, and from her father, Eddie Carson, she got her features, her tight wiring, and her nervous energy. To both her parents she owed her gift for dancing. Carrie had such good balance that, even seven months pregnant, she could dance with a glass of water on her head and not spill a drop. Eddie, who made his living as a drummer, loved dancing so much that he earned lessons at the local dance academy by playing the drums at the Friday-night socials. Eddie and Carrie had met as members of the cast of a production at a local black theater, and for a while they worked up a song-and-dance routine which they performed at bars and vaudeville houses.

When Josephine, her first child, was born, Carrie McDonald was twenty-one and not married to Eddie Carson. Sometimes, when she followed him to work, she carried Josephine with her, but often she left the baby with her mother and aunt. Family life was not appealing to the fast-talking, snappy-dressing drummer. He wanted Carrie young and free. With a baby in her arms, she was considerably less appealing.

Within a year after Josephine's birth, Eddie left Carrie, who blamed her child for making her lose her man. Josephine's resemblance to her father was just a distressing reminder to Carrie of the man who left her. In one twist of fate, Josephine lost both her father and her mother's love.

Carrie had three more children after Josephine—Richard, Margaret, and Willie Mae—whose father, Arthur Martin, lacked Eddie Carson's glamour but had the great virtue of sticking around. When Richard was born, sixteen months after her own birth, Josephine was sent to stay with Grandmother McDonald and Aunt Elvara. She didn't stay very long, but the brief, early exile made a big impression on her, convincing her that Richard—and the two girls who followed him— were wanted and she had not been. In another way, too, she felt like an outsider in the Martin family. Arthur Martin was dark-skinned and so were his children. Josephine was noticeably lighter, and although light skin was valued in certain black families, usually families with middle-class aspirations or pretensions, in the dark St. Louis ghetto and in the Martin family it had no value at all.

Arthur Martin was kind, but a poor breadwinner: he had a job for a while in a local foundry, then lost it. During Josephine's childhood, he spent more and more time at home, more and more time in bed. He made the children shoes from newspapers and coal sacking so they could walk in the snow. He papered the walls of their succession of rooms and shacks with newspapers and magazines to keep out the cold.

Carrie supported them all by doing laundry. As she subsided from aspiring dancer into domestic drudge, she became a demanding, disapproving mother who treated her children so sternly it verged on cruelty. Once, when she learned that Richard had taken someone's bicycle, she tied him up and beat him until Josephine and Margaret cried and begged her to stop. She told them she would rather beat him herself, even risk killing him, than have him be beaten and maybe killed by white men.

Cold, smells, bugs, and rats were the medium of Josephine's childhood. When Arthur Martin put his feet up on the table, the smell was so bad that Josephine would have run from the room except that the room was heated by a coal fire in a metal barrel and outside was freezing. For a while, Arthur and Carrie and the four children slept in one bed, children's heads at the bottom, parents at the top with their feet in the children's faces. Bugs were almost impossible to get out of the bedding, and many nights were made sleepless by bug bites. Sometimes, to get away from the bugs and the smell of her stepfather's feet, Josephine slept on the floor wrapped in newspapers.

Carrie McDonald did not allow any child the luxury of being an economic liability. She expected all her children to contribute to the family's support and made it clear to Josephine that, as the eldest child, more was expected of her. When Josephine was eight, she was sent to work in the home of a white woman named Mrs. Keiser. There she would get up at five every morning and work until eight, because the law required her to go to school, but she had to get all the morning chores done before leaving. She lit the fires, peeled potatoes, emptied chamber pots, scrubbed the steps, swept the rooms, and, once a week, washed the clothes. At night she slept in the basement with the dog, next to the stockpiles of wood and coal.

Josephine was slapped around routinely at Mrs. Keiser's and beaten when she got up late. She soon lost her appetite from terror and depression and gave her food to the dog. Although she had been a plump baby whose nickname was "Tumpie," for Humpty Dumpty, whom she was thought to resemble, she grew painfully thin. The dog and a chicken named Tiny Tim were her only friends, and one day, after Josephine had fed and fattened the chicken over months, Mrs. Keiser told her to kill him. Josephine obeyed mechanically. She put the chicken between her legs, stretched its neck downward, and cut it with scissors. She squeezed the headless chicken between her legs as the blood gushed out and the chicken stopped twitching. She held her breath so she wouldn't smell the blood. When the chicken was dead, she kissed it and plucked its feathers.

Eventually, Mrs. Keiser went too far. To punish Josephine for using too much soap in the wash, she shoved the little girl's hands into boiling water. She was burned so badly her screams brought neighbors, and she was taken to the hospital. The doctors called her mother, and she was carried home.

Even then she was not allowed to stay with her family. Her mother again found a white woman to give her room and board in exchange for chores. Josephine liked this job more. Mrs. Mason bought her clothes, fattened her up, and gave her time to play, but she eventually had to send Josephine back to her home again when Mr. Mason began showing an interest in her.

By this time, Josephine didn't know which direction exile was in. She wasn't sure whether she preferred being in the comfortable and pleasant house of Mrs. Mason or in the shack her mother lived in with her stepfather and the other children. When her mother sent her off again to Aunt Elvara's, she wasn't reluctant to go.

In Aunt Elvara and Grandmother McDonald, Josephine fortunately had alternative mothers. To them, in various ways, she owed her sense that life existed elsewhere, in other forms, in other times and places, and that a person didn't have to stay and suffer where she started out. Aunt Elvara had more money than anyone else in the family because her husband's death in the Spanish-American War had left her with a government pension. She was a formidable woman, severe and given to sudden rages, proud of her Indian background. She and Josephine's grandmother, her half sister, continued the perpetual ghetto bickering over skin color and blood, and who had how much of what kind, but with a twist. For Aunt Elvara it was Indian blood that counted most, and she looked down on Carrie's children with Arthur Martin, who seemed to her too Negro. Josephine, lighter, was more acceptable.

Because of Aunt Elvara's temper, Josephine was afraid of her. She was closer to her grandmother, and the bond between them counteracted in part her sense of being unwanted by her mother. Grandmother McDonald loved her in the less complicated way of grandparents and acted as her bridge to distant times. She told little Josephine stories about slavery, about her great-great-grandparents brought against their will from a faraway place. She sang her songs and hymns which promised freedom after oppression, release after constraint, joy after grief.

It was a message Josephine needed to hear. When she went home again she had to go back to work. She led her sisters and brother in scavenging for coal in the railroad freight yards behind Union Station.

The most agile of the children as well as the oldest, she jumped on the cars and threw down pieces of coal to the others, who waited with sacks. She also led teams of kids to the rich parts of town and went door to door asking for work. She offered to wash floors, scrub stoops, wax, or shovel. When they got no work, she took the others scavenging in the garbage. Josephine was meager-looking and scrawny, so people weren't eager to employ her. But she put on a smile and sold herself. "I know I look small, but I'm really fifteen" was a line she used over and over.

To a girl who had been doing hard domestic labor from the age of seven, the story of Cinderella seemed more like local realism than distant myth. She had scrubbed floors, cleaned out ovens, and ironed clothes until she wept from exhaustion. From an early age, she knew she'd have to be her own fairy godmother, her own Prince Charming. Any magic pumpkin was going to be paid for by money she had earned. When she was ten years old and supplying all the food and many presents for the family Christmas, someone mentioned Santa Claus to her and her reply was caustic: "There is no Santa Claus. I'm Santa Claus." The belief that Cinderella, through her own efforts, without Prince Charming, could make it from ashes to palace kept her going. Cinderella and the story of Christ's crucifixion and resurrection reinforced one another. They seemed to make the same point. Pain, hard work, and sacrifice will lead to triumph. But the imagery of the Cinderella story—clothing, from rags to ball gowns and elegant shoes—was the more congenial.

Images of palace life were provided in school by history books whose illustrations meant more to her than the text she could barely read. History presented itself as the story of kings and queens who were always changing costumes. Every time you turned the page, a century had passed and there was a new style of clothing. If there was something proto-Folies-Bergère about this way of looking at history, it was nonetheless inspirational, giving her something to aim for.

When she was eleven years old, a public nightmare, the East St. Louis race riot of 1917, stamped itself upon her memory of childhood alongside the private traumas. In one of the most vicious of the race riots which succeeded World War I, as whites tried to reclaim the ground blacks had won during the war, whites went rampaging through the black ghetto of East St. Louis, setting fire to buildings indiscriminately. Thirty-nine black people were killed and thousands left homeless. They scooped up what belongings they could and, afraid for their lives, fled across the Mississippi bridge to St. Louis proper. Josephine always remembered standing at the end of the bridge and watching them run across toward safety, abandoning their homes, as panic-stricken as stampeding animals. She heard stories of horrible atrocities, pregnant women ripped open, men burned. It made such an impression on her that when, later, she told the story of her life, she sometimes began with the East St. Louis race riot, as though it were her earliest memory.

That such a childhood produced an expatriate is not surprising. What better response to the fear of exile than voluntary expatriation? "They" might drive you out of your home any minute, whether "they" were your parents or rampaging white bigots. A person who fears being driven from her home when she doesn't want to go might understandably leave when she thought other people wanted her to stay. At thirteen, Josephine would leave St. Louis for the rest of America, and then at nineteen would leave America for the rest of the world. Whatever happened to her, she wanted to have happen, and to prove she had wanted it to happen in the past, she would voluntarily do it in the present. To show that she was in control, most especially when she was not, would turn out to be her deepest psychic necessity, and her favorite psychic maneuver was to anticipate a possible attack and claim it as her own initiative.

All these strategies showed on Josephine's mobile little face in the goofy cross-eyed grins for which was noted even as a child. Whenever she feared failure, as she feared it at school, where she did not do well, she hid behind that simultaneously ingratiating and subversive mask, as many black male comics had done before her.

Anyone who has ever been at a loss and forced a laugh to cover it, or who has noticed that the class comedian is rarely the most prepossessing kid, can understand how clowning is connected to low self-esteem. But making faces is something of a specialty. Jean-Paul Sartre, as a child, used to retreat to his room and make faces at himself in the mirror whenever he humiliated himself. It was, he said, his way of throwing acid on the smiles which had failed to please his elders. Anna Freud had a little patient who made faces, and she explained the way it worked as a strategy to defend the ego. The child, Freud speculated, had noticed how the faces of people angry at him became distorted, and as a way of protecting himself against their anger, he anticipated it, expressing it himself in facial contortions, "identifying with the aggressor."

For Josephine this defense mechanism worked brilliantly. She did to others, in the guise of humor, what she would not give them the chance to do to her—mocking, dismissing, rejecting. Even when it stopped being a way to ward off fear, she continued to rely on it to channel love. The cross-eyed, goofy, stereotypically blackface grin would become a kind of signature, even when—most effectively when—she was glamorously dressed, so that it seemed a parodic comment on her own beauty, on conventions of beauty, on the culture that had made her famous.

In 1918 the family's financial situation improved when Aunt Elvara died and left her government pension and insurance money to Grandmother McDonald, who then went to live with the Martins. They moved to a real house with a concrete basement, which the children quickly commandeered for play. The boy next door, who had been to the local black vaudeville house, the Booker T. Washington Theater, introduced such sophisticated touches as candles in tin plates for footlights, straight pins for tickets of admission, crates for seats, and rags for curtains. He served as producer and put on shows starring his sister and Josephine. Whatever siblings and friends could be rounded up paid a straight pin for admission to watch Josephine and Joyce McDuffy kick and strut. When the McDuffy children were not available, Josephine liked to get her brother and sisters to watch her parade across the stage in her grandmother's old dresses, making the same entrance over and over.

In later years, when she was the most famous American performer in Europe, she opened a wax museum of scenes from her own life which she called the Jorama. The Jorama's first tableau showed a little girl in adult clothes dancing in a basement. It was the image of her childhood that she wanted to present, the image she wanted to remember—a girl practicing what she would go on to do so well, a small version of the big Josephine Baker, a little girl in control, whose childhood was a rehearsal for the big show.

The Théâtre des Champs-Élysées is on the avenue Montaigne, in a neighborhood more associated with hotels and couturiers than with entertainment. Its out-of-the-way location hadn't helped business, and the theater was losing money when Rolf de Maré, who had brought the Swedish Ballet to Paris, purchased it in March 1925 and announced his intention of turning it into a music hall. High culture would not be excluded, merely democratized, so that it appeared as one variety act among others. Pavlova herself was booked there. She would follow the Revue Nègre, although she would not do nearly so well.

Some people bemoaned turning this elegant theater into a music hall, but Rolf de Maré simply shrugged. It was either that or turn it into a movie house. The franc after the war was worth a fifth of what it had been worth in 1913, when the theater was built, and now the only people who seemed to have money to spend on an evening out were foreigners. Music-hall entertainment appealed to them because you didn't need French to appreciate it. But with the Revue Nègre, de Maré was hoping to attract a more local audience, betting that Paris, the world's most exogamic city, was ready for a new infusion of fresh blood.

One had only to look at the bas-reliefs on the façade of the Théâtre des Champs-Élysées, a tribute to the American dancer Isadora Duncan, to be reminded that this happened periodically. Executed by the noted sculptor Émile-Antoine Bourdelle, the marbles depicted "Apollo and the Muses," and while the muses all had different faces, their bodies were all the body of Isadora, who dominated the inside of the building, too, in murals and frescoes by Maurice Denis. With her bare feet, her flowing toga-like dresses, her fluid gestures, her luxuriant body, and her radiant idealism, Isadora embodied an aesthetic of liquidity and unity, a modernism—Art Nouveau was part of it—whose development was interrupted by the war. The Théâtre des Champs-Élysées is a magnificent example of that aesthetic, as well as a monument to the woman who expressed it in dance.

To those who were aware of cultural history, the appearance of the Revue Nègre on the stage of the Théâtre des Champs-Élysées might have seemed particularly appropriate: if the building epitomized prewar modernism, the black revue came to symbolize postwar modernism—the new, Cubist sensibility which savored angles and fragments rather than curvilinear forms, juxtaposition rather than fluidity as a principle of coherence, frenetic energy rather than graceful lyricism. Isadora Duncan had refreshed European culture by bringing it the spirit of an Americanized Greece. Josephine Baker would refresh it by bringing the spirit of an Americanized Africa.

Opening night of the Revue Nègre was October 2, 1925. The program began at eight-thirty, but the Revue Nègre did not come on until two hours later, after the intermission. First there were dancers, Japanese acrobats, trapeze artists, and an urbane Parisian songster, Saint Granier, known for his excellent diction and charming personality. By the time the Revue Nègre came on, the auditorium, which had been filling up gradually, was packed. Chic Paris had not turned out in such numbers for any performance since the Ballets Russes before the war. Darius Milhaud was there. So was Jean Cocteau, and Janet Flanner attended to get material for one of her first "Letters from Paris" for *The New Yorker*. The great auditorium with its enormous murals of Isadora was filled with artists and society people, the city's tastemakers.

When the audience was somewhat settled, the regular music-hall orchestra stopped playing, and the black jazz musicians, led by Claude Hopkins, filed onto the stage, playing, and took up positions at the side before a striking curtain: a black man dancing on checkerboard squares. There was a drummer, a saxophonist, a trombonist, and a tuba player, in addition to Hopkins on the piano. When they reached the end of their first number and began the next, the curtain rose to reveal a backdrop of steamboats on the Mississippi at night, a levee, with cargo on the dock waiting to be loaded. Dressed in colorful plaids, men sat on bales, talking, listening to the music. Women strolled onstage in dresses that had been enlivened with ribbons and feathers. Maud de Forest, bizarrely outfitted in a pink dress and feathered hat, sang the blues, and the women started to dance.

Most people in the audience had seen one or two black performers on a stage before, but never so many together. The entire cast of twenty-five was onstage, and the audience was shocked and excited by their number. As their eyes became accustomed to the exotic sight, people noticed other things—the bright colors of the costumes and the sets, the abandon of the dancers, the women's loveliness, their perfect smiles (and knees and ankles), their liveliness, their vigor, how happy they seemed, the fact that, after all, they were remarkably light-skinned.

When the audience was fully enchanted by the energy and joy of the performers, Baker made her entrance—clowning. Like a strange creature from a distant world, she walked or rather waddled in, her knees bent and spread apart. Her stomach was sucked in, her body contorted. She looked more like an animal than a human being, a weird cross between a kangaroo, a bicyclist, and a machine gun. She was dressed in a torn shirt and ragged shorts. Her lips were painted large in the style of blackface. Her skin seemed to be the color of bananas. Her hair, short to begin with, looked as if it had been plastered down on her head with caviar. She screwed up her face, crossed her eyes, puffed out her cheeks, and made noises in a high-pitched voice. Then she did the split. She splayed her arms and legs as if they were dislocated. She shook and shimmied constantly, moving like a snake. Instead of her moving to the music, the music seemed to come from her body. Finally, she left the stage on all fours, legs stiff, rear end in the air, higher than her head, looking as awkward as a young giraffe. As abruptly as she went offstage, as quick as a one-step she came back on again. Her movements were all so fast no one had time to decide what was happening. "Is it a man? Is it a woman?" people wondered. Is she awful or marvelous? black or white? Is that real hair or has it been painted on? She epitomized ambiguity, new frontiers. She seemed something more fugitive and extravagant than a dancer—more like ectoplasm. She was a revelation of possibilities in human nature they hadn't suspected. The animal inside of every human being wasn't dark, tormented, savage. It was good-natured, lively, sexy rather than sensual, above all funny.

After the frenetically energetic opening, the next scene allowed the audience to calm down. Against a Covarrubias backdrop of a skyscraper, a peanut vendor came onstage pushing his cart. He began playing a melancholy plaint on the clarinet. Louis Douglas and Marion Cook, as a couple of lovers, walked on, danced to the music, disappeared, and the peanut vendor concluded his sad solo. The peanut vendor was Sidney Bechet, and his music was what Josephine Baker liked best about the Revue Nègre, although to some in the audience it was "tuneless." "Louisiana Camp Meeting," which followed, brought back Josephine Baker with Maud de Forest. They played two brides expecting to marry the same man. They fought. The man was left alone dancing around his top hat. It was Louis Douglas again, this time showing what an extraordinary tap dancer he was. He could shower the stage with taps without seeming to move any part of himself but his feet. Douglas, like Bechet, had performed in Paris before—at the Alhambra and the Ba-ta-clan music halls. Known locally as the man with the rubber legs, he was admired for his sheer physical dexterity, even though tap dancing was not a much appreciated art in Paris.

There were six more "tableaux" in the Revue Nègre. The sets were an anthology of visual clichés of black life—giant watermelons, jazz bands—executed with a certain vigor and invention. Two of Caroline Dudley's sisters, Dorothy and Katherine, were artists and had also worked on the sets. The next really stunning moment—like Baker's first entrance—came in the last scene, set in a Harlem nightclub. There was some singing, one-stepping, tap dancing, then Josephine Baker and Joe Alex, her partner, as though performing on the stage of the nightclub, did their Danse Sauvage.

Baker, bare-breasted, wore a satin bikini with a skirt of feathers over it and a collar of feathers around her neck. There were feathers in her hair and around her ankles, and—strange detail for a savage dance—she wore flat-heeled black shoes. Yet so strong was the impression she gave of nudity that keen-eyed Janet Flanner would remember her as having appeared with only one pink feather between her legs. Her partner carried her in on his back. He, too, had feathers around his hips as well as beads around his neck, knees, and ankles. A smiling giant of a man, he provided the perfect male counterpoise to Baker's good-natured energy. But savage? At least he wore no shoes, and the audience found him savage enough.

Baker was upside down and had her legs splayed. When he deposited her on the ground, she went into something Flanner called a "stomach dance," probably an improvised combination of various moves related to the Belly Dance—the Shake, the Shimmy, the Mess Around—which were popular with black jazz dancers in the twenties in New York. Not a Charleston, danced with the legs and arms, it was a dance for the rear end.

Hips, stomach, and rump had never moved so violently on a Paris stage. To the Parisian audience, the dance seemed close to obscene. Baker lifted her arms above her head and did a bump and grind— "a simple movement in front of the stomach and a tremor of the rump." Some people found it disgusting and whistled their disapproval. Some even got up and left. Others applauded to cover the whistles. This was the finale, the core of the program, the final drumroll and star burst at the end of these fireworks. The heart of darkness had been reached. The layers of civilization had been peeled back and the sexual center revealed. What else was left to see? Louis Douglas reappeared as a waiter in the Harlem nightclub, dancing frenetically around the edges of the Danse Sauvage, couples whirled around, Josephine Baker shook her feathers, and, to an enormous drumroll and definitive clash of the cymbal, the curtain came down.

The opening of the Revue Nègre was exactly the kind of Event that its backers had hoped it would be. It angered and irritated people just enough to guarantee that it would be considered significant. People agreed it was the sexiest thing they'd ever seen on a stage ("the triumph of lubricity, a return to the manners of the childhood of man"), only disagreeing—but disagreeing violently—over whether that was good or bad.

Jacques-Émile Blanche, a portrait painter of some renown, compared the opening night of the Revue Nègre to the first performance of *The Rite of Spring*, at which the old Countess of Pourtalès had stood up and said in disgust, "We are no longer in France!" Things were different in 1925 from what they'd been in 1913. The public was accustomed to the Folies-Bergère, ballroom dancing, Montmartre nightclubs, the exoticism of the circus and the music hall. They had seen the fakir Tara Bey stick daggers in his throat and not bleed. They were harder to shock than Madame de Pourtalès. Nevertheless, the Revue Nègre, like *The Rite of Spring*, shocked many.

Blanche, for one, registered the shock but was pleased by it. It did for him what he had hoped would be done by the Exposition des Arts Décoratifs, the Art Deco show, which was then taking place in Paris. He had looked in the Art Deco show for a "manifestation of the modern spirit," but he found it instead at the Revue Nègre. As time went by and people had more time to think of the Revue Nègre as a manifestation of the modern spirit, they did so. The French press turned out column after column about it. The Revue Nègre entered the *discours* of the capital, its perpetual verbal adjustment of what is interesting and meaningful. Consensus was quickly reached that the Revue Nègre was meaningful. But what exactly did it mean? What did Josephine Baker portend?

To read the reviews of the Revue Nègre is to immerse oneself in the fantasy life of the French male in the years between the wars. They are threaded with impassioned allusions to distant times and places. The names of the eighteenth-century French explorers Bougainville and La Pérouse turn up a lot, as do the names of Stanley and Livingstone. The South Seas mingle with the Congo. What matter? The natives are all black. Audiences of the Revue Nègre were looking at scenes that purported to represent American Negro life, but they were seeing in their minds' eyes the jungles of Africa and the palm-fringed beaches of the Pacific. They were reenacting Gauguin's escape from bourgeois morality, his nurturing plunge into color. They were white explorers voyaging to the edge of civilization, encountering the savage, incorporating it into themselves by making love with a savage woman.

If it may be harsh to call the fantasies racist, it is fair at least to call them colonialist. In the following year, the Folies-Bergère would make the colonialist fantasy even more explicit with Josephine Baker as Fatou, the native girl, clad in a skirt of fake bananas, who climbs down the limb of a tree and into the life of the white explorer as he lies dreaming under his mosquito net. Like the picture postcards of veiled but bare-breasted Algerian women that were popular in France in the early twenties, the Revue Nègre excited its audiences by reminding them of a world that was both mysterious and sexually available, alien yet subject.

The cast of the Revue Nègre, professional entertainers and products of big-city life whose art was perfected on Manhattan stages, had nothing to do with the tropics, bonfires, poisonous flowers, jungles, and turquoise waters. Yet people said of them, "Their lips must have the taste of pickled watermelon, coconut, sweet pepper, and guava. One sips in through the eyes the sweet saltiness of their perspiration, the sweat of a hamadryad bounding across jungles filled with poisonous flowers." An embarrassing example of the triumph of fantasy over fact would come in 1931 when Josephine Baker was initially selected to be Queen of the Colonial Exposition—until public outrage reminded the organizers that she did not come from a colony of France.

The smartest critics were aware of the sources of their reactions. "Our romanticism," wrote one, "is desperate for renewal and escape. But unknown lands are rare. Alas, we can no longer roam over maps of the world with unexplored corners. We have to appease our taste for the unknown by exploring within ourselves the lands we haven't penetrated. We lean on our own unconscious and our dreams. As for reality, we like it exotic. These blacks feed our double taste for exoticism and mystery. . . . We are charmed and upset by them, and most satisfied when they mix something upsetting in with their enchantments." Indeed, audiences of the Revue Nègre seem as a group oppressed by the weight of their own civilization, transportable at the least excuse to distant times or places, hungering for renewal in a way which, if your orientation was either Freudian or racialist, you might call regressive.

. . .

Almost everyone who saw Baker dance in her early years, when she did the Charleston and that "stomach dance," compares her to an animal. Some say a panther, some say a snake, a giraffe, a kangaroo. But a Russian-born dancer named Mura Dehn, who saw her dance in the Revue Nègre, said she moved like a hummingbird, and that seems to me the most accurate description. Dehn remembers her walking onto the stage with tiny quick steps, in profile, her rear end sticking out, "walking like a little hummingbird with her heinie moving so fast behind her like a hummingbird." Her heinie, as Mura Dehn called it, moved at incredible speeds and seemed to take on a life of its own in her dancing. She handled it as though it were an instrument, a rattle, something apart from herself that she could shake. One can hardly overemphasize the importance of her rear end. Baker herself declared that people had been hiding their asses too long. "The rear end exists. I see no reason to be ashamed of it. It's true there are rear ends so stupid, so pretentious, so insignificant that they're good only for sitting on." With Baker's triumph, the erotic gaze of a nation moved downward: she had uncovered a new region for desire.

She was also doing steps that were technically quite difficult, and making them look easy. When Europeans started to learn the Charleston, their faces twisted with the effort of turning their feet in and out. When Baker did the Charleston, she could throw herself completely into the dance. The metaphor of abandon was built into the Charleston. If you did it well, you threw yourself away, flinging out your arms and legs. You collected yourself, then let yourself go. The dance, in a sense, was *about* letting go. It meant liberty, freedom, the throwing off of old restraints, including, of course, sexual ones. And so it was appropriately the dance of the twenties.

In a Charleston step called "the fan," one bent at the knees and put one's hands on them, opening and closing the legs while switching hands from knee to knee. Baker could open the fan so wide that it made her legs seem endless. She went down and up; she slid; she turned sideways; she faced the audience; she crossed her eyes; she twirled, putting her finger on her head as though she herself were a top she was spinning; she sang in a man's voice. The next moment she dropped the contortions, the mugging, and reverted to beauty. You never knew what she would do from one minute to the next. Her dancing was a series of unexpected changes, and unexpected changes are the essence of jazz.

Not in fact tall, when Baker danced she seemed tall, with legs that seemed long but were not long. From nude photographs of her in this period you can see that her body was far from perfect. Her thighs may have been a little heavy, but when she moved you noticed none of this. So for an aesthetic that shunned the statuesque, that sought to show form in movement, hers was the perfect body in motion, offering relief from the usual frozen attitudes of beauty.

It was often said that Baker dancing looked like an African sculpture come to life. If you compare her in the stance of her banana dance, the descendant of the Danse Sauvage of the Revue Nègre, to an African statuette, you can see why: the knees-bent, rear-end-protruding posture is identical. How did the resemblance come about? The French may have been wrong to perceive this American woman as West African, but ironically they may have been right. Some of the principles of her dancing, as well as her posture and moves, stem from an African tradition which was in part preserved in America.

In the European tradition—in classical ballet as in the waltz—dancers, especially women, show the front, presenting the chest. In the African tradition, dancers, men as well as women, dance with the rear end. Moreover, one of the principles of African dance is the moving of various parts of the body according to different rhythms in the music. The hands and feet can move to one drum while the torso moves to another and the rear end to yet another. A master can move to four different rhythms at once. The body below the waist moves differently from the body above the waist, and various parts of the body are in fact "played" as though they were instruments. Western dancing, attempting to present the body as a unified line, knew nothing of this sort of segmented motion.

African dance is done with the feet flatly planted, whereas European dancers tend to move onto their toes. The one prefers stylized stability, the other stylized instability. European dancers reach, leap, stretch upward, and, especially in classical ballet, in their moments of greatest intensity and extension, seem to strive for something overhead, aspiring to a heaven metaphorically "above," like the soaring verticals of Gothic arches. But African dancers, in their most virtuoso sequences, tend to be closest to the earth. They "get down" to show the greatest respect and to perform their deepest moves.

African sculptures reflect this preference for stabilized balance. They represent weight as evenly distributed between right foot and left, whereas in the seminal posture of Western art, the Greek contrapposto, one leg bears the weight of the body. The basic postures of the human body differ from culture to culture. Instead of the Greek contrapposto, weight resting on one leg, in African art there is the squat. Paradoxically, the asymmetrical Western posture implies rest; the stolid African posture implies motion, energy massed at the knees and hips, waiting to be released.

Dance with bent knees, say the people of the Congo, lest you seem a corpse. In Liberia, Nigeria, and Zaire it is a great compliment to say that a dancer moves as if he or she had no bones. Extraordinary flexibility is a highly valued quality in African dancers, a sign of life, youth, and vigor, and the suppleness of its dancers is considered one of Africa's cultural resources. According to this tradition, Josephine Baker, in being almost double-jointed, possessed a great gift.

Her greatest gift, however, was her ability to seem to let herself go when she danced. She seemed able to tap at will sources of energy and spontaneity that for most people are protected by layers of self-consciousness and social prohibition. For this, she may have been at least in part indebted to childhood churchgoing, which filtered to her another aspect of African tradition. A choreographed emotional display was at the heart of many black church services, those in which the carryover from African religion was strongest. Certain movements, seeming to an outsider uncontrolled, almost wild, but in fact highly conventionalized, signaled possession by a spirit.

Baker had been brought up a Baptist, but for St. Louis churchgoing, she often preferred to attend the services of the Holy Rollers, which had more music, more movement, more of the "call and response" interaction between the preacher and the congregation, and which were, in general, less staid, more African, more "ecstatic" than those of the Baptists. It began, typically, with the singing of hymns. The worshippers tapped their feet, clapped their hands, swayed to the music. The preacher shouted in the rhythmic style of black sermonizing so close to chanted poetry, and the congregation answered back in unison, bearing him up: Amen, Hallelujah, Praise the Lord. In this hypnotic setting, with the rhythm strongly established, one person after another would jump up to demonstrate possession. They entered a kind of stylized trance whose excitement was contagious. The whole congregation stood, eyes closed, swaying, caught up in the ecstatic experience.

When little Josephine was in a serious mood, she joined in praying with the others, and when the Holy Spirit seized her, dizzy with excitement, she threw her legs up in the intoxicated dance. When she was feeling less pious and more irreverent, she just laughed at the people seized by ecstasy. But whether she laughed or prayed, she saw the twitching and swaying and spasms that signified possession by a spirit; she observed that stylized jumping, running, jerking, and screaming could be signs of something powerful going on inside, and highly acceptable to the group. In the white European tradition, the soul is a quiet thing, to be discovered in peace and through introspection. In the African tradition, the soul can express itself in motion and be discovered through motion. Childhood churchgoing gave Baker the gut conviction that it was good to move and that the soul could express itself through the body. She learned to let herself go in a way that was socially approved. Afterward, she always looked forward to the moment she went onstage to both lose and find herself in the dance, when she had, as she would put it in the French phrase, the devil in her body, *le diable au corps*.

Long before Baker hit Paris, the dancing black female body was associated in the French imagination with lewd invitation. From the earliest exploration of Africa, European travelers had been struck by African dances, and the dancing black came to hold a particular grip on the European imagination. To European observers, these dances expressed such indecency, such unbridled sensuality that they could only imagine them resulting from primitive inferiority—or, in kinder versions, primitive innocence. One traveler, describing his visit to Senegal in 1828, wrote: "The dance of the Negresses is incredibly indecent. They form a circle and mark time by a movement of the top of their bodies in front and by clapping the hands. Each of them leaves her place in the circle and takes her turn in the middle; she gets into positions so lascivious, so lubricious that it's impossible to describe them. . . . It's true that the Negresses don't appear to have the depraved intentions which one would imagine; it's a very old custom, which continues as it were innocently in this country; so much so that one sees children of six performing this dance, certainly without knowing what they're leading up to." The possibility that there was nothing innately lascivious about the dance and that it was not leading up to anything at all never entered the traveler's mind. As everybody knew, black women were sexier than white women, and dance was the supreme expression of black female eroticism, just as violence was that of black male eroticism.

The conventions of African dancing were no more familiar to Europeans in 1925 than they had been in 1828. Anything more spontaneous than the waltz was still likely to look like public lovemaking. Ballroom dancing had become acceptable in the Anglo-Saxon world only around World War I, through the efforts of that clean-cut couple Vernon and Irene Castle. The fox-trot and tango became popular then, but even these dances seem formal compared with the dances of the 1960s, beginning with the twist. At that point, black dancing finally began to triumph in the West, and our current model of social dancing tends to be individual and improvisatory, calling upon the whole body and not concentrating on the placement of the feet, demanding movement in the various parts of the body and not aiming for a beautiful line to be echoed by a partner. We are so used to this style of dancing that it has no capacity to shock us.

No filmed footage exists of the Revue Nègre; however, there is some film of Josephine Baker dancing as Fatou at the Folies-Bergère in the following year, a dance close to what she did in the Danse Sauvage, only without a partner. You'd think that would allow us to see what people saw in 1925, but it does not. The film shows that heinie moving as fast as a hummingbird. It shows a dancer who is energetic and contagiously happy, but not particularly sexy. The conventions of her moves being more familiar to us, we cross no boundary in watching her. She can delight us but not shock. Perhaps the best way to imagine how sexy she looked to people brought up on the waltz is to remember how and why Elvis Presley once seemed obscene. It was equally a matter of violating white conventions of movement.

The man who looked the hardest and most knowledgeably at Josephine Baker dancing in 1925 was the distinguished dance critic André Levinson, no fan of black dancing, indeed a man of almost flamboyant ethnocentricity in his view of art. But he had a historical sense and a broad knowledge of the dance, and he expressed better than anyone else what these new dances of the black Americans meant to classical Western dance.

For one thing, he understood where the dances he saw on the stage of the Théâtre des Champs-Élysées had come from, both that there was an African tradition and that it had come to Paris by way of New York—"though the road is long indeed from the valley of the Niger to the lights of Broadway." He had a sense of the historical moment: African culture, by whatever circuitous path, was coming into contact with classic European culture. He foresaw that black culture would be assimilated into the mainstream of American culture, if not of European culture. Black would get whiter, and white would get blacker. He thought he understood why the crossover was taking place at that moment.

Dance, he said, has a tendency to get ordered and intellectualized to the point where spontaneity is suppressed. What began as joyous tumult becomes mechanical exercise. Perfect form squeezes out spirit. Dance renews itself by going back to its historical roots, the sources of its spirit, which should be sought in distant places since we cannot travel back in time. The vogue in Paris for black American dancing had been preceded by the success of the Ballets Russes, with its self-conscious orientalism, and a vogue for Japanese and Balinese dance.

Levinson's landmark book, *La Danse d'aujourd'hui*, explored many of these exotic forms of dance, including even some acrobatics and other circus and music-hall phenomena, taking the widest possible view of French cosmopolitanism and cultural appropriation. He proposed, as other critics of culture since Matthew Arnold have proposed, that periods of expansion and ferment alternate with periods of refinement and distillation. French culture, exhausted for one reason or another, was in a period of gobbling up cultural food to prepare for a coming age of creativity. The model assumes a kind of ingestion of lower organisms by a higher one, plankton by a whale. Jazz and jazz dancing are viewed as raw materials for future higher cultural forms.

Levinson, with no compunction about using words like "savage," "primitive," and even "prehuman," saw the evolution of the dance very clearly. It began in rhythm and worked its way up to greater complexity. Rhythm is the great energy source which tends to get atrophied in "civilized" human beings. But this energy source has been preserved in the dances of blacks, who are in fact primarily concerned with marking rhythm, turning their bodies into instruments of percussion. Whereas the ballet dancer aims at lightness and silence—the ideal involves the dancer touching ground as little as possible—the primitive dancer pounds and thuds, in flamenco as in tap dancing. Compare, he asks of us, the flexible soft-soled satin shoes of the ballerina with the formidable patent leather shoes of the tapper. In *La Sylphide*, Maria Taglioni delighted her audiences by appearing to run over a field of grain without bending the stalks. "The Negro stepper, who pounds the platform with unremitting rigor, producing an infernal racket, is a no less sincere expression of another type." Another type, and a lower one. The European enthusiasm for it is a sign of decadence—a willed return to a lower form of life.

Despite his contempt for black art, Levinson reviewed the Revue Nègre favorably, largely because of his enthusiasm for Josephine Baker, who, in his view, transcended the character of her dance. As he went on thinking about black dance, he exempted Baker more and more from his repugnance and indeed idealized her as much as the most besotted hack writers and critics. His description of her dancing in the

Revue Nègre is one of the best, although it, too, shows the accumulated weight of French romanticism.

"There seemed to emanate from her violently shuddering body, her bold dislocations, her springing movements, a gushing stream of rhythm. It was she who led the spellbound drummer and the fascinated saxophonist in the harsh rhythm of the 'blues.' It was as though the jazz, catching on the wing the vibrations of this body, was interpreting word by word its fantastic monologue. The music is born from the dance, and what a dance! The gyrations of this cynical yet merry mountebank, the good-natured grin on her large mouth, suddenly give way to visions from which good humor is entirely absent. In the short *pas de deux* of the savages, which came as the finale of the Revue Nègre, there was a wild splendor and magnificent animality. Certain of Miss Baker's poses, back arched, haunches protruding, arms entwined and uplifted in a phallic symbol, had the compelling potency of the finest examples of Negro sculpture. The plastic sense of a race of sculptors came to life and the frenzy of African Eros swept over the audience. It was no longer a grotesque dancing girl that stood before them, but the black Venus that haunted Baudelaire."

Janet Flanner was in the audience, too. Not for her those fantasies of tom-toms and bougainvillea.

She made her entry entirely nude except for a pink flamingo feather between her limbs; she was being carried upside down and doing the split on the shoulder of a black giant. Midstage, he paused, and with his long fingers holding her basket-wise around the waist, swung her in a slow cartwheel to the stage floor, where she stood like his magnificent discarded burden, in an instant of complete silence. She was an unforgettable female ebony statue. A scream of salutation spread through the theater. Whatever happened next was unimportant. The two specific elements had been established and were unforgettable—her magnificent dark body, a new model that to the French proved for the first time that black was beautiful, and the acute response of the white masculine public in the capital of hedonism of all Europe—Paris. Within a half hour of the final curtain on opening night, the news and meaning of her arrival had spread by the grapevine up to the cafés on the Champs-Élysées, where the witnesses of her triumph sat over their drinks excitedly repeating their report of what they had just seen—themselves unsatiated in the retelling, the listeners hungry for further fantastic truths. So tremendous was the public acclaim that for the first week's run the cast and the routine of the performance were completely disorganized. Drunken on the appreciation they had received, and on champagne, to which they were not accustomed, the Negro choruses split up into single acts consisting of whichever males or females could still keep their feet, or had not lost their voices from the fatigues of pleasure, all of them nonetheless alive and creative with the integral talent of their race and training. Most of us in Paris who had seen the opening night went back for the next two or three nights as well; they were never twice alike. Somewhere along the development, either then or it may have been a year or so later, as Josephine's career ripened, she appeared with her famous festoon of bananas worn like a savage skirt around her hips. She was the established new American star for Europe.

Janet Flanner may have thought the Revue Nègre proved "black was beautiful," but the show acted like a litmus test for racial attitudes, and by no means everyone liked it. Robert de Flers, a member of the French Academy and prestigious reviewer for *Le Figaro*, the most important Paris daily, called the show a "lamentable transatlantic exhibitionism which makes us revert to the ape in less time than it took us to descend from it." The Baudelaireanism in which people had encased it, that tissue of references to distant places and times, was an outrage to Baudelaire, whose imagined paradise had consisted of *ordre et beauté, luxe, calme, et volupté*. Here was no order, no beauty, no luxury, no calm. Josephine Baker was the high priestess of ugliness. She put her body into awful contortions, deformed her cheeks and eyes, and delighted her admirers—deluded fools who would bring about the end of European civilization. Not without a sense of humor, de Flers said he was willing to bet that she had never thought of founding a new aesthetic on the mobility of her rear end. The people around her did not, as so many seemed to think, represent some earlier and purer state of humanity. These were not noble savages out of the jungle but poor people from the dregs of civilization—not primitive but degenerate. No theater in New York, he said, would present a show like the Revue Nègre except in Harlem, where white people never set foot. Maybe some French people thought their welcome of the Revue Nègre was polite to Americans. They should realize it was closer to an insult.

"Degenerate" is the word that places de Flers's fury in a context of European racial politics. "Degeneracy" was the rallying cry for attacks on blacks and Jews alike from early in the century straight through the Third Reich, a code word giving access to early-twentieth-century racism. In the famous exhibit of "Degenerate Art," the Nazis would gather and condemn much of the important work of the century.

Degeneration was the dark underside of Darwinian thought. For if it was possible for the race to evolve from ape to man, to grow ever more civilized, it must also be possible for the race to deteriorate. It might even be possible to return to the ape. Hence de Flers's taunt: the Revue Nègre "makes us revert to the ape in less time than it took us to descend from it."

His tirade hints at another common position: that a war between the races is in the making, and if whites don't "colonialize"—that is, dominate—blacks, blacks will colonialize whites. The Revue Nègre's popularity signaled to de Flers the beginning of black cultural hegemony and thus, to him, the end of civilization. To be logical, he said, we should burn our books and libraries. In the words of another writer who agreed with him: "All masterworks of the human spirit will be thrown into a great bonfire around which savages will dance naked." With racist fantasies like that on the one hand and colonialist fantasies on the other, it seems fair to say that Baker's impact on Paris in 1925 had as much to do with her color as her talent. She served as a focus for decades of theorizing about race.

In its golden age, the spokesmen for racism were not ignorant outcasts fighting to hold on to the only thing they had, a sense of superiority by virtue of race, but patricians who had inherited the world and didn't understand the terms of the inheritance. In the heyday of racism, white men had an epic historical vision in which civilization itself, the jewel of the white race, was threatened on every side by barbarian hordes.

Mankind had struggled up painfully from the animal kingdom to this point of civilization and now, unwilling to fight for survival against the engulfing people of color, civilized man was on the verge of extinction.

Madison Grant, the author of *The Passing of the Great Race*, a racist classic of 1916, exemplifies the patrician pedigree of early-twentieth-century racism. He lived on Park Avenue and was president of the New York Zoological Society and trustee of the American Museum of Natural History. His work is filled with half-understood scientific theories, echoes of Darwin and Mendel turned to his own ends, and with theories made up for the occasion but articulated with the unction and certainty of science. "The cross between a white man and an Indian is an Indian; the cross between a white man and a Negro is a Negro; the cross between any of the three European races and a Jew is a Jew." The classification of "the three European races" was one of Grant's scientific contributions. There were the dark and volatile Mediterraneans, the stolid, peasant Alpines, and the light-haired, light-skinned, intelligent, active, inventive, and responsible Nordics. The word "Nordic" became popular in the twenties to denote the highest form of white person. In New York, guides offered tours of Harlem "for Nordics."

Mendelian genetics had discovered the phenomenon of "reversion"—that in genetic crosses, an earlier trait sometimes reasserted itself—but Grant turned reversion into an invariable occurrence and a racial bugaboo. Certain races, he believed, are closer to the animal past, while others are further away, higher, more evolved. Darkness of feature is always a sign of the primitive, because animals all have dark eyes. In man, dark eyes are older, more basic, than light eyes. A broad nose is more ancient than a thin, long, aquiline nose. Dark hair is more ancient than blond. As man moved upward, "working out the beast," in Tennyson's phrase, he left these features behind. But being more ancient and rooted, the dark animal features predominate in a mix. The cross between a white man and an Indian is an Indian.

Everywhere Grant looked he saw the lower forms winning out. Why should this be if, as Darwin told us, the fittest survived? Wasn't the light-haired, aquiline, blue-eyed clearly better, fitter to survive, than the dark-haired, dark-eyed, broad-nosed? Grant played fast and loose with the theory of natural selection to explain it. Life itself, he argued, had gone downhill. Lower forms were more suited to the sweatshop reality of modern life than higher forms like himself, Anglo-Saxons whom he called "native Americans" and who he believed would be obliterated if the races continued to mix. Racial purity was the only way to save the white race. If it mixed with any other race, it lost out genetically, because its excellence was a delicate late bloom on the tree of evolution. The lower had the genetic power to destroy the higher.

Grant inspired another American, Lothrop Stoddard, to produce a book called *The Rising Tide of Color*, which had an even more immense success. Written in the aftermath of World War I, it saw that cataclysm as a weakening of white racial unity—a "white civil war"—of which other races would hasten to take advantage. Grant wrote an introduction to Stoddard's book in which he said the feared catastrophe—the end of civilization—would not take place "if the Nordic race will gather itself together in time, shake off the shackles of an inveterate altruism, discard the vain phantom of internationalism, and reassert the pride of race and the right of merit to rule." Some weak-minded sentimentalists, believing people could be improved by education and good living conditions, would let anybody at all emigrate to America. Racists, who saw themselves as hardheaded, had contempt for this fuzzy liberal optimism. It was a cardinal racist belief—if not the cardinal belief—that heredity was more important than environment, people were determined by the inner not the outer, the physical not the cultural, "blood" not experience.

The Rising Tide of Color, published in New York in 1920, appeared the same year in England and soon after was translated into French (*Le Flot montant des peuples de couleur*). There was an eager readership for such books on both sides of the Atlantic, and they passed back and forth quickly. Maurice Muret's *Le Crépuscule des nations blanches*, published in Paris in 1925, the year of Baker's arrival, was translated into English and published in New York the following year as *The Twilight of the White Races*. Émile Fournier-Fabre's *Le Choc suprême*, *ou la mêlée des races* appeared in 1921. They all shared a sense of impending doom. Pessimists thought the struggle had already been lost. Optimists thought the white race could hold on to its edge by scrupulously avoiding contact with the lower races.

In *The Great Gatsby* (1925), the wealthy Tom Buchanan was depressed by a book very much like *The Rising Tide of Color*. He told his guests, including Nick Carraway, about it after dinner one night.

> "Civilization's going to pieces," broke out Tom violently. "I've gotten to be a terrible pessimist about things. Have you read *The Rise of the Colored Empires* by this man Goddard?"
>
> "Why, no," I answered, rather surprised by his tone.
>
> "Well, it's a fine book, and everybody ought to read it. The idea is if we don't look out the white race will be—will be utterly submerged. It's all scientific stuff; it's been proved. . . . This idea is that we're Nordics. I am, and you are, and you are, and—" After an infinitesimal hesitation he included Daisy with a slight nod, and she winked at me again. "—And we've produced all the things that go to make civilization—oh, science and art, and all that. Do you see?"

It could be argued that the most important movements of mind in the twentieth century have been stimulated by racialist thinking, which produced on the one hand the vicious quest for racial purity of Nazi Germany and on the other an enthusiasm among whites for the nonwhite races which was a fertilizing force in much modern art. I call it racialist thinking to separate it from its evil child, racism, but also to suggest how racism and its siblings, either primitivism or exoticism, are connected. The primitivist shares the racist's belief that differences between races are meaningful and enduring, from which all the other nonsense follows, but the primitivist is enthusiastic about the characteristics of nonwhite races whereas the racist deplores them. The primitivist tends to believe in a mixture of various racial qualities as an ideal, whereas the racist is disgusted by the idea. But they are in the same ballpark. The very term "primitivism" suggests a hierarchy of racial values whose usual order the primitivist chooses to invert.

Most racialist writing descends from the mid-nineteenth-century *Essay on the Inequality of Human Races,* by a French count, Joseph-Arthur de Gobineau. Although he became the patron saint of Nazi racism through his disciple Houston Stewart Chamberlain, Gobineau had some ideas which would have horrified the Nazis. Gobineau thought each of the three races—white, black, and yellow—had some virtues, and that the greatest civilizations had to be mixtures of all three. Blacks had a force of imagination which whites did not. Although the white race was objectively the most beautiful of the three, still the most beautiful people of all were mixtures of white and black. Ancient Greece was a great civilization because all the racial qualities had been in perfect balance. A little racial mixing created vigor, superior hybrids, but too much produced degeneration, and to Gobineau's pessimistic temper, it seemed that racial mixing always tended toward imbalance. Decline was inevitable. The blood of Europe had already been too much adulterated. "We do not descend from the ape but we are headed in that direction."

It is useful to see the enthusiasm for African art and culture which developed in Europe in the early part of the century with this racial thinking in the background, as in this passage from D. H. Lawrence's novel *Women in Love.* Gerald Crich, Lawrence's antihero, manager of a coal mine, exemplar of the efficiency and emotional sterility of his class, encounters some "primitive" sculpture in the apartment of some trendy friends in London. He asks the novel's hero, Rupert Birkin, for his opinion of an Oceanic piece of a "savage woman in labour." "It is art," says Birkin—daringly, at a time when such pieces were still generally regarded as curios—and his opinion irritates Gerald Crich.

"Why is it art?" Gerald asked, shocked, resentful.

"It conveys a complete truth," said Birkin. "It contains the whole truth of that state, whatever you feel about it."

"But you can't call it *high* art," said Gerald.

"High! There are centuries and hundreds of centuries of development in a straight line, behind that carving; it is an awful pitch of culture, of a definite sort."

"What culture?" Gerald asked, in opposition. He hated the sheer barbaric thing.

"Pure culture in sensation, culture in the physical consciousness, . . . mindless, utterly sensual. It is so sensual as to be final, supreme."

But Gerald resented it. . . .

"You like the wrong things, Rupert," he said, "things against yourself."

Gerald has the classic racist's attitude: whatever is different from himself is threatening. Birkin, on the other hand, represents the artistic avant-garde in his race enthusiasm.

Birkin's racial theories, which we may assume are Lawrence's, are more complex than the simple opposition between black sensuality and white rationality that they first appear. Mixture and purity figure, as they do in most racialist thought, except that Lawrence reverses the usual racist polarity: for him, purity is decadent and dangerous. The black race, as Lawrence mythicizes it, was originally both sensual and intellectual, but for thousands of years now the race has been in a sense "dead," having become one thing only, sensual. The white races are on the verge of an analogous death, a death not into the senses but into the mind, unless they give themselves up strategically to the sensual qualities of the black. "The white races, having the arctic north behind them, the vast abstraction of ice and snow, would fulfil a mystery of ice-destructive knowledge, snow-abstract annihilation. Whereas the West Africans, controlled by the burning death-abstraction of the Sahara, had been fulfilled in sun-destruction."

Such ruminations make Birkin think of Gerald, fair, blond, blue-eyed, industrious, quintessentially Nordic, "one of those strange white wonderful demons from the north." "Was he fated to pass away in this knowledge, this one process of frost-knowledge, death by perfect cold? Was he a messenger, an omen of the universal dissolution into whiteness and snow?" The answer is clearly "yes," and it is no surprise to the attentive reader when Gerald freezes to death on the top of an Alp, while on vacation. However statistically improbable such a death, it was metaphorically inevitable.

Lawrence's frozen Alp may be extreme, but he was not alone in fearing racial death by cold—more usually represented as the cold efficiency of the industrial system. The pervasiveness of the fear may be gauged, in popular culture, by the names of the nightclubs popular in Harlem in the 1920s and 1930s which catered to whites seeking regeneration: the Cotton Club, the Plantation Club. They evoked the warmth of the South and the metaphorical warmth of a pre-industrial system of production which depended, coincidentally or not, on slavery. When they were not evoking the Old South, these nightclubs purveyed jungle imagery which would be equally successful in Europe. For the metaphorical opposite par excellence to Lawrence's frozen Alp was the jungle, where death came through surrender of reason, surrender to the senses.

There are many early-twentieth-century writers besides D. H. Lawrence whose themes are primitivist—E. M. Forster, for example, who opposes unendingly the overbred gentility of the North to the passionate emotional authenticity of the South, whether of Indians, Italian peasants, or the English lower class. But D. H. Lawrence is a better example of a literary primitivist because with him it isn't just a matter of themes. Primitivism informs his technique. He wants to bypass conventional realism in order to bring deeper, darker parts of the soul into fiction. He does this in part by symbol and in part by the bludgeoning effulgence of his prose when he talks about important things like sex and race.

Modernist literature—whether primitivist or not—experimented with new forms, not for the sake of experiment, but out of the conviction that old forms did not capture something important in life, a "spirit," a force, a religious or spiritual dimension existing somewhere below or above consciousness but beyond the purviews of traditional art which concerned itself too much with surface. In the primitivist writers, artifacts of primitive cultures offered quasi-magical access to these other realms of feeling, realms beyond thought. The Malabar caves in Forster's *Passage to India* or the southwestern cave dwellings in Willa Cather's *Song of the Lark* are locales where the spirit world is more easily entered by modern people. Even drained, overbred, urban people adopt, in those locales, the spirituality of the primitive peoples who inhabited them.

From a certain perspective, the greatest and most influential literary primitivist of all was Freud, who can be seen as internalizing the racialist myth. Within each individual soul was located this conflict between archaic, primitive forces, thought of as dark and deep, and the closer-to-the surface, more tenuous forces of civilization. The energizing, fertilizing id, whose repression caused neurosis, was a kind of black race even middle-class Viennese Jews, even "Nordics," carried within themselves.

Josephine Baker's body should be understood as one of many African "objects" which suddenly seemed beautiful to a Parisian avant-garde whose enthusiasm for African art had been developing for two decades. The story of how such objects—for years viewed as curiosities at best—all of a sudden moved into the category of "art" is fascinating, and only beginning to be told.

Since the late 1800s, Paris had been the city above all others— challenged only by Berlin and London—where the West was fertilized by African art. Art and artifacts acquired by French trade and scientific expeditions had been sent home in sufficient numbers so that by the second quarter of the nineteenth century people were beginning to think of building places to put them. In 1874 E. T. Hamy of the Musée d'Histoire Naturelle conceived the idea of gathering in a single museum all the tribal objects scattered in various institutions in Paris. The Musée Ethnographique des Missions Scientifiques opened in 1878. It was the immediate ancestor of the Musée de l'Homme in the Trocadéro Palace, which was to play such a large part in the history of modern art. Various World's Fairs, notably in 1878, 1889, and 1900, displayed the fruits of France's colonial exploits. The figures and fetishes, however, were seen by most people as evidence of backwardness rather than as the wave of the future.

In about 1906 Matisse, Derain, Vlaminck, and Picasso began collecting tribal objects from Africa—masks, figures, and ornamental objects. Extraordinary collections were amassed from objects brought to Paris by colonial officials and travelers. Photographs of the studios of these artists in the early years of the century show them filled with tribal objects. These men who changed the way we saw were themselves changed by their contact with African objects. What exactly did they see in them? A formal vocabulary which was simpler, more abstract, more direct than the classical visual vocabulary of the West. A vocabulary that eschewed illusionism and a fidelity to particular facts which had come to seem empty pyrotechnics to some. Above all, the African objects represented a magical relationship with reality which was—to Picasso—deeper and more significant than the connections Western scientific thinking trained us to see and revere as fact.

His passionate response to African art changed the course of his work on that seminal painting *Les Demoiselles d'Avignon*. When he began working on it in March 1907, it was to be a brothel scene— five naked prostitutes surrounding a sailor and a medical student. By June, the medical student and the sailor had been dropped. The encounter with female sexuality in its seductive and terrifying forms would take place directly between the viewer and the five female figures. But Picasso was not completely satisfied with the way the painting was going, and he went to look at Romanesque sculptures in the Musée de Sculpture Comparée in hope of getting inspiration. That museum was in the Trocadéro Palace. When he was there, Picasso remembered that André Derain had suggested he take a look at the African pieces in the Musée Ethnographique, which occupied the Trocadéro's other wing.

Picasso had seen African masks and figures before this, in the studios of some of his friends, but they were isolated objects held up for aesthetic admiration. In the Trocadéro, he encountered a jumble of objects whose ethnographic interest and ritual purpose was paramount. They suggested another relation between the visible world and the world of the spirits than that of the West, which had, in fact, largely ignored the spirit in favor of the representation of the visible. They were not tastefully displayed on black velvet or in glass boxes or against neutral carpeting. They were jammed together on hastily constructed tables and in cases. The place was badly lit and evil-smelling. There was something horrifying about the setting which helped create the epiphany Picasso apparently had there. It was a shock, a revelation. He was repelled by the place, but couldn't leave. "It was disgusting. The Flea Market. The smell. . . . I wanted to get out of there. I didn't leave. I stayed." He felt something important was happening. He realized why he was a painter: not to represent the visible world, but to evoke and deflect psychological forces, spirits; to enchant, release, be a priest, perform exorcisms. The African masks were tools and weapons with which man waged his war on demons within and without. "Magical things," they mediated and interceded between man and the forces of evil.

The Trocadéro rooms, with their jumble of alien forms which threatened and scared him, seem also to have aroused a kind of envy in Picasso. That was the kind of impact he wanted his work to have. He did not want to paint pretty pictures, hung on walls for admiration, a trick at which he had matched his father by the time he was fourteen. When he finished *Les Demoiselles d'Avignon* in July 1907, the faces of the two prostitutes on the right and one on the left resembled African masks.

It used to be thought that Picasso was incorporating into his painting a purely formal tribute to African sculpture and gesturing toward his own future Cubist style, itself an analytical and intellectual development. But more recently people have begun to realize that the African masks were painted in for their emotional impact—to express the terrifying aspects of female sexuality. Thus the painting in its final form expresses the contradictory attraction and repulsion which was handled narratively and somewhat conventionally (through the images of sailor and medical student—the latter presumably warning about disease) in the first version. Picasso turned to the African imagery because he thought it expressed something Western art could no longer express. He used it to get at a world beneath or above the world we can see and usually represent in art.

Such a reading usefully shows us that Picasso's enthusiasm for African art was not just formal, but it doesn't go far enough in suggesting how ideologically charged that enthusiasm was. In the case of *Les Demoiselles d'Avignon*, Picasso's belief that the African masks would arouse terror in everyone depended on a long European tradition of associating the African with the terrifying. More specifically, he was calling upon an association between female sexuality and blackness which exists only from a white perspective. He had alluded to it before—crudely—in his 1901 parody of Manet's *Olympia*, in which the reclining odalisque is redrawn as a black woman. Female sexuality and the black were for Picasso visual analogues.

The 1984 "Primitivism" show at New York's Museum of Modern Art announced with great fanfare the inspiration provided by tribal art (what used to be called "primitive" art) to the early modernist masters. The show was organized in terms of correspondences— "affinities," the curator called them—between tribal art and modern art. They were stunning. A Max Ernst sculpture stood next to an African sculpture of which it looked like a copy, the kind art students used to make of masterpieces in the Louvre. Giacomettis stood beside similarly elongated tribal pieces. A photograph of Picasso in his studio surrounded by African sculptures stood as an image of the appropriation of non-Western art by Western art.

One cultural historian criticized the Museum of Modern Art show for aestheticizing issues that should have been treated in terms of race, sex, and power. Art is not a universal category, he argued, but a changing, Western cultural category, an honorific Western culture bestows on objects that interest and promise to nourish it. "The fact that rather abruptly, in the space of a few decades, a large class of non-Western artifacts came to be redefined as art is a taxonomic shift that requires critical discussion, not celebration." He has a point. Why were objects that had been relegated to ethnographic museums suddenly "art"? Why was the Revue Nègre as exciting as the Ballets Russes? He points to the posture of Josephine Baker in her savage dance, rump out, knees bent, back straight, looking exactly like an African carving, as an example of an "affinity" unexplored by the "Primitivism" show. "The black body in 20s Paris was an ideological artifact." The enthusiasm wasn't just for art; it was for race.

In the Renaissance, African blacks were a rarity in Europe and consequently valued. Italian courts in the sixteenth century had blackamoors in residence, like pets. They were hard to come by and virtually irreplaceable when they died, so they were well treated. An enthusiasm for African statues is one thing, for black flesh another. I would call one primitivism and the other exoticism.

Nella Larsen, a Virgin Islands-born writer of African and Danish descent, portrayed what it felt like to be on the receiving end of European exoticism in a 1928 novel called *Quicksand*. According to Larsen's autobiographical heroine, Helga Crane, "the advantages of living in Europe, especially France," was among the favorite subjects of cocktail chatter in Harlem in the twenties. Sick of always having to think about race in America, sick of always being perceived only as a member of a group and that a despised one, Helga goes to visit her relatives in Copenhagen, where she has an enormous social success. Her relatives dress her up and introduce her to the most interesting people in the city. Rich, ambitious people, they use Helga to help them move into artistic circles. "She was incited to make an impression, a voluptuous impression. She was incited to inflame attention and admiration. She was dressed for it, subtly schooled for it. And after a while she gave herself up to the fascinating business of being seen, gaped at, desired." But happy as Helga is to have escaped the ignominy of being a black woman in America, much as she loves being made much of, she can't repress the feeling that she is "a decoration, a peacock, a curio." True, they appreciated her beauty and her rarity, but "she wasn't one of them," and in some fundamental way she didn't really count.

Compared with racism, exoticism is merely decorative and superficial. It doesn't build death camps. It doesn't exterminate. Exoticism cares mostly about its own amusement and tends to find differences of color amusing where racism finds them threatening. Exoticism is frivolous, hangs out at nightclubs, will pay anything to have the black singer or pianist sit at its table. Racism is like a poor kid who grew up needing someone to hurt. Exoticism grew up rich, and a little bored. The racist is hedged around by dangers, the exoticist by used-up toys.

If one is to be treated as a thing, one would rather be treated as a rare and pretty thing than as a disgusting or dangerous one. But that is still to be treated as a thing.

. . .

The art dealer Paul Guillaume was outraged by de Flers's attack on the Revue Nègre, and in his role of cheerleader for primitivism in the arts, he listed all the painters and writers who had been inspired by African art: Picasso, Derain, Matisse, Segonzac, Vlaminck, Laurencin, Braque, Léger, and Modigliani, and, among writers, Cendrars, Apollinaire, Breton, Éluard, and Cocteau. "We who think we have a soul will blush at the poverty of our spiritual state before the superiority of blacks who have four souls, one in the head, one in the nose and throat, the shadow, and one in the blood." He accepted, if only at the level of metaphor, the notion of a war between black and white, but prophesied—and reveled in—the triumph of the blacks. "The intelligence of modern man (or woman)," he taunted, "must be Negro." It was as though the racial conflict were a kind of oedipal conflict. Other modernists, too, rejoiced to ally themselves with the children against the fathers, which may explain the fervor of their embrace of black culture.

A reporter asked Caroline Dudley what she thought of causing, indirectly, the end of Western civilization. The sensible woman shrugged her shoulders and had her troupe do a benefit for war wounded, orphans, and widows on the stage of the august Opera House. That would show them who was civilized.

And, of course, there were some people in Paris to whom Josephine Baker and her savage dance meant nothing. Maria Jolas, wife of Eugène Jolas and one of the pillars of the expatriate literary community, made a point of not going to see the Revue Nègre. Sixty years later she was still irritated by Baker's success. "She just wiggled her fanny and all the French fell in love with her."

CHAPTER 2
BLACK BROADWAY,
BLACK PARIS

Josephine Baker had learned to dance on the streets and in the houses and yards of black St. Louis. There, as in Harlem and other black urban centers, new steps spread quickly. Dances came in from out of town, were mastered, were outgrown. She liked to say later in life that she learned to dance by watching the kangaroos in the St. Louis Zoo, and after seeing her films, you might believe that she got a lot, too, from chickens and camels, even giraffes, but she invoked the zoo and the animals no doubt to please an audience that loved her as a child of nature. Animal dances have always been part of the black vernacular dance tradition and indeed can be traced back to Africa. Similarly hiding the traces of a dance tradition and playing up the image of herself as a natural, Baker would say that she learned a lot from mimicking rag dolls whose arms flopped around at wonderful, awkward angles and in odd, unpremeditated gestures. But the rubber-legs dancing and so-called legomania, which made Baker look like an unstrung puppet on Parisian stages, were movements known to twenties jazz dancers in America. (One of her strangest moves, in which she half crouched, bent at the waist, and pulled each leg forward while seeming always about to fall on her face, was a step called Through-the-Trenches, which surfaced after World War I and mimicked the way soldiers moved in a crouch to avoid sniper fire.)

By the time she was thirteen, Baker had built up an enormous repertoire of moves. She knew them so well that when she started to dance professionally, it could look like she was making it all up as she went along. But underneath the seemingly total spontaneity were known steps and dances—the Mess Around, the Itch, Tack Annie, Trucking—and years of daily practice. When she seemed most unstrung, there had been the most careful preparation. Even her eyerolling was something she worked at.

That she should make her way into show business seems inevitable now, but didn't when she was growing up in St. Louis. She was on her way to being a drudge. Her mother did laundry, her sister did laundry, the aunt for whom she was named did laundry. After a bigger than usual fight with her mother, when she was thirteen, she moved out and began supporting herself as a waitress. She worked at the Old Chauffeurs' Club, a hangout for jazz musicians on Pine Street. It was next door to the Pythian Hall, where her father's band was playing. Living to music, surrounded by musicians, suited her better than living with such bitter disappointment as her mother's and stepfather's.

After eight months at the Chauffeurs' Club, she suddenly announced that she was getting married. Her family never knew much about Willie Wells except that he didn't last long as Josephine's husband. They had a traditional wedding, with wedding gown and guests who were served pork ribs. Josephine played married lady with enthusiasm, quitting her job, staying home in the room they had to themselves in the McDonald house, making baby clothes. She wanted to give up, relax, and let herself be taken care of. Although she could see that neither her father nor her stepfather had supported his family—the women had done all the supporting—she nevertheless hoped for a different way and took it out on Willie Wells when he wasn't the man she thought he should be. He left her in fury, the marriage ended, and Josephine went back to waitressing. But she wanted to get even closer to the music.

Soon she joined up with a group of street performers who called themselves the Jones Family Band. Old Man Jones played a horn, Mrs. Jones the trumpet, and their daughter, Doll, a fiddle. Mrs. Jones taught Josephine to play the trombone, which she did doing quick dance steps and crossing her eyes. They played ragtime outside bars and pool halls, anywhere people gathered, passing the hat for money. Among other places, they played on the street outside the Booker T. Washington Theater, St. Louis's black vaudeville house. When a traveling troupe called the Dixie Steppers played the Booker T. Washington, they were down an act and the manager hired the Jones Family to fill in. That was how Josephine Baker made it onto her first stage.

As she liked to tell the story, with her old-fashioned taste for drama and clear-cut decisions, leaving less to chance and more to her own initiative, she and her half sister Margaret were standing outside the theater when suddenly it came into Josephine's mind to ask for a job. She invited Margaret to join her, arguing that they had to earn their living somehow: at least show business would be fun. But Margaret didn't like the idea. Josephine alone went in the stage door and managed to talk herself into a job. Even though the story was not as clear-cut as Josephine wanted it to be—the two sisters at the stage door, one with dreams, the other without—it is true that Josephine took action and the rest of her family did not, and that is always something of a mystery. Talent can be a lever for moving the world, but first you have to want to move it.

A certain type of woman finds her most powerful sources of energy in resisting her mother. Whatever Josephine wanted to be, she did not want to be like her mother. She did not want to be sour and disapproving, or to trust a man who would leave her, no more than she wanted to love a man she'd have to support. She did not want to give up on her dreams and endure life in a state of embittered resignation. Carrie McDonald seemed to want Josephine to do something Josephine didn't think she could do: to live and suffer within familiar limits. Since she had never really succeeded in pleasing her mother anyway, why not go further afield? At some level she chose to reject her mother before—once more—her mother rejected her. If there was a woman in her family she identified with, it was Grandmother McDonald, who had left home in search of a better life.

Josephine was optimistic. Her imagination was filled with stories of oppressed children who triumphed in the end, stories that suggested, in various ways, that even after a long time of stagnation or misery, a better life could begin: Sleeping Beauty and Cinderella on the one hand, the story of Christ's crucifixion and resurrection on the other, plus the illustrations from history books. She wanted to be a queen, to wear splendid clothes and walk down a grand staircase while everyone watched. It all began with desire. Everything does.

It wasn't immediately clear what thirteen-year-old Josephine could do for the Dixie Steppers. She was too small and scrawny to be a chorus girl. Her first performance was an accidental comic sensation. Assigned to play Cupid in a love scene, she glided on pulleys above a pair of lovers. But the wires got caught and Josephine merely dangled overhead, obviously in distress, to the delight of the audience at the Booker T. Washington Theater.

Because she made the Dixie Steppers' manager laugh, he agreed to keep her with the troupe when they left St. Louis, but he could never find anything for her onstage and she became a dresser. Principally, she dressed and tried to take care of the troupe star, Clara Smith, one of several unrelated Smiths (the best-known now being Bessie) who sang the blues in that heyday of blues singing.

The female stars of the black vaudeville circuit, the blues singers knew that part of their job was to offer offstage a spectacle of glamour for their audiences, living lavishly, dressing splendidly, spending lots of money on themselves and turning themselves into symbols of their own success which they could offer, vicariously, to their audiences. They loaded on the ostrich feathers, the beaded headbands, and the heavy gold jewelry. Clara Smith felt the responsibility to dress up for her audience. She wore a red wig and, even though she was very fat, gauzy dresses over pink tights. She tried to increase her stature by balancing her weight on high-heeled shoes. She must have looked ridiculous. Nonetheless, she introduced Josephine to black glamour by showing her pictures in magazines of other, more successfully outfitted stars, and her voice, Josephine said, gave you chills.

The southern black vaudeville route—raucous, makeshift, indomitable—was Josephine's first real school. As she traveled around the South with the Dixie Steppers, she earned nine dollars a week as Clara Smith's dresser, ironing clothes, sewing on buttons, wrestling her into her costumes, trying to keep her from eating too much. At the same time she was learning the ethos of performance: that real life is lived on the stage and the rest of it exists so you can give your best for those few minutes a day when you're really living and what you do really counts. She was learning discipline, for which there are few better schools than the theater: if it is a demanding parent, it is a chosen one, and while it is immensely authoritarian, it rarely provokes rebellion.

They got as far south as New Orleans and as far north as Philadelphia, where Josephine married a second time, a man named Willie Baker, who was built something like her father, compact, wiry, and energetic. Formerly a jockey, he was now working as a Pullman porter. They lived with Willie Baker's family in Philadelphia, where Josephine's position was uncomfortable. Her mother-in-law felt her son had made a bad match—a third-rate chorus girl and dark-skinned to boot, for if Josephine looked light-skinned in the Martin family, she looked dark among the lighter-skinned Bakers.

Josephine's difficult childhood had left her thirsty for love, but the love she got from one man never seemed enough to satisfy her. She needed love on the grand scale—that is, the kind of multiplied approval a person gets onstage from an audience. Very likely she found it easier to give love that way as well, to many people rather than one. It spread out the risk of not being loved in return. Unsurprisingly, the second Willie lasted little longer than the first.

Her dream was to play on Broadway, but in 1920, when she was touring with the Dixie Steppers, there had not been a black show on Broadway for ten years. Black entertainment and white were totally separate spheres. Blacks performed for blacks and whites for whites. At that time, if whites wanted to see black faces onstage, they went to see white performers in blackface. Sometimes they even liked to see blacks in blackface. The makeup made the performers somehow less black, more a white-oriented caricature of blackness, with the exaggerated lips and eyes as well as the burnt-cork complexion. If blacks wanted to see whites onstage, they could manage it in sophisticated cities like New York, but unless they wanted to sit in the remotest balcony (called "nigger heaven"), it took a thick skin—and a light one. It involved getting the lightest member of a group to buy the tickets and distract the usher while the rest took their seats. But blacks in white theaters, like whites in black theaters, were the exception. In New York, black shows played mostly uptown in Harlem, at the Apollo or the Lafayette. Out of town, there were two separate vaudeville circuits: the Keith circuit for white performers and the TOBA circuit for blacks. TOBA stood for Theater Owners' Booking Association, but insiders like Josephine knew the joke that TOBA meant Tough on Black Asses.

The one exception to the rule that blacks played for blacks and whites for whites was in the area of music, and this was thanks largely to the exertions of a single man, James Reese Europe. A managerial genius, Europe had seen that organization was necessary if black musicians were to make any money from music. He gathered many of them into an organization, part social club, part booking agency, called the Clef Club, with headquarters on West Fifty-third Street. Anyone in New York City who wanted to hire a band with black musicians had to go through the Clef Club, which boasted it could supply any size group, from three to thirty, at the briefest notice. Europe held his musicians up to standards of dress and professional responsibility, and the composer Eubie Blake, for one, never ceased to be grateful. He said that before Europe, black musicians had been no better off than wandering minstrels.

Europe turned music into a serious profession for blacks, getting them jobs with good pay in New York's best hotels and at the private parties of the rich. Since promoting black music meant popularizing jazz, he was responsible for the first jazz concert at Carnegie Hall, in 1912, with 125 instruments, including ten pianos. Europe went on to supply the music for Vernon and Irene Castle as they spread the gospel of ballroom dancing in the years before World War I.

Like many black performers in the early part of this century, James Reese Europe had a sense of racial mission—a belief that he had to succeed professionally in order to prove the value of his race. His dream was to put blacks on Broadway. Killed by a knife-wielding drummer in 1919, he did not live to realize his goal, but he had passed it on to others. Eubie Blake got from Europe a lofty sense of theater as a tool of integration which he in turn handed on to everyone connected with *Shuffle Along*, the show that brought blacks to Broadway in the 1920s and changed American musical theater.

In April 1921, Josephine Baker was playing the Gibson Theater in Philadelphia with the Dixie Steppers. She had finally made her way into the chorus, filling in for a dancer who had hurt herself. Physically, she stood out from the other girls: she was lighter and smaller than the rest. Also, they looked bored, as though they were merely doing a job, whereas when she came onstage, she came alive. Black vaudeville had a role for her—the comic chorus girl, the one who stood at the end of the line and pretended that she couldn't remember the steps or keep up with the others.

By that time *Shuffle Along* had played one-night stands in New Jersey and Pennsylvania and two weeks at the Howard Theater in Washington, D.C., and looked as if it had a chance to get to Broadway. Audiences loved it, but to say the show was radically undercapitalized would dignify its financial status. It had no money at all. Everything was makeshift. The costumes were leftovers from two old flops, with sweat stains under the arms. Eubie Blake, the composer, and Noble Sissle, the lyricist, had written some of the songs to fit the hand-me-down costumes. The standard plantation plaids had produced "Bandanna Days." Oriental clothes had produced "Oriental Blues." For the out-of-town tryouts, the company had had to hitch rides, cadge places to sleep, and borrow from whoever would lend, even cabdrivers, in order to keep going from one place to the next. They were unable to pay the chorus and dancers until the play opened, which may be one reason they found themselves short of chorus girls in Philadelphia. Members of the company were bringing in for auditions friends or people whose work they'd happened to see.

One rainy day, Wilsie Caldwell brought a thin, high-strung fourteen-year-old girl with big brown eyes to the Dunbar Theater, where *Shuffle Along* was installed. Wilsie, a chorus girl, and her husband, a dancer, had either met her in a bar (according to Josephine) or seen her perform at the Gibson and thought she was terrific (according to Noble Sissle). She was interviewed by three of the four men who created the show, Noble Sissle, plus Flournoy Miller and Aubrey Lyles, the authors of the book. She made a big impression on all of them, but she was too funny-looking for the chorus: too thin, too small, and darker than the other girls they'd hired. There was no question of hiring her, in any case, because she was clearly too young. New York State had a law forbidding the employment of chorus girls under sixteen. They asked Josephine how old she was, and for about the first time in her life when asked her age, she didn't lie enough. She said fifteen, whereas in fact she was a couple of months shy of fifteen. Accustomed to her own line, "I know I look young, but I'm really fifteen," she might have thought fifteen was old enough for anything. But she had to be sixteen. They had no choice but to let her go.

It didn't register on Josephine that she had been rejected because of her age. She only heard, "Too thin, too small, too dark," and the last rankled. It rankled to be rejected as too dark by the New York show and by the Baker family when she was disliked in her southern vaudeville troupe and in her own family for being too light. Wilsie Caldwell tried to explain it to her. Sissle and Blake were trying to succeed with white audiences. They had to produce a visually acceptable cast, as light as possible. If Josephine could understand the magnitude of what Sissle and Blake were trying to do and appreciate the odds against them, she might be able to accept her personal disappointment more easily.

It was true that Sissle and Blake were nervous. They had written some great songs for the show, including "I'm Just Wild About Harry" and "Love Will Find a Way." But naturally they did not know what a hit "Harry" would be—nor, certainly, that Harry Truman, a quarter century later, would use it as his campaign song, thus endowing it with close to eternal life and Blake with unending income. At the time, Blake was not feeling good about the song. He had written it and loved it as a waltz, but when he played it for Lottie Gee, the show's star, she insisted that he speed it up into a one-step. In a colored show, she said, a waltz would never do. Too beautiful. Since Sissle agreed with her, and his commercial instincts were good, Blake reluctantly transformed his beautiful waltz into an upbeat one-step.

"Love Will Find a Way" was worrying him, too. It was a romantic ballad, and romantic ballads sat no more comfortably in black musicals than waltzes did. Jesse Shipp, who had written the book for *In Dahomey*, ran into Blake on the street one day. Told about "Love Will Find a Way," he predicted disaster. White audiences didn't want love duets between blacks. On opening night, Sissle stood backstage with Miller and Lyles. They were filled with apprehension as Lottie Gee and Roger Matthews started to sing the ballad. They felt sorry for Blake, stuck out in front leading the orchestra, exposed to the audience's anger. To their amazement, the audience threw no tomatoes but clapped contentedly. In fact, they demanded an encore.

The book of *Shuffle Along* concerned small-town politics. Two partners in a grocery store (Miller and Lyles in blackface) were both running for mayor of Jimtown. In one of the most popular bits, both partners are stealing from the till, each hires a detective (the same man) to check up on the other, one is told the other has stopped stealing. "Oh yeah?" comes the reply. "When did he die?" Miller and Lyles wrote some of the early Amos 'n' Andy shows. Their jokes were largely based on ineptitude, verbal and otherwise. "You gotta be repaired [i.e., "prepared"] for that," and so on. Like Miller and Lyles's blackface vaudeville routines, based on stereotypes of black venality and stupidity, the book of *Shuffle Along* would seem excruciatingly racist and caricatured to a contemporary audience. Even in 1952, when an attempt was made to revive the show, the book had to be scrapped, so badly had it already dated. For example, in the original show, the newly elected mayor of Jimtown could not spell "cat," and that was supposed to be funny. ("Nowadays," said a solemn newspaper piece in 1952, exploring the changes in the show, "when most colored people can read even in the deep country, the joke would fall flat.") In another grocery store scene, the owner-clerks are so lazy they tell the customers to take care of themselves. ("In this age of the supermarket, everybody serves himself, and an audience would be left cold by the dated wisecrack.")

Shuffle Along was the product of two teams of unequivalent talent. Miller and Lyles were good at what they did, but not on the level of the vastly more gifted team of Sissle and Blake, whose songs had something that transcended the moment. The show was hoisted to success by the music and the dancing. For if the book purveyed the old caricature of the black as shuffling, lazy, and venal, the musical part of the show embodied a new image: the black as source of energy.

It featured jazz dancing such as had never been seen on Broadway before. White revues tended to use chorus girls as displays: they stood there and looked lovely. A pretty girl was like a melody. She didn't move much. She walked only to show off her body and her costume. The *Shuffle Along* chorus line amazed white audiences because the women in it actually danced. The most influential review of the show, by Alan Dale of the *New York American*, contrasted the wild energy of this performance with the tameness of white Broadway: "Every sinew in their bodies danced; every tendon in their frames responded to their extreme energy. They revelled in their work; they simply pulsed with it, and there was no let-up at all. And gradually any tired feeling that you might have been nursing vanished in the sun of their good humor." According to Blake, it was this review, with its promise of a renewal of energy, that really brought in the audiences.

They opened at the Cort Theater on West Sixty-third Street, just off Central Park West, on May 23, 1921. On the first night there were empty seats, and *Variety* noted that "colored patrons" were seen as far forward as the fifth row when the upper floors did not sell out. But as word spread, the 1,100-seat house was filled nightly. They started doing a Wednesday midnight performance, so other entertainers could come, and that helped the word of mouth about the high quality of the performances. Since capitalization had been slim, and the salaries were low, the cast of sixty drawing about $3,300 weekly, they could make a profit on a fairly small weekly gross. Soon the show was doing so well it was thought a road company could succeed, too, doing one-night stands around the country.

Josephine Baker could not put *Shuffle Along* out of her mind. She wanted to be part of what she knew was *the* great black theatrical enterprise of the moment. When the Dixie Steppers finally folded in Philadelphia, she took what money she had and went to New York, leaving another husband behind. It took a lot of courage, because she was fifteen and knew no one in New York except the Caldwells, who were casual friends at best. Still, in some ways, it took less courage than going back to St. Louis.

Carrie McDonald, without being a monster, merely because she could so strikingly withhold approval, was the only person Josephine feared in her life. She was also afraid that if she got near her again, Carrie would—like some mythical creature—snatch her back, not allow her to escape a second time, turn her into the unsuccessful drudge she had been before. In New York, she was virtually a runaway. She went there fleeing poverty and rejection, which she associated with her mother, and seeking the kind of love she had only felt performing.

When she got to the city, she slept on park benches for a couple of nights until she located the Caldwells at the theater. Wilsie was cordial. She told her she might be able to get a job with the touring company, which they were in the process of forming. Josephine auditioned for Al Mayer, the company's white manager, not for Sissle or Blake. This time she prepared. She put some of Wilsie's lightest powder on her face, and when asked how old she was, was ready with her reply—seventeen. (She was actually fifteen.) Nonetheless, she didn't get the job. "Too small, too skinny," said Al Mayer. He had a point. When you see photographs of the chorus line of *Shuffle Along*, Josephine Baker stands out even if you don't know her face. She is by far the darkest and, if you look closely, the skinniest, too.

A job was offered her as a dresser with the road company. She didn't want it. She'd been a dresser and hated it. But Wilsie argued the classic show business scenario: someone was sure to get sick, and if Josephine learned all the songs and dances, she might get a chance to go on. It had happened to her before. So she took the job as dresser. She learned the songs and dances, and when one of the chorus girls got sick, Josephine filled in for her.

Onstage, the old magical transformation took place. She burst into frenetic action. She seemed to move every part of her body in a different direction at once. She clowned outrageously, unable to stop herself. She crossed her eyes. Her feet tripped over each other while the other girls were kicking neatly in step. The effect of her performance was to mock the very idea of a chorus line, a row of people mechanically repeating the same gestures. The chorus line hated her. They had a simple term for what she was doing: scene stealing. But audiences loved her.

She began to get a reputation of her own and soon became a box-office draw. People buying tickets asked about the little chorus girl at the end of the line who crossed her eyes. Was she still in the show? She was singled out in reviews, and eventually Sissle and Blake, in New York, became aware that a phenomenon had developed in their touring company: a chorus girl who stopped the show night after night with her ad-lib clowning. They arranged to have the touring company play Brooklyn one Wednesday matinee and went across the river to see the wonder, whom Sissle recognized as the girl who had auditioned for him six months before in Philadelphia.

When they went backstage to talk to her, Josephine was afraid they had come to fire her. "I'm sixteen now," she said. "Please don't fire me." Of course she wasn't sixteen. But Sissle and Blake did not need to worry about the minimum-age law's being enforced for the touring company; it was a state law only. Far from firing her, they told her she could join the main company when the touring company folded for the summer.

By the summer, as it happened, *Shuffle Along* had reached the end of its fourteen-month run in New York, and it was the main company that went on the road, Josephine Baker with it. She stayed with the show for almost two years, until it closed for good in January 1924. She had managed, in her teens, to get herself into the middle of the most exciting black theatrical enterprise in over a decade and into exhilarating proximity with Noble Sissle and Eubie Blake.

The great black bandleaders of the twenties and thirties served as leaders and educators for the members of the organizations they headed, and so did theatrical entrepreneurs like Sissle and Blake. The musicians, dancers, and comedians around them were often pitifully untrained, uneducated, young. They taught them discipline and professional standards.

Eubie Blake was caustic about how much *more* discipline and training black performers needed than white ones in order to achieve the appearance of spontaneous performance that white audiences expected of them. When he had played for big dances, with a white band at one end of the room and a black at the other, the white band was provided with music stands and the black band with none, because blacks were not supposed to be able to read music. They were supposed to make music spontaneously, from their souls. Therefore, black musicians had to get the music for the new songs quick as a flash and memorize it completely so they could emit music like songbirds. Whereas, of course, there were men in the band who could play flies if they happened to settle on the page of music.

Sissle and Blake made Baker their particular protégée. They tried to teach her to sequence her act, to build effects, to employ tricks of showmanship. But it was hard going. The minute she was onstage, she seemed to forget. Sissle worked out routines with her and watched her performance from the wings, taking notes so he could go over it with her afterward. But there was simply no correspondence between what they had worked out and what she did. Under the pressure of the magical stage moment, she forgot the routines and made up sequences of her own. According to Sissle, her improvisations were even more spectacular than what they'd worked out, the dance steps wilder, the antics funnier. "She would come offstage with the audience screaming and applauding and with her face lighted up with joy," he recalled. Once she came offstage to find him scowling. "Did I do the steps right that time?" she asked, and was told she hadn't done them at all. She widened her eyes, put her hand over her mouth, giggled, and promised to do better next time. "Her emotions were beyond her control," Sissle said. It wasn't that she wanted to be contrary. But youth, high spirits, and her excellent instincts for getting a laugh were controlling her body.

Still, she was learning. Even before she joined the main company of *Shuffle Along*, she had learned to do the great American end run: If the main company won't take you, try out for the road company. If the road company doesn't want you as a chorus girl, take the job as a dresser. Work your way in. Make yourself familiar. Don't give up. Don't take no for an answer. At least, try to change it to "not right now."

For over a year, the *Shuffle Along* company toured America. This was an education, too, in more ways than one. To see America as a black performer in the twenties gave you a special perspective. Few hotels or restaurants were open to you. You had to make special arrangements everywhere you went just to eat and sleep. Billie Holiday, touring the South in 1937 with Artie Shaw's band, said the worst part was finding a place to go the bathroom. Every time, she said, it was an "NAACP-type production." Signed to do two weeks at the Selwyn Theater in Boston, *Shuffle Along* ran almost four months. It also ran fifteen weeks in Chicago, where it was hailed as Ethiopera, "the real colored thing." It played Toledo, Grand Rapids, Detroit, Buffalo, Rochester, Atlantic City, Milwaukee, Philadelphia, Peoria, Des Moines, Indianapolis, and St. Louis.

It was in St. Louis in 1922 that Baker had a chance to see how far she had risen. Elegantly dressed, she went back to her mother's house and was horrified by the filth. There were even dirty dishes under the bed. She had the satisfaction of being able to feel ashamed of her mother. She gave her family some money and promised to come back for the following Christmas, but she didn't. She continued to send money, more and more every year, but she didn't see her family again for fourteen years. The visit to St. Louis served to underline how successfully she had cut herself off from her beginnings. She was not yet the star her brother and sisters thought she was, but she wasn't doing badly in the big-city theater world. She had a reputation as a performer and a good income. She could afford to take a taxi back to the neighborhood she'd grown up in—and a taxi away from it.

Sissle claimed that by the time *Shuffle Along* closed, Baker had begun to develop some discipline as a dancer and could stick to a routine. "She began to realize," he said, "that a finished artist always knew what to do next and could weave a pattern of tricks and effects into an interesting sequence." He was trying to teach her the difference between talent and art. He wanted her to be able to imagine a future in which she didn't have to clown, didn't have to go crazy whenever she hit the stage. Nonetheless, what made her special was not routine but improvisation. She was a jazz artist, and her inspired solos, while they took place in a context that had its own discipline, were great because of her gift for spontaneous invention.

When *Shuffle Along* closed, Baker went almost immediately into Sissle and Blake's next show, originally called *In Bamville* and eventually *The Chocolate Dandies*. By now she was one of the principals, and, not including Sissle and Blake, she was the fifth-highest-paid performer in the company, making $125 a week. In the chorus of *Shuffle Along*, she had been making $30.

In the new show a part was created especially for her. Most of the time, wearing bright cotton dresses, oversize clown shoes, and blackface makeup, she crossed her eyes and performed the Sambo antics for which she'd become famous. But she also had an elegant white satin dress slit up the side in which she got to vamp the clowns, Lew Payton and Johnny Hudgins.

The Chocolate Dandies was a much more ambitious undertaking than *Shuffle Along*, and perhaps for that reason, not as successful. The costumes this time were elaborate and the cast larger. Twice as much business was needed to cover expenses and make a profit. It couldn't be done. As he had worried about the waltz and love duet before, Blake now worried about a scene in which the chorus girls wore lovely hoopskirts, like southern belles. "The scene is too beautiful for a colored show," said Blake to their producer, B. C. Whitney, who replied staunchly that it was a Sissle and Blake show—not a colored show— and insisted on keeping the scene. The set featured trees hung with

Spanish moss. The moon rose slowly as the Harmony Kings, including Paul Robeson, sang "Dixie Moon." The men wore pongee suits. The girls entered in their white hoopskirt dresses and broad hats. Applause died. Even favorable reviews of *The Chocolate Dandies* found the production "pretentious."

One reviewer complained about "the fatal influence of the white man" on the production. According to this view, civilization was a kind of contagious disease which Sissle and Blake had caught. They themselves were bitter about the show's reception. Blake thought he'd never written a better score. They had tried to move beyond what was traditionally possible in a black revue and found they could not. "People who went to a colored show expected only fast dancing and Negroid humor," said Blake, "and when they got something else they put it down." Josephine Baker was an exception. With her clowning and her energy, she was seen as "the real colored thing." The same reviewer who complained about the fatal influence of the white man on *The Chocolate Dandies* said that civilization had spared "the comic little chorus girl whose very gaze was syncopation and whose merest movement was a blues."

The reception of the new Sissle and Blake show crystallized a dilemma for black theater which was also a personal dilemma for Josephine Baker. On the one hand, if you aspired to a generalized excellence that transcended race, you lost what interest you had to the white audience and perhaps betrayed your black audience as well. On the other hand, if you supplied the "fast dancing and Negroid humor" you were reinforcing dumb stereotypes and killing your own artistic growth.

Back in the first decade of the century, when a group of black writers and composers had gathered at the Marshall Hotel to discuss how to get blacks on Broadway, this quandary had come up and caused dissension between the suave and elegant Bob Cole, a talented performer as well as a writer of songs, and the irascible composer Will Marion Cook. Cook was a violin prodigy who had been trained in Germany and who, upon his return to New York, gave a debut concert which was generally well received. But one reviewer called him "the world's greatest Negro violinist," and this made Cook so angry he vowed never to play again, saying, "I am not the world's greatest Negro violinist. I am the world's greatest violinist." There are other accounts of why Cook abandoned the violin; all agree he was a difficult man, but a musical genius.

Cole believed that any black artist should "strive for the fine artistic effect, regardless of whether it had any direct relation to the Negro or not," although naturally his efforts would all be informed by race pride. Cook, by contrast, believed that the black performer "ought to be a Negro, a genuine Negro." He should eschew white patterns and not employ his efforts in doing what "the white artist could always do as well, generally better." Constantly thrust back into the role of "Negro performer," Cook thought others were naïve to imagine they would ever get beyond race. But most of what passed for "genuinely Negro" on the stage at the turn of the century consisted of grotesque stereotypes. With the best of intentions, Cook played into the hands of white theater critics and audiences who wanted black performers to offer exaggerated images of "darky" life. What was black? What was "genuinely Negro"? Plantation life, the Mississippi, levees, bright-colored cottons and turbans, cotton pickers, pickaninnies, and cannibals.

A Cole and Johnson operetta, *The Red Moon*, provoked a put-down in 1908 that proved to be recurring: not black enough. "Although the company is made up entirely of colored performers," said the *New York Sun* critic, "there were times when one fairly ached for the sight of a man or woman who was black and wasn't ashamed of it." It was the same story in 1919 with a show called *Put and Take*. "Only at the very end does it become the novelty that it should be if it wants to survive at all and have any excuse for invading Times Square. Colored performers cannot compete with white ones, and colored producers cannot play within an apple's throw of Ziegfeld and try to compete with him," said a New York newspaper confidently. "Here colored folks seem to have set out to show the whites they are just as white as anybody. They may be good, but they're different—and in their own entertainment, at any rate, they should remain different—distinct—indigenous." (This problem of having to fulfill a standard of negritude and not just of art continues to haunt some black artists and intellectuals—for example, Alvin Ailey, some of whose dances have been criticized for not being black enough.)

There was a collective yearning on the part of the elegant black performers of the early part of the century to display even more of their elegance onstage, but elegance conflicted with what much of the white audience thought of as their distinctive racial appeal. For Baker, clowning her way to success was a joy, a kick, but she could see how clowning of that sort might become a convict's task. Although she wanted to be a queen, she could be forever the jester, the funny girl who crossed her eyes. The world can never have too many inspired eye-crossers, but who wants to spend her life being one?

After *The Chocolate Dandies* closed, Baker went to the Plantation Club, a copy of the Cotton Club—a large-scale nightclub featuring a black revue—at Broadway and Fiftieth, over the Winter Garden Theater. In the summer of 1925, the regular star, Florence Mills, was on vacation, and Ethel Waters was taking her place. Baker was in the chorus but stepped out of the line every night to do a specialty dance. One night Caroline Dudley came backstage after the show to recruit for the black revue she wanted to take to Paris.

Caroline Dudley was a young society woman originally from Chicago. She was married to the commercial attaché at the American embassy in Paris, Donald Regan, but the marriage was not a happy one and would not last much longer. With three sisters who were all in some way distinguished, all beauties, all talented, she was looking for a way to claim distinction for herself. She considered herself the only one with no gift, just some ideas, some energy, and some money. So she became a producer.

She got the idea of bringing to Paris a black revue like *Shuffle Along, Runnin' Wild*, which had succeeded it on Broadway, introducing the Charleston, *The Chocolate Dandies*, or another called *Dixie to Broadway*. She went to New York and put together her inspired package.

It was not as easy to persuade people to go to Paris as she would have thought. Ethel Waters, then slim and sexy, was the singer whom

Dudley went to the Plantation Club to recruit. Waters had just made "Dinah" a hit. She had a great voice and a good shimmy, but she didn't have the nerve to leave America. She handled the offer like a street fighter, showing no fear, but demanding a ridiculous amount of money, $500 a week. That was her way of saying she didn't want to go.

When they met at the Plantation Club, Josephine Baker saw immediately that Caroline Dudley had things to teach her. She was impressed by Dudley's looks and her clothes. Such was the glamour Baker yearned for. More adventuresome than Ethel Waters, she had already risked a couple of departures, and each had turned out well; but this was more radical. She would be leaving America, leaving the English language, leaving—except for the two dozen members of the troupe—the black world. However, she had heard that life was actually better for black people in Europe, and she liked the French waiters she had met in New York.

For Dudley, the hiring of Josephine Baker was a sudden inspiration. She had admired Baker in *Shuffle Along*, but then had lost track of her. Stumbling across her at the Plantation Club was a wonderful accident. She had come in search of a singer but it struck her now what a valuable addition to the group a comedian like Baker would be.

Baker wanted to sing. Not only did the singer have more status than the comic dancer, she was sexier. She reminded Dudley that she was Waters's understudy and had performed for her a couple of times, but Dudley said no: Josephine would do her funny dancing, and she would hire someone else to sing. She knew she could find a much better singer than Josephine, with her thin, high voice, but she'd never find a better comic.

She offered her $125 per week, but Baker held out for $200 and then agreed to go.

At some level, she was aware that the glamour she wanted was not possible for her in New York. Her role in show business would never be more than antic clowning. What Caroline Dudley was offering—besides an attractive salary and a chance to get even farther from St. Louis—was a way out of the dilemma of the black performer in America.

. . .

The troupe that sailed on the *Berengaria* landed in Cherbourg on September 22, 1925, and proceeded to Paris the same day by train. All the black performers noticed that they were not told the dining car was filled but were served in the same car as whites with what seemed like enthusiasm. Sidney Bechet told them, not for the first time, that this was one of the reasons he had wanted to come back to France.

Paris seemed small to Baker compared with New York, but she knew immediately she would love it and set out to conquer it, like a hero in a Balzac novel. Her strategy from the first was to think of the city as a lover and try to seduce it. The French waiters in New York had told her how: be chic and make them laugh. It took her a few weeks to learn to be chic—the first time she went sightseeing, she wore golf pants—but she certainly knew how to make them laugh.

In some ways Paris was closer to New York in the twenties than it is now. Of course, it took at least a week to get there by steamship, but when people had plenty of money, they had time. Rich people went to Paris for the races, for the social season, for the shopping, and after the Volstead Act made the public consumption of alcohol illegal in the States, for the booze. For those who took pleasure even semi-seriously, Prohibition made America a land of repression and hypocrisy. Paris became the playground annex to New York and the American myth of Paris was born, to remind a puritan society that work is not all there is to life, or that the American way of working hard and relaxing violently is not the only way. Work, admittedly not as much of it as in America, and pleasure, admittedly more, can be mingled throughout the day. *Ninotchka*, in which Greta Garbo plays the stern, ascetic Russian commisar who visits Paris and is emotionally reborn (she laughs), may be the quintessential film about Americans in Paris.

In the aftermath of the war, Americans filled Paris, taking advantage of the sustained beauty of daily life and of the rate of exchange, which was wildly in favor of American dollars and got more so as the decade advanced. Young scapegraces like A. J. Liebling, who dropped out of college and was at loose ends, or Flora Lewis Mayo, who became Giacometti's mistress, could be supported quite nicely in Paris for $200 a month. People with more money could live as if they were truly rich, giving them a heady sensation of power all the sweeter because it hadn't been worked for. The less money people had, the longer they tended to stay. The young Canadian writer John Glassco described his experiences in one of the most likable of the many memoirs of expatriate Paris life in the twenties: "To be able to live well on very little money is the best basis for an appreciation of beauty anywhere, and I think we admired the city all the more because we could now eat and drink almost as much as we liked."

In Malcolm Cowley's account, *Exile's Return*, cultural imperatives drove young Americans to Europe. Artists and intellectuals, sensing the mediocrity and banality of American life, went to Europe seeking cultural renewal. Not everyone, of course, could go. Some had jobs. "But the younger and footloose intellectuals went streaming up the longest gangplank in the world; they were preparing a great migration eastward into new prairies of the mind."

There were other Americans in Paris in the twenties who were there for still other reasons and about whom we tend to hear less than we do about Scott and Zelda Fitzgerald, Ernest Hemingway, Gertrude Stein and Alice B. Toklas, and the intellectual pilgrims of Cowley's imagining.

Black soldiers had crossed the ocean to fight in the Great War, the first transatlantic war in which they had the opportunity to serve. Whether or not they should do so had been the subject of considerable debate when war was declared. Some people felt that until blacks were fully enfranchised and entitled to the same rights as white Americans, they should not be asked to fight for their country. But W. E. B. Du Bois threw his enormous prestige behind the position that if black soldiers fought loyally and bravely—as he knew they would—a grateful government would surely redress the injustices which all black Americans suffered. After war was declared in 1917, more than 370,000 black men joined the armed forces. James Reese Europe, always alert for ways to advance the race through a mixture of music and public relations, organized, recruited, and led an all-star military band. He even got Noble Sissle to join as drum major. Europe's was not the only black group to play for the troops in World War I, and of all black participants in the war the musicians arguably had the greatest cultural impact. They left behind on the Continent the legacy of jazz, whereas the black fighting troops, by and large, were not allowed to fight. Segregation followed them to war, and they were assigned to labor and transport details, unloading ships and burying the dead.

The black regiment from New York, known as the Harlem Hellfighters, got itself attached to the French Army rather than the American Army so it could see combat. They wore American khaki uniforms but had French rifles, bayonets, helmets, gas masks, knapsacks, food, and ammunition. Hamilton Fish, Jr., one of their white officers and a fervent believer in his men's fighting ability, thought they would make themselves as well known as the Rough Riders in the Spanish-American War. But a secret memo from General Pershing to the French command warned against allowing any fraternization between French soldiers and American blacks. The shaking of hands, for example, was to be strongly discouraged.

The Harlem Hellfighters certainly distinguished themselves. They were the first Allied unit to reach the Rhine. They served longer than any other American unit. They were, as a unit, awarded the Croix de Guerre by the French and 171 of their officers and men were awarded that treasured medal individually. But no black American troops were allowed to march in the great victory parade of the Allies up the Champs-Élysées, even though France and Britain were represented by dark-skinned colonial soldiers. Moreover, the War Department requested that no black troops be portrayed in the Pantheon among the heroes. Despite their distinguished service, the Harlem Hellfighters did not become as well known as the Rough Riders.

They had one day of glory, and again music had a lot to do with it. On February 17, 1919, when they returned to New York, the entire regiment, line after disciplined line, paraded the length of Manhattan, up Fifth Avenue, behind James Reese Europe's magnificent jazz band—sixty brass and reed players, thirty trumpeters and drums. Crowds cheered them all the way up Fifth Avenue. At the top of Central Park, they marched a block west and then continued parading up Lenox Avenue to 145th Street. In Harlem, the band started playing "Here Comes My Daddy Now" and the crowds and soldiers both went wild with joy, the strict order of the marching columns dissolved.

Some of the black soldiers who had served in Europe, returning home to a racial situation worse than ever, decided to go back again to countries without segregation. The question of the popular postwar song was particularly pointed for blacks. How ya gonna keep them down on the farm after they've seen Paree? Will Marion Cook provided an opportunity for many black musicians to get to Europe in 1919 when he organized a European tour for a group he called the Southern Syncopated Orchestra, consisting of thirty-six instrumentalists and twenty singers. One of the people he recruited, first to go to New York from his native New Orleans and then to go to Europe, was Sidney Bechet.

It was June, before what would be a bloody summer of race riots, when they left in a boat which took fifteen days to make the crossing to England. Bechet brought boxes of soap with him, because someone had told him there was soap shortage in Europe. The Southern Syncopated Orchestra was a great success in London, playing for four months, with a command performance before the King, who Bechet said was the first man he recognized from having seen his picture on money. Bechet was a particular success. Ernest Ansermet, the Swiss conductor, came night after night trying to figure out how Bechet got the effects he did. He wrote about "the extraordinary clarinet virtuoso who is, so it seems, the first of his race to have composed perfectly formed blues on the clarinet."

Bechet, who was often drunk, found England too confining. England found Bechet too often drunk and deported him for his part in a brawl. Crossing the Channel to France, Bechet threw his English money overboard, sick of seeing George V's face: it now reminded him of the cops. Paris was more to his taste for many reasons, not the least of which was that his mother was French-speaking. He liked Montmartre because it seemed to him a kind of musicians' colony. He couldn't walk down the street without seeing four or five people he knew, performers, entertainers, people "with real talent to them" and everyone "crazy to be doing." He'd start home and never get there.

There was always a singer to hear, a musician playing somewhere. People were always about to do something amusing, and he always felt like joining them. When the Southern Syncopated Orchestra split up, Benny Payton, the drummer, formed a smaller group, including Bechet, which stayed on in Paris.

Some black musicians had gone to Europe before the war to play for Vernon and Irene Castle on one of their tours and never returned to America. Buddy Gilmore, the drummer, was one, and Louis Mitchell, also a drummer and a singer, was another. Mitchell saved the money he made playing music and eventually bought himself a little nightclub in Montmartre.

Gene Bullard went to France in 1914 because he wanted to be a flier and couldn't be trained in the States. He served in the French Foreign Legion, then flew with the Lafayette Escadrille in World War I, winning fifteen medals. Later, he, too, gravitated to the Montmartre nightclub scene and became the manager of the Grand Duc, a well-known French-owned cabaret at the corner of the rue Pigalle and the rue Fontaine. There, by the spring of 1924, he had installed the only black female entertainer in Paris. Florence Embry, pretty, perky, and arrogant, was the singer, hostess, and all-around star of the Grand Duc. Parisians loved her style and the beautiful way she wore clothes, and because of her the Grand Duc was an enormous success, nightly filled with celebrities.

Not all the black Americans in Paris were musicians or connected with entertainment. Rayford Logan, an Amherst graduate, Phi Beta Kappa, later a history professor at Howard University, was one who had stayed in France after serving in the war so as not to "run the risk of humiliating experiences." Still, so filled was France with Americans that humiliating experiences were unavoidable—especially because, with his light skin and carefully cultivated manner, he was frequently taken for white. One woman, married to a German, stimulated to chat by the sight of his Phi Beta Kappa key, told him her husband had been a professor in the States before the war. Her husband was not bitter about the war itself, only that the United States had allowed black troops to fight against white ones. And now, ever since the war, Vienna was flooded with them. "We are hardly able to live from hand to mouth while these jazz band players strut around in fur coats and diamonds." She was looking forward to going back to the United States, "where they know how to behave themselves."

Except that he subscribed to *The Crisis*, the magazine of the NAACP, and was there to avoid humiliation, Logan was no different from many Americans living privileged lives in postwar France. In 1920, he went to Dax to take a rest cure. He enjoyed the theater and the bullfights, dressed for dinner, spoke French and German like the other guests. The bank phoned him the daily stock-market quotations from Paris. He played billiards and bridge. One night before dinner he began chatting in French with a lady whose accent he couldn't place. Nor could she place his. "Pardon me, but is Monsieur Polish?" "No, Madame, I am American," he said. Out of deference to his reply, she switched to English, but she refused to believe he was an American. "You can fool these Europeans but you can't fool me. Whoever saw an American who looked like you? You are Polish, a Polish prince." He assured her again that he was American, "an American Negro." This answer she found even more charming than his previous one. "You a Negro! A Negro here in Dax, staying at this hotel, speaking French better than I do, eating in the first-class dining room while I eat in the second! That is the cleverest disguise I ever heard in my life. A Polish prince passing for a Negro! That is *too* funny."

Langston Hughes, young but already a published poet, worked his way across the Atlantic as a cabin boy, landing in Rotterdam in 1924. From there, with seven dollars in his pocket and knowing no one in all of Europe, he went to Paris. That first day, like so many other Americans in Paris for the first time, he walked compulsively. Checking his bags, he took a bus to the Place de l'Opéra, walked to the Place de la Concorde, walked along the Seine, went to the Louvre. He slept in Montmartre and discovered next day from a black doorman that he'd stumbled into the right quarter: many black Americans, almost all musicians and performers, lived there. All the nightclubs in the area of Pigalle had at least a few blacks in their orchestras. At the Casino de Paris, a leading music hall, the orchestra was entirely black. The dancers Joe Alex and Louis Douglas were there, working in the music halls. The doorman was discouraging about getting any other kind of work. "Less you can play or tap dance, you'd just as well go home."

It took him more than a month to find a job. He became himself a doorman, at a club on the rue Fontaine, where Josephine Baker would later have her own club. He got five francs a night, at about twelve francs to the dollar, plus food and tips. It wasn't much. Nor did he care for the work. He was part greeter, part bouncer, and the clientele of this place consisted largely of hookers who got into fights. He was happy when he found another job, as dishwasher, backup cook, and waiter at the Grand Duc. Rayford Logan, who had read Hughes's poems in *The Crisis* and to whom Hughes had an introduction, helped him get the job at the Grand Duc. Gene Bullard, the manager, was a friend of his. It was a small world. They said it took two days to get to know every black American in Paris.

Not only did Logan help Hughes get his job, he introduced him to Anne Coussey, an English girl of African descent who was in Paris studying at Raymond Duncan's school for arts and crafts. Anne was beautiful, cultivated, charming. She charmed Hughes into the one heterosexual romance of his life, and although it only lasted a month, it provided the inspiration for a lot of later writing. She was "Mary" of his autobiographical *The Big Sea* and of many poems, including "Fascination" and "Spring for Lovers." The charm of being in love in Paris in the spring was not lost on the poet. He and Anne walked hand in hand through the Luxembourg Gardens and the Tuileries. The romance ended with little anxiety when Anne's father, worried that she would marry a good-for-nothing, demanded she return to London or have her allowance cut off.

Hughes worked from eleven at night to seven in the morning and breakfasted with the musicians on champagne. The Grand Duc was a center for the black musicians of Montmartre: when they finished their work at other cabarets, they gathered at the Grand Duc to eat, drink, and play some more music. Since Hughes worked at night, he wrote during the day, in his garret room (*chambre de bonne*) at 15 rue Nollet. He didn't write as much as usual because he was so happy, but one of the poems he wrote in this period was "Jazz Band in a Parisian Cabaret."

One afternoon, on a raw sunless day in May, the kind of spring day in Paris that so dismays Americans, accustomed to brighter spring skies, he heard a woman enter the Grand Duc, talk to Gene Bullard, and then start to cry. He knew it had to be the woman Bullard had brought over from the States to replace Florence Embry, who had moved down the street to Louis Mitchell's place, which would be renamed Chez Florence. The replacement's name was Ada Smith. She had been a partner of Florence Mills's in a singing-dancing group called the Panama Trio. More recently, she'd been singing solo in nightclubs in Harlem. Florence Embry's husband, Palmer Jones, who had recommended her, said she didn't have much of a voice, but her personality was irresistible, and for a place like the Grand Duc, personality was crucial. Bullard had persuaded her to come to Paris for a salary of $75 a week. She was light-skinned, twenty-nine but looked younger, and she had red hair, which gave her her nickname, Bricktop.

Bricktop was crying partly because she'd just had an eleven-day crossing in which she was constantly seasick, but also because she'd just had her first look at the Grand Duc. The place held twelve tables and there was room for six more people at the bar. She could hardly believe this was the nightclub she had crossed the miserable ocean to work at. She was used to the big and exciting New York clubs, the Cotton Club, Small's Paradise, Connie's Inn. "Do you mean to say this is the whole place?" she asked Bullard. "It's about the size of a booth at Connie's Inn." That was when she burst into tears, and Bullard had no idea how to comfort her, but a handsome young man came running out of the kitchen and said, "You need something to eat."

Langston Hughes took Bricktop into the kitchen, fed her, and assured her she would come to love Paris and the Grand Duc. And so she did. When Josephine Baker came to Paris in 1925, Bricktop, already at home, would be her best friend. She had a quick wit, which served her well for her nightclub repartee as for the business of daily life. She was much more practical and down-to-earth than Baker, less given to fantasy. Warm, solid, stable, competent, she allowed people to turn to her for help, and Baker, among many others, did.

. . .

Harold Stearns, the quintessential expatriate, according to Cowley, believed that only in Europe could an American live fully and richly. He developed this theme with grace and ingenuity in his "Letter from Paris" which he wrote for the society magazine *Town and Country* from 1922 to 1925. He watched young Americans pour into Paris, saw them rise to opportunities, fall to pieces, or remain untouched, leading oddly detached lives, with no responsibilities, in which some found personal happiness and some found nothing at all. He considered Paris "the greatest testing ground of character in the world," all the more bracing and morally provocative because Paris didn't care what you made of your life. "Paris does not reproach the person bent on going to the devil—it shrugs his shoulders and lets him go." Many young Americans, he observed, free from their families and a closely observing society, proved unable to discipline themselves. Sadly, Harold Stearns himself proved to be one of the "morally malnourished" he described whom Paris ruined. He drank and, panhandling in a genteel way, became a "character." His last "Letter from Paris" for *Town and Country* was written in October 1925, just about when Josephine Baker hit Paris and Janet Flanner began to write her enduring "Letter from Paris" for *The New Yorker*. Broke, he eventually borrowed the money to get back to the States, married a wealthy woman, and lived a compulsively scheduled and disciplined life thereafter.

Gertrude Stein, in a book she called *Paris France*, explained with carefully nurtured paradox why Paris, in the early part of the twentieth century, was exactly the right place for an American artist to be. Because innovative artists need a daily life of beauty combined with regularity, the fundamental classicism and conservatism of the French allows an avant-garde to flourish. Stein herself lived placidly in a bourgeois neighborhood. When her dog Basket died, she replaced him with another French poodle who looked just like him and she called this one Basket, too. The king is dead? Long live the king. That is the French way. Tradition: the steady continuity against which violent artistic gestures can be played. Of course, it was nice, too, that the French had such a special respect for artists that her car got a place in the garage while millionaires and politicians had to wait outside.

Jimmie Charters, the barman of the Dingo Bar, a favorite watering place of the Montparnasse artists, had his own explanation for what all these folks were doing in Paris, which he described as "the greatest wild-oats field the world has ever known!" Jimmie was convinced that alcohol was the catalyst in the flowering of Montparnasse in the twenties and, for his memoirs (for such was the self-consciousness of this place at this time that even the barman at the Dingo wrote his memoirs), he got mischievous Marcel Duchamp to back him up: "Liquor was an important factor in stimulating the exchange of ideas between artists." So young Americans gathered at the Dôme, the Coupole, and the Select. The Rotonde, also on the Boulevard Montparnasse, was out of favor because its management had refused to allow an American girl to sit in public without a hat smoking a cigarette. If she couldn't do that, why be in Paris? It was too bad, because the Rotonde got the morning sun and the Select did not, but sacrifices were sometimes necessary for principle!

It's easy to mock the notion of expatriation as escape from a philistine culture by invoking the very different motives of most blacks who left America in the twenties. Did Bricktop leave Connie's Inn for the Grand Duc seeking "cultural renewal"? Did Josephine Baker go to Paris to find new prairies of the mind? This is partly a trick of rhetoric. No Malcolm Cowley has yet dignified the black exodus to France.

James Weldon Johnson said that the moment he set foot in France—it was 1905—he "recaptured for the first time since childhood the sense of being just a human being." "I was suddenly free; free from a sense of impending discomfort, insecurity, danger; . . . free from special scorn, special tolerance, special condescension, special commiseration; free to be merely a man." Years later Richard Wright would say virtually the same thing: that France was the only place he'd found on earth which allowed him the chance to live in "a normal human atmosphere." It was the diminishment, the constant specialization of identity in America, as much as overt discrimination that black Americans hoped to escape. They wanted to go where they could be people, not black people.

Joel Augustus Rogers, a journalist who sent dispatches from Paris to the black Chicago newspaper *The Defender*, compared the American Negro in Europe to a canary released from its cage or a lifer on parole. "No more bars to beat against; they have disappeared as if by magic." Trained either to resist race prejudice or to accede to it, the black American has neither an enemy to fight nor a fetish to bow to, says Rogers, and watches for a sign of discrimination with even a bit of hope—"something that will make him feel at home"—so close to alarming can be the sense of freedom. Many other black Americans who visited Europe before World War II testified to the exhilaration of escaping America's prevailing racial awareness. For them, the historical American pilgrimage route was reversed. The land of opportunity and freedom lay east not west.

Bricktop had been in Paris a year and a half when Josephine Baker arrived, and by that time she was as well-established as Florence Embry had been. For a while, however, the Grand Duc was not small enough. Bricktop kept singing to empty tables while patrons flocked to Florence, down the street. Her luck did not turn until Jack Dean, husband of the movie star Fannie Ward, wandered in one night when it was unpleasantly crowded at Florence's. He was surprised and delighted to see there was another black woman performing in Montmartre. The Wards thought Florence was getting uppity with success and welcomed the chance to stop patronizing her. They filled the little place night after night with their friends from the theater and fashion worlds; Bricktop and the Grand Duc were launched. When the Wards moved off to other discoveries, writers and artists, led by Scott and Zelda Fitzgerald, took their places at the tables of the Grand Duc, which soon became known as Bricktop's.

Bricktop adored Scott Fitzgerald, whom she saw as a boy in a man's body, irresponsible but irresistible. She treated him like a baby, and he treated her like a mother. One night, when he jumped into a fountain near the Champs-Élysées and was arrested by the police, he invoked the name of "Madame Bricktop," and, dripping wet, was deposited by two policeman at her door. She wouldn't let him in because he'd make a puddle on her floor, but put him in a taxi and sent him home. He was back within five minutes. He had kicked out all the windows in the taxi in order to get her to take him home personally.

Bricktop herself didn't understand why she was taken up so strongly by these white compatriots—especially Cole and Linda Porter. Porter wandered into the Grand Duc one slow morning and heard her sing one of his songs. Although he didn't leave, as he sometimes did when people sang his songs in a way he didn't like, he wasn't very interested in her singing. It was late fall or early winter of 1925, after Josephine Baker had brought the Charleston to Paris, and he wanted to know if Bricktop could dance. He was giving Charleston parties two or three times a week at his fabulous house on the rue Monsieur, and he wanted her to teach people the steps of the newest dance rage. She was happy to. Through the Porters and their friend Elsa Maxwell, Bricktop met dozens of important people who wanted to Charleston. Soon she was getting $50 a night plus a $50 tip to do parties—more than her weekly salary—and $10 each for private lessons.

In the summer of 1926 the Porters invited Bricktop to join them in Venice. Ostensibly it was to give more people more Charleston lessons. But Bricktop came to think that the real reason for Porter's interest in her was his shyness. He got along with people with the help of his impeccable manners. But he envied (or so Bricktop thought) her easy camaraderie, her spontaneity in conversation, her ability to express her own personality informally, authentically. He fantasized a person he could not be and called it Bricktop.

In 1925, just a few months before Josephine Baker arrived in Paris, a young black woman named Gwendolyn Bennett went there to study art. Bennett had published some poems in *Opportunity* and taught art at Howard University, from which she had a one-year leave of absence. With a fellowship of a thousand dollars from a sorority and no other income, she would be living on $83 a month, less than half what A. J. Liebling or Flora Mayo had, 8.3 percent of Josephine Baker's salary from the Revue Nègre. She approached Paris with suspicion and timidity. That and her poverty shaped her reaction to Paris. This was Sin City. Robbery and rape would not have surprised her. On her first day in Paris, June 25, 1925, the hotel clerk sent a male visitor directly up to her room. She was shocked.

Whereas at home it had been a lovely spring, in Paris it was raining, "a cold rain that eats into the very marrow of the bone, . . . and I am more alone and homesick than I ever believed it possible to be." She had a lunch date, but the taxi took her to the wrong Hotel d'Angleterre and she missed it. At night, she went to the movies, but she got lost and panic-stricken returning to her hotel room. In the dark, all the horrible things she had heard about Paris came to mind. She was afraid of men attacking her. She had no umbrella and no coat, except the jacket of her suit.

The next day she gave herself the task of finding Anne Coussey, who was back in Paris and whom Langston Hughes had told her to contact. Walking on the Boulevard St.-Michel, she saw "a young nice-looking colored girl." They caught each other's eyes. "Are you from America?" asked the other. "Yes." "You're not by any chance Gwendolyn Bennett?" It was Anne, which gives some idea of how few "young nice-looking colored girls" must have been walking around Paris. Taking an immediate liking to each other, they walked to the Boulevard Montparnasse and had tea at the Rotonde. They watched artists hiring models. Anne introduced Gwendolyn Bennett to Gwendolyn Sinclair, who was studying fashion drawing. The two Gwendolyns talked of getting a studio together.

Gradually she began to have friends, almost all of them black Americans abroad. She went shopping with Alston Burleigh and his father, the famous composer and arranger of spirituals, Harry T. Burleigh. She took them to the Magasins du Louvre to buy velvet trousers, which all the artists in Montparnasse were wearing then. After a month, she had settled in, but she was "infinitely weary of hearing so much French and understanding so little." The Fourth of July made her particularly homesick. "All day long I did not see or speak to a single one of my compatriots, nor did I hear a word of English spoken." She noted the growth in herself of a "strange new patriotism" because of her stay in France. "There are times when I'd give half my remaining years to hear the Star-Spangled Banner played. And yet even as I feel that way I know it has nothing to do with the same 'home' feeling I have when I see crowds of American white people jostling each other about the American Express."

Like other black Americans in Paris, Bennett regarded white Americans as not quite compatriots and, with reason, was wary of them. White American tourists frequently did not scruple to object to the presence of blacks in Paris hotels and restaurants, and although the hotels and restaurants sometimes stood up for their black patrons, sometimes they bowed to the pressure. One day Bennett was dancing at the Acacias, a popular *thé dansant* near the Bois de Boulogne. It was a chic place that made her feel like "a dream-girl in a land of dreams." She was dancing with Louis Jones, a musician at Florence's whom she had started going out with. He was a splendid dancer and had taught her to tango. They looked good together on the dance floor of the Acacias, and she was happy until she heard some white Americans commenting on their "native rhythm." Her comfort then was to think how it must gall them to see her and Louis "on a par with them" at the Acacias.

One Thursday, August 6, 1925, Gwendolyn and eleven of her friends had a celebration, the kind of night Paris in the twenties was famous for. It began with late dinner at a Chinese restaurant on the rue de l'École-de-Médecine. It was eleven-thirty, late even by Paris standards. At a quarter to two they went to the Royal in Montmartre for champagne, smoking, and dancing. When Louis finished work at Florence's he joined them there and danced with Gwendolyn. At four-fifteen they moved on to Bricktop's. The Grand Duc was particularly crowded that night with American blacks. Lottie Gee, the star of *Shuffle Along*, was there and sang "I'm Just Wild About Harry." She'd had too much champagne for top-notch singing but there was something very sweet and personal about her singing that song, said Bennett, "and we colored folks just applauded like mad." Bricktop sang "Insufficient Sweetie" and "I'm in Love Again" and teased Louis about

Gwendolyn. They ate hotcakes and sausages at the Grand Duc and got home at six-thirty, when the sun was barely up and they could admire the lovely gray light of the morning sky.

Bennett lived a bohemian life in Paris, but not a carefree one. She felt keenly how much her poverty was keeping her from. Also, she came to France with a burden of anxiety, and she went home with it. Back in the States, she gave a typewritten page of advice to a friend who was going to Paris. She gave her a list of hotels and warned against taking a room in Montmartre. Eat only *prix fixe* meals, she advised, not à la carte. The Café du Dôme is the artists' hangout, but "beware of adventurers and adventuresses." "Do not call on anyone who is not recommended. Don't display a lot of money or tell anyone where your bank is. Give ten per cent on the bill for a tip but never less than fifty centimes in a first class restaurant." When Bennett got back to the States, she moved from Washington, D.C., to Harlem, wrote poetry, taught art, had a hard and interesting life, and is remembered as a minor figure in the Harlem Renaissance.

Her Paris was not the Paris of the Fitzgeralds, Gertrude Stein, and Hemingway, although the two cities touched at some points: Bricktop's and Florence's in Montmartre, the Rotonde and the Dôme in Montparnasse, the Acacias near the Bois, Shakespeare and Company, the bookstore and expatriate gathering place in St.-Germain, where Gwendolyn Bennett bought a copy of *Ulysses* from Sylvia Beach, who had Bennett and Paul Robeson for Thanksgiving dinner in 1925.

When Josephine Baker came to Paris with the Revue Nègre, Bennett went to see her perform. But she meant something different to her from what she meant to the white Americans like Fitzgerald's Charlie Wales, who distantly admired her "chocolate arabesques." Bennett was proud of her, as she was proud of the black musicians of Montmartre, because they were so good and they were hers.

Will Marion Cook also caught the Revue Nègre in Paris, and he hated it for different reasons from those who saw it as an attack by black culture on the supremacy of white. "With Europe begging us for a Negro novelty, first Arthur Lyons took that awful 'Chocolate Kiddies' to Berlin—and now this Paris abortion." Exempting Josephine Baker and a couple of other performers, he blamed the disaster on

Caroline Dudley, who, he said, knew nothing about genuine black culture. He lumped the revue with *Shuffle Along, Runnin' Wild, The Chocolate Dandies,* and *Dixie to Broadway,* which were all equally betrayals of real black culture, "all rank and weak imitations of sordid, unfunny white plays." "The prostituting of Negro talent by encouraging imitation of all that is weak, low, and vicious must stop. Let Broadway wallow in its own filth! . . . From now on let's have the real thing!"

The vitality of Harlem spread to Paris and was fed by Paris. Other figures of the Harlem Renaissance who spent significant amounts of time in twenties Paris were Jean Toomer, Jessie Fauset, and Walter White. Alain Locke, the Howard University philosophy professor who, by editing the book *The New Negro,* popularized the idea that there was, in fact, a black American cultural flowering in progress, visited Langston Hughes in Paris to collect some poems, although he, like Du Bois, was more at home in Germany. But the real renaissance in Harlem was taking place in Small's Paradise, Connie's Inn, and the Cotton Club, and the real innovators and cultural giants were Duke Ellington, Louis Armstrong, and Fats Waller. Not only was jazz the best thing in black cultural life in the twenties; jazz may have been the best thing happening in American culture. From the point of view of most informed Europeans, it *was* American culture. When Europeans thought of America, they thought of black musicians, black singers, and black dancers—certainly not of Hemingway, Fitzgerald, and Stein, who lived in their midst without affecting them. Until the twenties, as far as the rest of the world was concerned, with a few picturesque exceptions like Buffalo Bill and Mark Twain, America had no culture. When it finally turned a face to Europe, that face was black.

CHAPTER 3
TOP BANANA

The Revue Nègre was a sensation, and Baker was amused by all the fuss. She read her press clippings. In fact, she used them to learn French. She was too smart not to realize how high-flown the prose was and how far from reality. Primitive instinct? Madness of the flesh? Tumult of the senses? "The white imagination sure is something," she said, "when it comes to blacks." They thought she was from the jungle. She knew very well she was from St. Louis. She went to parties all over Paris with Caroline Dudley or Paul Colin, and to ward off the feeling that she was on display, like a circus animal, she put on her most fashionable dress, then spent the evening as near as she could to the food.

Soon after the opening of the Revue Nègre, she got an offer to join the Folies-Bergère in the following season as the star of a new show. She went to the current show, *Un Soir de Folie*, and liked what she saw. She was pleased there were some black dancers, and asking that they all be kept on for the next show, she accepted the Folies-Bergère's offer. This meant disregarding an obligation to Caroline Dudley.

After its run at the Théâtre des Champs-Élysées had been extended twice, the Revue Nègre moved in late November to the smaller Théâtre de l'Étoile on the avenue des Champs-Élysées, where it ran through December. After that, Caroline Dudley had planned to tour Europe as far as Moscow. But the new Folies-Bergère revue was scheduled to open in April, and Baker had to be back before that for fittings and rehearsals. So the European tour of the Revue Nègre consisted only of Brussels and Berlin.

Dudley, who claimed she lost money on the show because of Baker's defection, said, "Josephine, you will hurt your soul." Bitter not to have been consulted about the offer from the Folies-Bergère, she warned her that if she went to the Folies she'd amount to nothing more than a feathered mannequin. Baker replied, "Missus, I'm feeling fine."

For the first time in her life, money was being showered on her. Who knew how long it would last? Moreover, she already had developed such a strong sensitivity to exploitation that now, and for the rest of her life, she could not see a contract as anything but an attempt on the part of a powerful organization to bind a weaker individual to disadvantageous terms. This meant that she was not very cautious about what she agreed to, and not cautious at all about breaking her word. In the first of what would prove to be a string of lawsuits which Josephine's fast-and-loose attitude provoked, Caroline Dudley sued her for breach of contract.

According to Bricktop, Josephine was too young to handle her sudden stardom. Realizing she was in over her head, she turned to Bricktop, who was ten years older. "She wouldn't go around the corner without asking my advice." She was always dropping in at the Grand

Duc and saying, "Bricky, tell me what to do." She was badly educated, barely able to sign her own name. Bricktop sensibly advised her to get a rubber stamp made for autographs.

She didn't have much trouble deciding to stay in Paris. She had never been so happy. She stood in front of the mirror in the apartment she now shared with Maud de Forest looking at her body. Before, people had told her it was too dark or too light, too skinny or too short. In Paris, everyone was wild about it. She had one admirer who was not only French but an artist, who drew her over and over again. For the first time in her life, she felt beautiful.

Thus, when the Revue Nègre left the Gare St. Lazare in the winter of 1926, Josephine had a feeling she'd never had before. She was sorry to leave.

Berlin at that time was easily as exciting as Paris, a super-metropolis where gifted and ambitious people gathered from all over Europe. The ruinous inflation of the early twenties was over, leaving behind a heritage of recklessness. People who had seen their savings wiped out by inflation, now that they were making money again, had no inclination to save it. New factories, schools, and theaters were being built—some designed by the brilliant architects of the Bauhaus, including Ludwig Mies van der Rohe and Walter Gropius. There were three opera houses open ten months a year supported by the city of Berlin and the state of Prussia. Alban Berg's *Wozzeck* had premiered at the State Opera Unter den Linden in 1925. Bertolt Brecht had come in from Bavaria and was working on *The Threepenny Opera*. Stage designers came from Greece, conductors from Poland, publishers from Russia, playwrights from Budapest, composers from Spain and Italy, pianists from Latvia and Switzerland. Lavish musicals came from Vienna, Budapest, and even America. *The Chocolate Kiddies Revue*, the black show Will Marion Cook detested, had preceded the Revue Nègre from New York. With it came a good jazz band, led by Sam Wooding.

Theater in Berlin was particularly vital. Erwin Piscator was putting on his strange productions at the Volksbühne, a theater founded and maintained by Berlin's labor unions. Tickets were all one price and people drew their seats from a jar as they entered. Half the audience were students and workers and half people who had been driven there by chauffeurs. Max Reinhardt was running four theaters, including the Deutsches Theater, where he did innovative productions of Shakespeare, and the Grosses Schauspielhaus, a cross between Madison Square Garden and St. Patrick's Cathedral.

In one of the revues on the Kurfürstendamm, Marlene Dietrich was lying on her back and doing bicycles in the air with her gorgeous legs. The nightclubs of Berlin were famous—Cabaret of the Comedians, Kata Kombe, the Blue Angel, Sound and Smoke, Megalomania—as were its homosexual and lesbian cafés. Sexually, Berlin was a much wilder city than Paris. Homosexuality was totally in order. Booted prostitutes of both sexes abounded. Both cities were cheap for foreigners, but because of the sexual climate the less adventurous Americans tended to go to Paris whereas the English preferred Berlin.

If Max Reinhardt had had his way, Josephine Baker would have become another of the out-of-towners absorbed by the dazzling city who helped make it even more dazzling.

One night she was told that the most famous director in Germany was in the audience. She was inured to these superlatives. Everyone she met was "the greatest this" and "the most distinguished that" and "the best-known other"—and perhaps they were, in their countries. But she had already seen enough to be unimpressed by local celebrities, or at least to know how local celebrity was. "Fame is a ladder with many rungs," she said, "and there is one for each of us. Back in St. Louis, everyone knew Mrs. Nichols's cat because one of its ears had been ripped off by a dog!"

Usually she said, "Everyone tells me you're the most famous writer (or painter or journalist or director, or the most beautiful woman) in the city," for she saw how well people responded to this treatment. But when she was introduced to Reinhardt, she knew that he really was special. Moreover, he didn't give her time to produce her standard line. He asked her to stay in Germany and let him train her at the Deutsches Theater. He would turn her into a great actress.

Reinhardt had seen *Shuffle Along* on a visit to New York in 1924 and been convinced that black vaudeville could help renew European drama. Even though in shows like *Shuffle Along* it was prostituted to farce, the body language, especially of the black comedians, was a revelation to him. Now he tried to explain to Josephine why her talents were important.

"The expressive control of the whole body, the spontaneity of motion, the rhythm, the bright emotional color. These are your treasures—no, not yours only—these are American treasures. With such control of the body, such pantomime, I believe I could portray emotion as it has never been portrayed."

Josephine didn't take the offer seriously at first, but she was flattered by it and took to Reinhardt as immediately as he did to her. She noticed his intensity, the way certain gifted people have of bringing all their attention to bear on you, as though nothing else, for the moment they were talking to you, existed. She loved his articulateness. Nobody had ever spoken to her as he did about the theater or taken her so seriously or understood so well what she was doing. Caroline Dudley's warning rankled. "Feathered mannequin?" Never amount to anything? Not if she were an actress trained by Max Reinhardt.

She began hanging around after the performances with the director and his friends, including Karl Gustav Vollmoeller. Vollmoeller was a well-known playwright, whose *Achtes Wunder der Jungfrau Maria* (translated as *The Miracle*), directed by Reinhardt, was a hit in Britain and America as well as Germany and made a star of Lady Diana Cooper. He lived a bohemian life, giving parties which were known for their surprising mixes of people. His mistress was young Fräulein Landshoff, who liked to wear men's clothes.

Through Vollmoeller, she met Count Harry Kessler, a diplomat, art collector, publisher, biographer, and inspired diarist. He knew everyone from Einstein to the Kaiser, and wrote about them all. His father had been ennobled for making a fortune as a banker, and he was called the "Red Count."

At one in the morning in February 1926, Max Reinhardt called Harry Kessler, who had just closed the door on the last of his dinner guests, and asked him to come over to Vollmoeller's place on the Pariser Platz. Josephine Baker was there and the fun was just starting.

Kessler had already seen the Revue Nègre, and loved its tautness, the
tension between its "ultramodern and ultraprimitive" qualities. In comparison, German works seemed to him to hang like a limp bowstring.
He was eager to meet Miss Baker.

He arrived at Vollmoeller's to find his host surrounded by naked
women. Baker, wearing only a pink apron, was dancing a solo with
what seemed to Kessler brilliant mimicry and purity of style, doing
an intricate series of improvisations on a basic pattern. He was told
that she did this for hours, without getting tired, continually inventing
new figures like a happy child at play. He noted that she did not seem
to get hot or perspire, and he found her bewitching but unerotic.
"Watching her inspires as little sexual excitement as does the sight of
a beautiful beast of prey." But nonetheless, something in the situation—perhaps the men in dinner jackets surrounded by naked women
—threw him into a reverie about masters and slaves. Baker seemed
to him an ancient Egyptian dancing girl come to life again, and he
felt as he imagined Solomon or Tutankhamen must have felt looking
at their dancers.

By now Baker's dance had brought her into the arms of Miss
Landshoff, who was dressed in a tuxedo, and Kessler was getting the
idea for a pantomime or ballet based on his fantasy. It would feature
Miss Landshoff and Baker as Solomon and his Shulamite, the Shulamite dressed (or not dressed) in ancient style and Solomon dressed
in a dinner jacket, the whole to be set to music "half jazz and half
Oriental, to be composed perhaps by Richard Strauss." Kessler was
not the sort of man to have an idea like that without acting on it, so
ten days later he gave a party at his place to discuss the project further.

When the evening performance of the Revue Nègre was over,
Kessler sent Miss Landshoff and a gentleman to pick Baker up at the
theater. He expected that she would dance for his dinner guests and
a few other people he'd invited—many gentlemen and a few ladies.
It was a formal group, not like the irregular gatherings at Vollmoeller's;
nor was his splendidly appointed home anything like Vollmoeller's
bohemian digs. He had an art collection, of which his current favorite
piece was Maillol's sculpture *Crouching Woman*. This was in the library,
which he had otherwise cleared so Baker would have room to dance.

But when Baker arrived she didn't feel like dancing. She sat in the corner, saying she was embarrassed to appear nude in front of ladies at such close quarters. Kessler did not press her. With exquisite tact he described instead the first scene of the ballet he imagined for her about Solomon and the Shulamite. His plans had become more ambitious, and now he envisaged Serge Lifar as Solomon and Baker as the dancer he buys and showers with gifts. The more he gives her, the more she eludes him. He grows daily more naked and the dancer grows harder and harder to see. At the end, she disappears in a tulip-shaped golden-colored cloud composed of all the jewels and rich fabrics he has given her.

Josephine, who loved fairy tales, listened enthralled. She had felt extremely unhappy when she arrived at Kessler's house and discovered a party of elegantly dressed men and women waiting for her to dance. She had been expecting something more like Vollmoeller's lunatic and déclassé establishment. She was intimidated by Kessler's gorgeous rooms and his works of art and the fact that he was a count. And she was tired of being expected to entertain people. There was not much she could do to redress the balance of advantage between these people and her except refuse to dance. Then, to her astonishment, the count told a beautiful story about someone just like her, a dancer for a king, whom the king showered with gorgeous presents. She was given more and more jewels, more and more clothes, while the king lost everything he had to her. This was the kind of story she liked. She cheered right up, undressed, and started dancing.

She danced in front of Maillol's *Crouching Woman* without at first seeing it. When she got into a rhythm, she noticed the sculpture. She stared at it, copied and then parodied its pose. It became the theme for her dance. She talked to it. She seemed to savor its shape and its monumentality. She pretended it was an idol and worshipped it. Then she made fun of herself as priestess and the statue as goddess.

Had she thought about it in advance, she could have paid Kessler no greater compliment than to dance to his sculpture. He thought it appropriate that the sculpture should be more real and interesting to her than himself and his friends. Genius, as he saw it, was addressing genius.

Josephine began to feel comfortable with her new German friends. Another time at Vollmoeller's, she sat on a sofa all night and ate sausages, pretending they were hot dogs. In some ways she liked Berlin more than Paris. The lights were brighter and denser at night, the great cafés with their lights blazing looked like ocean liners in the dark, and people were looser. She didn't have to worry all the time if her clothes were perfect or if she was doing something ridiculous, like eating the shells of the *crevettes* when she was supposed to peel them off. Here they didn't care. They were kinkier. Aberrance amused them. The Folies-Bergère seemed very far away.

It is extraordinary how important an institution can be if you are a member of it and how unimportant if you are not. The Folies-Bergère was a great Parisian institution, but Josephine Baker was not particularly impressed by it until she became a part of it. The authority of its director, Paul Derval, immense inside the Folies and the Parisian show business community, meant nothing to her yet. She began to think of accepting Reinhardt's offer to stay in Berlin and work with him.

One night at a party, she met a Frenchman who said he was looking forward to seeing her in the Folies-Bergère. She replied, "Don't count on it." The Frenchman, who knew Paul Derval, immediately reported back to him that his star might have changed her mind. This was horrifying news to Derval, who had already commissioned a show built around her. The producer, Louis Lemarchand, had already hired designers, including Georges Barbier and Erté. The costumes were being sketched by Max Weldy. The sets were in the works, and music had been commissioned from a half dozen songwriters, including Spencer Williams and Irving Berlin. In those days a Folies shows was no flimsy affair. It took months to prepare and involved hundreds of people. Derval sent an agent to Berlin as quickly as possible to speak to Baker. He tried to impress upon her the grandeur of the enterprise with which she would be involved and the enormous number of people she'd be letting down if she didn't appear. Did she realize each show took three months to rehearse and involved three hundred people and twelve hundred costumes? Did she realize how many people had already been hired? Did she understand that music had been com-missioned from Spencer Williams and Irving Berlin?

Baker later said that at last Derval's agent had hit names that meant something to her. Spencer Williams! Irving Berlin! "It didn't take long to make up my mind," she wrote. "Herr Reinhardt hadn't men-tioned Irving Berlin." There may be more truth in this story than at first appears. Her thoughts raced ahead and she often made up her mind on the basis of such seemingly by-the-by details. Irving Berlin meant music, which meant jazz, which meant such pleasures as Sidney Bechet on the clarinet, such as herself dancing. What would it feel like never to dance onstage to great music again? This was a small, decisive moment. She would go back to Paris not to be a "feathered mannequin" but to dance—to be, in however strangely packaged a fashion, what she chose to make of herself, and not what a German director could make of her.

However, she could not help but notice that the situation had some advantages for her. Both her account of this incident and Der-val's agree that she got him to pay an extra four hundred francs per performance before she agreed to return to Paris. He had already invested so much money in the show that he had to give her whatever she asked. It came to another hundred dollars a week. Baker was candid about her greed: if he needed her so much, why not make him pay? She could remember what it had been like to be poor, and she could never get enough to make her feel safe from returning to that poverty.

Everybody seemed to want to use her. Artists wanted to use her for their art, entrepreneurs wanted to use her to make money, more ordinary men wanted to use her to make love to. A hard core of sense in her recognized that however fervent her admirers were, in some way they all wanted to exploit her, and so it seemed only fair that she should be able to exploit them in return. From this wary perspective, Max Reinhardt was little different from Paul Derval, and neither were that different from the young men who came backstage begging her to go out with them. Once, in Paris, she had simply snatched a thou-sand-franc note from the hand of such a young man—not a particularly rich one—as he was going to pay the bill for their drinks. When he looked startled, she'd told him that if he wanted to go out with actresses, he would have to pay the price. Many years later she remembered this as an instance of racial revenge—revenge for what his ancestors had done to hers. Her determination not to be taken advantage of was connected to an awareness of the oppression of her race—in practice, a racial touchiness. If these Solomons wanted their Shulamite, they would have to pay.

If *Shuffle Along* was Josephine Baker's college, the Folies-Bergère was her graduate school. Here she learned the art of illusion, from masters. Here she learned what she owed her audience in taking up the role of "star."

Look for the Folies-Bergère in a contemporary guide to entertainment in Paris like *Pariscope*, and you will find it listed under "Erotic Spectacles." This was not always the case. It used to be considered a music hall, and Folies shows were reviewed by music-hall critics, a respected subspecies of drama critics. Founded in 1869, the Folies-Bergère was the first of the Paris music halls, as it is still the most famous outside of France. Others are the Casino de Paris and the Moulin Rouge.

What goes on on the stage of a music hall is *le music-hall* (that is the French word, spelled with a hyphen), stage entertainment of varying kinds: comic acts, singers, acrobats, dancers. The American equivalent would be vaudeville. Music-hall entertainment was born in London in the nineteenth century, but it developed into something peculiarly French and remained popular in France long after it had been driven under by the movies and television in other countries. Some of the most beloved French stars of all time were stars of the music hall: Maurice Chevalier, Mistinguett, Yves Montand, Arletty, Edith Piaf, Georges Brassens, and Yvette Guilbert, in addition to Josephine Baker. They may have gone on to theater or film, but their beginnings were music-hall.

Rapport with the audience was always the key to their success. Music-hall performers made a personal appeal for love, and if they were successful they were loved like members of the family, so that once they were stars, they were stars for life. They endured, they continued, and their audiences stayed with them, amazed at how gracefully they grew old and how far back they went together. If they were clever, like Maurice Chevalier, they didn't try to hide their age but rather flaunted it and played with it.

Personality counted at least as much as talent in this business. Mistinguett, the other great star besides Chevalier and Baker of the period between the wars, had neither an outstanding voice nor great dancing ability; nor was she particularly beautiful. But when she came onstage, she electrified the audience. "She was Parisian in tone, elegance, and allure. No one knew better than she how to wear those feather gowns and headdresses or how to maintain, under that stupefying headgear, the smiling ease and good humor which made her whole audience happy." She had wit, charm, vivacity, versatility— qualities much admired in Paris, qualities which in a sense *were* Paris. Indeed, it seems to me that Mistinguett and the other greats of the music hall, including Baker, occupied a special place in the national consciousness: wherever they came from, they were seen as embodying the spirit of Paris, putting the best face on things—and the best leg. They were a national heroic type, like the cowboy for Americans, but, unlike him, embodying the urban virtues of sociability and panache. One of Mistinguett's headdresses weighed more than fifteen pounds. (Imagine her carrying three five-pound sacks of potatoes on her head.) Another of her favorite costumes had a twenty-one-foot ostrich-feather train. It was not just a question of being plucky. That might be the spirit of London. The trick was to look plucky and gay under that ridiculous burden, the feathered glory of civilization.

In the late nineteenth century, the Folies-Bergère featured great artists like Yvette Guilbert and great beauties like La Belle Otéro and Liane de Pougy, along with wrestlers, singers, mimes, and acrobats, but the nude tableaux over the years became more and more the focus of the spectacle. Nudity on the Parisian music-hall stage began in the nineteenth century with an annual contest of artists' models, which developed into the Quatz' Arts Ball, an annual dress-up and undress night involving artists and art students. This once-a-year saturnalia found its way with astonishing rapidity into the mainstream, so that female nudity—above the waist—became a Parisian tradition. In March 1894 a small music hall on the rue des Martyrs presented a skit called "Yvette Goes to Bed," which created a vogue for gradual onstage disrobing. "Suzette and the Heat Wave," "The Maid's Bath," and "Liane at the Doctor's" quickly followed. Angèle Hérard packed them into the Casino de Paris with a vulgar piece called "The Flea," in which she examined her own body for the source of her itch. She took this immensely popular piece on tour throughout Europe, going further in some places than others. In Berlin she could remove her corsets, but not in Vienna. In Munich she could scratch her knee but not in Budapest.

On the stage of the Folies-Bergère, nudes—that is, bare-breasted women—first appeared in 1894. They always wore bikini pants or, at the very least, a G-string. A prefect of the police had to preview each show to make sure it didn't go beyond the bounds of decency. Still, the Folies were fairly vulgar at the turn of the century, and the lobby of the Folies-Bergère was one of the most active cruising grounds in Paris. The audience walked in and out of the theater—often coming in hours late, often leaving hours early, and moving around quite a bit in between. They could pick up prostitutes in the lobby on the way out. Things were later cleaned up considerably, but nonetheless, by 1918, the tableaux of nude girls had become the principal box-office draw and the variety acts secondary. For true fans of le music-hall, the emphasis has always been the other way around, and the nudes continually provoke resentment from the connoisseurs as a vulgar intrusion into a great native art form.

The Parisian intelligentsia had been interested in the life of the music halls since Toulouse-Lautrec frequented them and drew what he saw. He saw cancan dancers and the ancestor of the music hall, the café concert, where singers stood and performed in the middle of a group of people drinking at tables. After World War I, there was a resurgence of interest in music-hall life on the part of intellectuals looking to popular culture to reinvigorate high art. Jean Cocteau, a notable proponent of this view, saw the music-hall, the circus, and jazz as the most fertilizing contemporary influences on art, music, literature. To prove his point, he incorporated various images from popular culture into *Parade*. In the same spirit—whose effect after all these years seems more academic than it does vigorous—he made one of the characters in his 1920 collaboration with Darius Milhaud, *Le Boeuf sur le toit*, a black American boxer, and the whole piece was set in an American speakeasy.

One of Cocteau's favorite music-hall acts was the acrobat Barbette, who performed at the Casino de Paris in 1920 and the Alhambra in 1923 and continued to perform in Paris for years with great success. Barbette came onstage elaborately gowned in a metallic dress and feathers. Stripping that off, she climbed onto a trapeze and performed various acrobatic feats almost nude. Having wowed the audience with her gymnastic skill, Barbette, taking her bows, suddenly reached up and snatched off a wig to reveal that she was in fact a man. It was the kind of androgynous act the twenties loved, and no one loved it more than Cocteau. Barbette, in reality a Texan named Van Der Clyde, became one of his close friends.

Not content to be amused, the French, an intellectual people, philosophize about their amusements. Which is more vital, the music-hall or the theater? Which is the art form of the future? These were questions which engaged many fine and some not so fine minds, including some who considered film as a possible competitor to the music-hall—but rejected it. In the fifties, Roland Barthes wrote an appreciation of the music-hall aesthetic, participating in a conversation that stretched back over thirty years. Colette is another who wrote notably, although not theoretically, about the music-hall, in her novel *The Vagabond* (1910), which is based on her own experiences on the music-hall stage, and in "Backstage at the Music Hall" (1913). Her music-hall experience was one of her bonds with Josephine Baker, and when they met, Colette asked Baker whether there was an English chorus girl at the Folies who spent her backstage time knitting for her baby. "Yes, do you know her?" asked Baker. "There is always one," replied Colette, student of enduring types of femininity.

To Cocteau and many others, the music-hall appeared a serious formal alternative to theater, offering liberation from stale theatrical formulas. Theater dealt eternally and tediously with love. Music-hall

treated everything. Theater was limited by text and text by the traditional development in three acts, whereas music-hall lived without
structure from moment to moment, act to act. E. E. Cummings,
another music-hall enthusiast, called it "plotless drama." The most
extreme devotees of music-hall seemed to feel that it was life itself,
whereas drama was just a diminished stylization of life.

Less sophisticated theorists glorified music-hall escapism, sometimes
by calling it realism. "The whole world is at our disposition: Hawaii
with its nostalgic guitarists, the Orient with its jugglers and disturbing
balancing acts, America with its eccentrics, its dancing girls and its
dancers, India with its charmers and magicians. The limits of the
possible are pushed back." In the days before film and television, access
to the world—even in this shallow and stereotyped fashion (the snake
charmers of India, Hawaiian guitarists)—came in some strange ways,
from institutions like department stores and music halls.

The Paris music-hall was entering its golden age in the twenties. It
offered visions of a wider world that were still at least minimally
convincing. It had full command of resources that would later go into
movies and television. The sets had become lavish, the costumes were
frequently as well made as clothes by the great couturiers, and the
entertainment was better for the influence of jazz, which took the
emphasis of music-hall performance away from singing and static display of the body and put it on dancing. "The voice has to be in the
legs today," as one student of the genre put it. Many people had their
first electrifying view of jazz dancing in 1918, when Gaby Deslys
danced with Harry Pilcer on the stage of the Casino de Paris. She had
come back from America the year before with her hair bleached, with
body paint for the nudes, with her American dance partner, and with
a jazz band. Benefiting from their Americanization and from new
money, music-hall productions of the twenties were as elaborate and
inventive as they would ever be. The people who thought that music-
hall was the great art form of the future saw the form at its height
and thought it was just the beginning.

Today the Folies-Bergère plays to half-empty houses. It is best appreciated as one of the last places to catch a real vaudeville show, a museum of entertainment. The night I went, the first act consisted of a woman who made her trained French poodles jump through hoops. It was far from the least amusing act of the evening. The nudes, who are by no means nude, stand like statutes and display their bodies, which are by no means perfect. The Folies-Bergère is in this respect, and this respect only, shocking. Americans are accustomed to a harsher ideal. The Folies believes in a range of ages—something for everyone. It is also heterodox about color. The star of the Folies when I saw it was Lisette Malidor, a statuesque black woman who had been the Folies star for fourteen years.

The Folies-Bergère remains devoted to an ideal of glamour constructed of feathers, sequins, and rhinestones, which has become terrifically out of date. Hipper "erotic spectacles" run to leather and rubber. But never mind. The Folies keeps on fulfilling the ancient functions of music-hall—to entertain, to show another world ("Love in Hungary" was the climactic number the night I went), to dazzle with splash and color. It carries on this way as though it were not possible, any night of the week, to see more distant places and more amazing feats on television in even the most isolated French hamlet.

Paul Derval, the director of the Folies-Bergère, was a forty-six-year-old former stagehand and vaudeville actor who had taken over in 1919 and made the Folies a household word the world over, a synonym for naughtiness. In fact, the secret of his success was to pasteurize the naughtiness. One of the first things he did was to put an end to the Folies as a cruising ground, banning hookers from the theater. Then he conceived the dream of outwitting prudishness and spreading female nudity to the masses. His brilliant solution was to treat the female nude as an art object, not an erotic one. He recognized he could get the audience off the defensive through the right sequencing. "A gradual buildup and perfect timing are needed for the proper display of the nude female figure," he wrote. Before the first nude of the evening was brought on, the audience had to be thoroughly warmed up, relaxed and at home.

The star, or *vedette* was to the Folies what the anchorman is to the evening news: the kingpin on whom everything depended. Derval believed that the star set the whole mood of an evening at the moment of her entrance. She could make or break the show by what she was able or unable to communicate to an audience as soon as she looked at it and they looked at her. Her business was to win them over by her personality and bubbling vitality. Yvonne Menard, one of Derval's favorite stars, used to get four men from the audience up on the stage as soon as possible to ride wooden horses. This was her icebreaker. Physical contact with the audience, getting them to touch each other or to touch the people onstage, breaking down in any way the psychological barrier between performers and spectators, was the best way to warm them up. (Passing flowers from stage to audience was a trick of Josephine Baker's.) Breaking down that barrier—warming up the audience—was the star's business. So "star" is a job description as much as it is an honorific.

Derval was in charge of a formidable organization, with a staff the size of the faculty at a respectably large university. There were musicians, machinists, wardrobe people, dressers, prop assistants, electricians, embroiderers and beaders, milliners, jewelers, specialists in feather headdresses, fans, and trains, carpenters, scene painters, metalworkers, ticket sellers, ushers, administrators. To make a feathered costume took four dressmakers more than a week. The beading for a typically elaborate dress, done by hand, took a specialist two days. The fabric required for the costumes of any revue stretched five hundred kilometers, the distance from Paris to Lyon, New York to Boston. The support crew numbered in the hundreds. To say nothing of the performers onstage. There was the star, who had to be a dancer, sixteen show girls (who didn't have to dance), ten chorus boys, and sixteen nudes (at least two of whom had to dance); there was also the chorus line of dancers, traditionally English, who lived a different life from the others and even had their own Anglican clergyman. In his career at the Folies-Bergère, this devotee of illusion, who aspired to give his audiences "three enchanting hours of fantasy and beauty and fun, an evening's escape into the land of dream-fulfillment," would put on thirty shows. He was superstitious about the shows' names: each had to have the word *folie* ("madness," "folly") in the title, and each title had to consist of exactly thirteen letters. His early show *Coeurs en Folie* featured nudes swimming in a glass pool onstage. He half drowned in his bathtub testing underwater techniques. His was an extraordinary devotion to craft.

The show in which Josephine Baker made her debut as star was called *La Folie du Jour*. It opened with a series of tableaux about Paris shopwindows. Eight girls representing Americans in Paris arrive on-stage scantily dressed. Before them is paraded the wealth of Paris: clothing and luxury goods of all sorts. In a reverse strip, they leave much better dressed than when they arrived. This skit went on for forty minutes and presumably served to reassure the audience, according to Derval's theory, about the nudity to follow. It also served as thematic introduction to a show which for all its frivolity was remarkably coherent, juxtaposing images of civilization at its most contrived with images of civilization's radiant opposite, Josephine Baker.

She made her entrance through an electric twilight walking backward on her hands and feet, arms and legs stiff, along the thick limb of a painted jungle tree and down the trunk, like a monkey. A white explorer was sleeping underneath by the side of a river. Barely dressed black men sang softly and played their drums. She was wearing nothing but a little skirt of plush bananas. It was the outfit she would be identified with virtually for the rest of her life, a witty thing in itself and wittier still when Baker started dancing and set the bananas in jiggling motion, like perky, good-natured phalluses. She came onstage laughing, laughing at everything. She seemed to be everywhere. She danced, miming sex. She offered herself, withdrew the offer, offered again, drew back again and burst into laughter. Morose people came to life. "O magic, O joy, absent till that moment," said one man in the audience. She shook and shimmied. It was her savage dance from the Revue Nègre done solo and in the setting which the designers of the Folies-Bergère thought appropriate: the African jungle which men had merely dreamed of while Baker danced onstage at the Champs-Élysées Theater.

Some people thought it changed the effect to have the underlying fantasy brought to the surface in this way. It was perhaps too obvious.

Baker had looked different when she really was surrounded by other blacks and not, as on the stage of the Folies-Bergère, by a few tokens. You can fantasize about being an African explorer confronted with a native woman dancing, or about being Solomon with a dancing girl at his command, but if your fantasy is packaged and you have to confront it, you may confront its tackiness as well. However, for others, the image of Baker in the jungle was persuasive and unforgettable, staying in the mind as it was meant to, through all the other complicated silliness of the Folies—an image of something stark, unified, uncomplicated, joyous.

It stayed in mind through "Whose Handkerchief Is This?" "Oh, the Pretty Sins," "Bewitched," and "A Feast at Versailles." The Versailles skit is a good example of how silly the Folies was and how evenhanded in its travesties: French monarchs were treated with no more respect than French colonials. Three of Louis XIV's mistresses descended the giant staircase of the Folies bare-breasted, to thunderous applause. Since the Folies stage was only twenty feet deep, there was no place to go but up, and the incredibly steep staircase was a feature of every performance. The mistresses were followed down the stairs by the Sun King himself, played by a woman. The scene was set in a château where portraits of ancestors hung on the wall, one of which came to life and, clad in armor, also descended the great staircase, reciting ironic alexandrines:

> Et pendant que d'argent vous emplissez vos poches,
> Nous sommes chevaliers sans peur et sans reproche.

(And while you fill your pockets up with gold,
We, your ancestors, have dignity untold.)

It was a satire of the nouveau riche who buy their way into high society. With society like this, who wouldn't long for the jungle?

The jungle—in the person of Baker—came back an hour after her first appearance, inside a huge ball covered in flowers like a Fabergé egg, which descended slowly from the top of the theater to the stage and opened to reveal "a wand of golden flesh" lying on a mirror. When the flower ball rested safely on the stage, Baker stood up, this time in a grass skirt and with feathers around her neck, and did a Charleston, madly, distressingly, as though she were possessed by a demon, or as though she were having an epileptic seizure. The lights reflecting off the mirror threw dozens of shadows of her figure onto the backdrop and around the theater, so there seemed to be six shadow versions of her dancing. This was by many accounts the best thing in the show. The refracted image of the dancing woman was genuinely exciting, genuinely Cubist. And if it worked for you completely, as it did for E. E. Cummings, the ridiculous, extravagant, elaborate flower ball containing that elemental wad of vitality was a resonant image.

There were other moments in this Folies show of 1926: the Tiller Girls, precision dancers, appeared dressed as dinner-jacketed men, as flagellants, as Pacific prawns, as transported slaves, as rabbits. Nevertheless the reviews were mixed.

The show brought to the surface considerable irritation about matters that might seem rather far away from the Folies-Bergère: the war, the devaluation of the currency, the fact that Paris was filled with foreigners, the fact that the foreigners had money and the French didn't. Many Parisian critics resented what they saw as a patent bias in the show. There was less text than ever, more display of flesh. The spectacular clothes, the colorful sets, the obtrusive nudes, were all geared to foreigners' tastes and not to the tastes of Parisians, who enjoyed verbal repartee. Mr. Music-Hall himself, the critic Gustave Fréjaville, took that harsh and chauvinistic stance. "There's no need to regret that the text of this revue is not always of the highest quality: its audience hears badly, understands little, and the French ears destined to receive this trash are so few in number that there's little need to worry about them." A furious attack on the 1926 Folies show came from an anti-pornography group which regretted that foreigners would think badly of France because of the nudity. Simultaneously, it blamed foreigners for debasing French entertainment: they alone could afford it and their taste was so appallingly low. "How long will this go on?" It was all the fault of the exchange rate, which put all wealth in the pockets of foreigners. It had started in 1921 and would end with the stock-market crash in 1929, but in 1926 the American influx was at its height, and many French people resented it.

None of this made any difference to people's reactions to Josephine Baker. Her personal success was as strong as ever. People who hated the show made exceptions for her. And she went on winning new fans and new admirers. Alexander Calder, inspired by the independent mobility of her various parts, went back to his studio on the rue Daguerre and made a wire sculpture, *Josephine Baker*, which was a prototype for his later mobiles. Society rebel and avant-garde culture vulture Nancy Cunard, who was engaged in a highly visible affair with a black pianist, Henry Crowther, reported on the show for *Vogue*, saying it "might very easily be called rotten, but can be sat through, even to twelve-thirty, because of the perfect delight one gets from Josephine Baker. She makes all the nudity and glitter of the rest (even the so well-drilled Tiller Girls) curiously insipid by comparison." E. E. Cummings saw the show with more enthusiasm and much greater subtlety. For him, it offered proof of how successful the Parisian "revue" could be. "By the laws of its own structure, which are the irrevocable laws of juxtaposition and contrast, the revue is the use of everything trivial or plural to intensify what is singular and fundamental. In the case of the Folies-Bergère, the revue is a use of ideas, smells, colours, Irving Berlin, nudes, tactility, collapsible stairs, three dimensions and fireworks to intensify Mlle. Josephine Baker." He remembered her from *The Chocolate Dandies* as a "tall, vital, incomparably fluid nightmare which crossed its eyes and warped its limbs in a purely unearthly manner." It might seem preposterous that this nightmare could become the most beautiful star of the Parisian stage. "Yet such is the case."

By the fall of 1926, her vogue was extraordinary. There were Josephine Baker dolls, costumes, perfumes, pomades. Only in the provinces did women wear the curls that had been fashionable in Paris not long before. In Paris women's hair was slicked down like Josephine Baker's, and to help achieve this look, they could buy a product called Bakerfix. "Small, brown and rather plump" was the winter's ideal. Women who, the summer before, had still been protecting their white

skin from the vulgarity of sunburn now put walnut oil on their skin
in lieu of weeks in the sun. "All that remains now," said a black
American who saw Baker at the Folies in the summer of 1926 and
delighted in her success, "is for her to try on the glass slipper and
marry the prince."

PART II
CHANGING

1927-38

The new Josephine, 1931.

Keystone, Paris

CHAPTER 4
FRESH BLOOD

A year after her arrival in Paris,
Josephine Baker still spoke only a few words of French, which she
mixed up with English in a way that journalists who flocked to interview her found irresistible. "Très sweet, le public, and it's grâce à les
journalistes that I have a life aussi agréable, understand?" She received
them with American informality, not at all the great star, often in a
messy dressing gown. She smiled that ravishing smile, and they were
hers. She seemed different offstage, physically smaller, less noisy, even
a bit timid, but nonetheless welcoming, gracious, and candid.

Her freedom from pretension was the most irresistible thing about her, and perhaps her most important "statement," if the way a person says something is deeper, more nearly his or her meaning, than what he or she consciously says. She mocked authority by mocking herself —her own beauty, her body, her face, the public, publicity. Tricked out in ridiculous costumes, waving her feathers behind her in comic majesty, gyrating close to epileptically, Baker spoke of pleasure in the body, of sane, lighthearted sensuality.

She moved often and liked every neighborhood she lived in. When she first arrived, she lived in a Left Bank hotel with the rest of the troupe. Then, to save money, she shared an apartment in black Montmartre. From the raffish rue Fromentin she moved to the bourgeois rue Henri-Rochefort near the Parc Monceau, and as her fortunes continued to improve, to the posh avenue Pierre Ier de Serbie. She filled her rooms with pets—dogs, rabbits, cats, and birds—and bought a phonograph. She listened to music constantly. When she went on a shopping trip, she made up her mind about what to buy as quickly as she did everything else.

Couturiers sent clothes for her to wear and she wore them with pleasure, then left them lying around her room in heaps. Bricktop, still her closest friend, rebuked her. The clothes were expensive. "Hang them up or have your maid do it," said Bricktop. "Oh, Bricky, they'll take them away and bring me a new pile tomorrow." She was feeling that heady sensation Americans had in Paris in the twenties. Fitzgerald evoked it in "Babylon Revisited": the snow of the twenties wasn't real snow. If you didn't want it to be snow, you just paid.

Marcel Sauvage interviewed her for L'Intransigeant on the occasion of the publication of Le Tumulte noir, a portfolio of lithographs by Paul Colin. She was the model for some of the pieces and the inspiration of others. Moreover, she had written an introduction in the form of a poem, called "Topic of the Day," about the rage for black culture in Paris. She recalled how "dark" Broadway had become in the early twenties. Now "it's getting darker and darker in Paris," she said. Another introduction rang other ironic changes on the theme of the black conquest of Paris. People whose ancestors were slaves have succeeded in enslaving Europe. Parisians have adopted their clothes and their dances. Paris boasts of black orchestras, black fetes, black balls, expositions of black art. "We negrify ourselves" ("nous nous négri-fiâmes"). Alongside the fashionable irony, some of Colin's illustrations have real vitality.

Sauvage arrived at noon, and she was still sleeping. She usually got up at four. She was living in two large rooms in a pension near the Parc Monceau. She cheerfully got up for him and threw on a rose-colored bathrobe with slippers to match. She didn't bother to tie the bathrobe tightly. Her hair was slicked down, and her nails were painted silver. She smiled and talked to him in English. She had only a few French phrases—among them, *pauvre oiseau.* That was for two parakeets in a cage next to a bust of Louis XIV, at whom, every now and then, they spit seeds.

The interpreter was late, but Baker had a knack for getting along with men whose language she did not speak. He asked her if she thought of doing her memoirs. She replied that the preface for *Le Tumulte noir* had taken her twenty-five minutes to write, and she could never bring herself to duplicate the effort. "You don't know what it's like to write," she said to the journalist. "I dance. That's what I do. I love that, and I love only that. I will dance my whole life." She threw herself into a leather chair, hunched her head between her shoulders, and flung off one of her slippers, giving herself over to unabashed flirting with Sauvage. What resulted from this was a charm-ing piece in *L'Intransigeant* and her first "autobiography," *Les Mémoires de Joséphine Baker*, published in 1927, when she was twenty-one.

When in doubt, she clowned. When at leisure, she danced. When attracted to a man, she made love with him. Particularly in this foreign place, sex seemed to have no strings. She made love with the room service waiter in the first hotel she stayed in, eager to see what French-men were like in bed. She seems to have been willing to try almost anyone, and men liked her so much at least in part because they could see that they were not, in making love to her, involving themselves in a soap opera. Many sex queens seem to suggest this comic sense of sex, even Marilyn Monroe, who managed to project a lightheartedness about sex which she disastrously lacked. For Josephine Baker, sex was a pleasurable form of exercise, like dancing, and she wasn't notably fussy about her partners.

She had the flapper mentality. She was one of those liberated women of the twenties who did not submit to the old moral codes, like the fictional Lady Brett of *The Sun Also Rises*, like the American model and photographer Lee Miller. The ground rules for their promiscuity involved a split between love and sex. For the flapper, sex was fun but had nothing necessarily to do with love. The result of thinking this way was that sex could be fun but it really didn't signify love. The besetting problem of the flapper mentality was that eventually sex could come to seem drained of all meaning, rather than happily freed from oppressive, limiting meanings. It took a while for this to happen to Josephine Baker, in part because her freedom was unlike that of women in conscious rebellion against bourgeois morality. She had never been bourgeois.

The bourgeois way is to save and accumulate. Sexual potential is a woman's capital. Starkly put, she saves herself to get herself a man who will support her in return for sexual services, including childbearing. She invests in a breadwinner. But Baker, from childhood experience, had little faith in men as breadwinners. Also, her sexual potential had not been a valued commodity. As a result, she could afford to please herself. Bent on her own pleasure, she didn't expect as much as a more bourgeois woman might, and for bourgeois men, her insouciance was a refreshing change. Pleasure-seeking was met by pleasure-seeking, not by the anxiety-producing rhetoric of romantic love. But despite Baker's enthusiasm for sex and her lack of the usual inhibitions, some of her lovers spread the word that she was so shy you would have thought her inexperienced. She came on strong, but at some point even *her* inhibitions were mobilized.

Her promiscuity was very likely a mask for a deep-seated distrust of intimacy. It seems to have been easy for her to go to bed with many men but hard to trust one completely. Making love, she had trouble being passive. She liked to set the pace, run the show, and turned sex into something more like a gymnastic exercise than a sensual experience, according to one of her lovers.

For all her seeming freedom and exhibitionism, she protected herself in some ways, of which lightheartedness was one and clowning another. From the later twenties date the striking photographs of her in glamorous designer dresses crossing her eyes, and at this stage of her life, the eye-crossing seems to me to function like a magical gesture of self-defense in a specifically erotic arena. It wards off the relentlessly erotic gaze of whoever might have been looking at her as, mythically, one warded off vampires by making the sign of the cross. Afraid in some way of evoking undiluted sexual excitement, she thwarts the deeply provocative contact of eye with eye not just by averting her own eyes but by jamming them grotesquely up against one another.

One of Baker's lovers in her early years in Paris was Georges Simenon, who later became famous as the author of the Inspector Maigret series. One of the most prolific writers of all time, Simenon was as prodigious in his appetite for sex as he was prodigious in his imaginative output, making love sometimes to four or five different women a day, by his own testimony. He said that Josephine Baker was the only woman who matched him sexually. He responded to her speed, intensity, and energy. Simenon would have married her, but he was only a fledgling journalist and she was already too famous to suit his masculine pride: he did not want to be Mr. Baker. He was also married, but that doesn't seem to have hindered his freedom of action or thought. To support himself and his wife when they first came to Paris, he had taken jobs in the mail room of a right-wing organization and later as private secretary for a marquis. Now, for love, he handled Josephine Baker's mail. It was Simenon, at least for a while, who arranged for the transmission of the two hundred dollars Baker sent home to her mother every month—a transaction she found too complicated to handle herself.

Whether it was goods or services, she didn't hesitate to accept presents from men. Gifts were a form of tribute she enjoyed and occasionally demanded. The jewels, furs, and other expensive presents had in some way no reality for her. They seemed like props in a fairy tale, emerald leaves on magical trees. While the line may seem fine between expecting tribute and asking for payment, there was a great deal of difference between her helter-skelter sex life and that of the dedicated courtesan. A man could earn his way into her favor one way or another, if not by looks, wit, and brains, then by position, money, utility. Like most people, she preferred to be in love, but when she wasn't, there was always sex. Even being in love didn't end adventures with other men. It wasn't the same thing.

What she really needed was someone to manage her—to take her in hand, run her career, make her decisions. She was making money and spending it like water. She was only twenty and had no head for business. Despite the fact that Europe was at her feet, perhaps even more so because of it, she had a sense of herself as a commodity whose value was precarious. "A violinist had his violin, a painter his palette. All I had was myself. *I* was the instrument that I must care for, just as Sidney fussed over his clarinet." She fussed over her body, rubbing it with lemon every day in a misguided effort to lighten her skin. She had a manicurist, a pedicurist, and hairdressers, in addition to the dressmakers she quickly got addicted to. They provided her a second skin. She couldn't shed her black one despite the lemons, but she could clothe it in a Schiaparelli, a Vionnet, or a Poiret.

A man who knew her slightly in 1926 said she had a manager then named Bondon, an older man who slapped her around and whom she addressed formally as Monsieur Bondon yet, like a child, called by the familiar *tu*. At the same time she was unsatisfyingly in love with an automobile manufacturer who loaded her with presents but would not marry her. Then she found exactly the man she needed.

"A frequent visitor to Paris, the Count was known in café society circles as Pepito and his wit and elegance made him a popular member of the nightclub set," Baker wrote of him. "I'll never forget that face. How could I? The delicate features, the lively, thoughtful eyes, the glinting monocle, the sensitive, sardonic mouth." He had, she said, a successful administrative career in Rome and a distinguished Italian family.

Bricktop said, "His real name was Giuseppe Abatino and he was working as a gigolo at Zelli's." She invoked the old gag and called him the "no-account count." According to Bricktop, Josephine had not been seeing as many men as "the Josephine legend" would have it. Most of the time, she hung around with a man name Zito, who worked as a caricaturist at Zelli's, a popular bar. Pepito was Zito's cousin, and her first date with him came about one night when Zito was sick. Bricktop was horrified when Josephine started going out with Pepito.

She thought he was a freeloader, a parasite. He couldn't buy himself a glass of beer. Perhaps she was a little bit jealous. After this, Josephine did not ask her for advice anymore. She also began to cut herself off from the black community in Montmartre.

It is too bad that Pepito's style of looks have passed out of favor. To us, he looks like a pimp. To Baker, he looked like Adolphe Menjou. His looks color one's view of their relationship—that, and the fact that there was so much of the pimp in Baker's model of a manager. He even had a pimp's name—Pepito Abatino—and a pimp's suave charm. There were many people who said he used her and bilked her of money. In fact, he did her lots of good. He was a full-time press agent for her, formulating the myth of her past that proved most useful. He shaped her stage career for the long haul. He put her financial affairs in order. He gave her a home. She adored him, clung to him—literally; photos of them together show it—and allowed him to make her over. He was seventeen years older than she was and could also serve as the father she had never had.

He went into action immediately, setting up a deal for the hair pomade Bakerfix and arranging an endorsement for Pernod. He secured a film contract and encouraged the project of her memoirs with Marcel Sauvage. In October, Baker had taken a second job, dancing in the early hours of morning at a nightclub in the rue Pigalle owned by two gentlemen named Harot and Léonard. The place had been called the Impérial, and they changed the name to Josephine Baker's Impérial in her honor. But what she wanted was a place of her own, and Pepito saw that she got it. He arranged for one of her admirers, Gaston Prieur, to finance it for her.

Prieur was a doctor who ran three clinics supposed to treat workers for illness and accidents on the job. Actually, it was a thriving insurance fraud. Every day hundreds of workers checked into these clinics. Prieur saw almost none of them, and in any case, few of them were sick. He paid them a bonus for giving him their business, sent them on their way, and then collected from their insurance companies for treatment. Thus financed, Chez Joséphine on the rue Fontaine opened on December 10, 1926.

The owners of Josephine Baker's Impérial, who had changed the name of their nightclub for her and then been abandoned by her, sued. She was also being sued by Paul Poiret, the couturier, for nonpayment of 5,000 francs out of 285,000 francs' worth of clothes she had bought in October, but this suit may well have been a Poiret publicity stunt, to draw attention to how much money she'd spent with him. Hating to be tied, she tended to provoke lawsuits, and in another litigious maneuver she tried to get out of her contract with the Folies-Bergère by saying she had been underage when she signed it. But Derval, who understood how to deal with his contrary star, told her she could leave if she wanted to, so she stayed.

To Josephine, all the suits were tedious paperwork. Pepito took care of them, as he now took care of all her problems. "At last I had someone to help me fight my battles," she said of him.

She danced at Chez Joséphine every night after she was finished at the Folies-Bergère, arriving at one in the morning. A writer from *Vogue* described her sweeping in one night, accompanied by maid, chauffeur, Eskimo dog, and several "nondescript people." "She came in without a wrap, and the length of her graceful body, which is 'light sealskin-brown,' was swathed in a blue tulle frock with a bodice of blue snakeskin, worn with slippers to match. The frock was cut excessively low in back, with a huge diamond ornament at the waist." After she danced, the *Vogue* writer went back to her dressing room so the illustrator with him could finish drawing her. There were photographs of her from all the newspapers stuck up around the room. She had kissed the dog on the top of his head, so he bore a big lipstick mark.

Chez Joséphine was another Montmartre hole-in-the-wall, the size of the Grand Duc. It charged outrageous prices, forty-five francs (about $45 in current money) for a dozen oysters—and for the chance of seeing Josephine Baker up close and at her best. She danced, clowned, and teased her clients, pulling the men's mustaches and stroking their bald heads. She acted as though everyone there was her personal friend, a style which Florence Jones had introduced to Paris and Bricktop perfected.

She had become La Baker—as the French say it, "Bakhair." When she walked into a room, the room suddenly seemed the right place to be. She drew all eyes. She was a great star, so luminous her presence that she lit up any occasion and so kind her heart that she lit up many. She kissed babies in foundling homes, gave dolls to the young and soup to the aged, presided at the opening of the Tour de France, celebrated holidays, went to fairs, joked with workers, and did charity benefits galore. She was all over Paris, always good-natured and exquisitely dressed.

At Christmas, she gave a special free matinee performance at the Folies-Bergère for the children of traffic cops in all the twenty arrondissements of Paris. She was, of course, suitably dressed as Santa Claus. She danced a Charleston and was joined onstage by an acrobatic horse ("the elastic Pegasus of the Folies-Bergère") and a magician. She gave each child a toy appropriate to his or her sex, and there was cake for everyone. The idea had been Baker's, and people loved it. "Mlle. Baker has come amongst us to civilize the Parisians." But no one could understand her odd choice of charity, and finally someone asked. "Why, among all the other functionaries who are equally worthy, have you chosen the traffic cops?" "Oh," she said, with Josephine logic, "it's because they're blacks." She meant that they were badly paid, overworked, underesteemed—which they were not—and perhaps, with their dark uniforms, stiff-sided little hats, and white gloves, they reminded her of Pullman porters.

The new year brought new projects. She bought a car, a Voisin painted brown, to match her skin, she said, and upholstered in snakeskin, of which she was fond. In June, when she was twenty-one, she got her driver's license. As though it wasn't enough to be doing the Folies and her own club, she began dancing at the Acacias, the fashionable *thé dansant*, in the afternoons. She sometimes danced over twelve hours a day. She said she ate herself fat and danced herself thin, but she was not yet thin by contemporary standards. In the spring of 1927 she weighed about 135 pounds.

The new show at the Folies-Bergère opened in April and Josephine was again the star—the black star. Pépa Bonafé was billed as the "white star." She had refused to work without star billing, and star billing had already been promised to Baker. This was the compromise: separate but equal.

To aficionados of the music-hall, the 1927 Folies-Bergère show represented either a high point or a low point, depending on their tastes. The old tradition of comic routines had by now been totally expunged. The show was purely visual, with its changes of tempo finely calibrated. The producer and writer, Louis Lemarchand, claimed he had been convinced years before that the comic bits were vulgar and he had sought, year by year, to eliminate text and create a spectacle woven purely of music, costume, sets. "But how much resistance to conquer from those around me!" At least some of whom thought he was pandering to foreign taste. Lemarchand was making his way toward what we would call a multimedia concept of stage entertainment, such as Piscator was experimenting with in Berlin. One of the show's innovations was its use of film. Behind Baker dancing a Black Bottom, they projected a film of her dancing a Black Bottom.

For Josephine Baker the 1927 show was little different from the one the year before. In one scene, "Plantation," she wore a version of the ragamuffin outfit she had worn in the Revue Nègre. In another, she did a Charleston in a skirt of billowy marabou feathers. In another, she wore a metallic bathing suit which outlined her bare breasts in rhinestone straps. She wore the banana skirt again in a more spangled, hard-edged version. It was the fate of those bananas to become ever harder and more threatening with the years, so that at last they looked like spikes. For her finale, she appeared with diamond balls dripping off the tips of her red-gloved fingers. Visually, she was as striking as ever, and her dancing was as good as ever. But people were getting a little tired of her act. The only thing new about her in this production was the spit curl in the center of her forehead—in French it's called an *accroche-coeur*, a heart hook. It wasn't enough. Some critics even complained her skin had changed color: she was too white. She was too afraid of falling out of favor not to notice that she was.

If nothing was really changing, she could at least make up a story of change. When Pepito entered her life, her habit of making up her life became even more exaggerated. She tried on different pasts as though they were dresses, to see which suited her. "Fifteen years ago

Baker in blackface for Sissle and Blake's second Broadway show, *The Chocolate Dandies*, 1924.
Billy Rose Theater Collection, Performing Arts Research Center, New York Public Library at Lincoln Center; Astor, Lenox, and Tilden Foundations.

The *Shuffle Along* chorus line, 1922. Josephine Baker is ninth from the right.
Billy Rose Theater Collection, Performing Arts Research Center, New York Public Library at Lincoln Center; Astor, Lenox, and Tilden Foundations.

Baker in satin for the glamorous side of her role in *The Chocolate Dandies*, with Lew Payton and Johnny Hudgins.
Billy Rose Theater Collection, Performing Arts Research Center, New York Public Library at Lincoln Center; Astor, Lenox, and Tilden Foundations.

LEFT: Paul Colin's poster for *La Revue Nègre*.
Bibliothèque Nationale, Paris; courtesy of Posters Please, Inc., New York.

Rehearsing on the roof of the Théâtre des Champs-Élysées, with the Eiffel Tower in the distance, 1925.
Roger-Viollet, Paris.

The banana skirt, first worn in
the Folies-Bergère, 1926–27.
Bibliothèque Nationale, Paris.

Baker and Joe Alex in the Danse Sauvage of *La Revue Nègre*. *Bibliothèque Nationale, Paris.*

On a Paris street, 1927. She
liked good shoes.
Roger-Viollet, Paris.

Photographed by Lipnitzki,
circa 1926.
Photo Lipnitzki, Roger-Viollet, Paris.

1927
Keystone, Paris.

Postcards of Josephine Baker
were favorites of tourists in
the 1920s and 1930s.
*James Weldon Johnson Collection,
Beinecke Rare Book and Manuscript
Library, Yale University.*

Josephine Baker, an iron-wire construction by Alexander Calder, 1927–29.
Collection, Museum of Modern Art, New York. 39 × 22³/8 × 9³/4″. Gift of the artist.

A new Josephine Baker begins to emerge in the 1931–32 Casino de Paris show, *Paris Qui Remue.*
Courtesy of Mr. John Brady, Jr.

Displaying her engagement ring, with Pepito Abatino.
Roger-Viollet, Paris.

In her dressing room at the Casino de Paris.
Photo Lipnitzki, Roger-Viollet, Paris.

No more bananas.
Bibliothèque Nationale, Paris.

The private Josephine, playing with her dogs at Le Vésinet.
Keystone, Paris.

Distributing pot-au-feu to the aged.
Keystone, Paris.

The *Ziegfeld Follies,* New York, 1935. The bananas have evolved into tusks.
Wide World Photos; courtesy of Performing Arts Research Center, New York Public Library at Lincoln Center; Astor, Lenox, and Tilden Foundations.

in California, my sister said to my father, 'Josephine must dance.' When I was nine, I studied with an old lady in my village. At ten, I was with a black troupe from New York. Ever since then. I've done nothing but dance. I took the boat for France with that troupe." She began to say her father was Spanish; her parents fell in love in school; when their parents tried to stop them from marrying, they ran away together; they had to separate because their work took them in different directions. Pepito's life was equally plastic. He was a count because he said he was.

It was a freewheeling time as far as the story of one's life went. Stars and their agents were do-it-yourself biographers, and the press collaborated. No one cared so much whether something was true as whether it made a good story. "Si non é vero, é ben trovato," as the Italian saying goes. The business of a press agent was to get his client's name in the newspapers, no matter how, and the business of newspapermen, whose lofty self-image was not yet in place, was to fill up newspapers. Two of the favorite ploys of twenties publicists were the stolen pearl necklace and the marriage with European nobility. Thus evolved the story of Josephine Baker's marriage to the Count di Albertini.

It was a good story to begin with. Henry James used it over and over. Sweet little girl from America goes to Europe and marries ancient European nobility—a marriage of the best of both worlds, American energy and European sophistication, American talent and European status. But what made the story irresistible in this case was color. "Negro Dancing Girl Bride of Roman Count" was the headline in the *New York World*. "Josephine Baker, of Harlem, adds a noble husband to conquests abroad."

He had given her a sixteen-carat diamond engagement ring, which she flashed at every opportunity. They had been married, they said, on Josephine's twenty-first birthday. "That ain't all he gave me either. I got all the family jewels and heirlooms that have been in the Abatino family for generations." They gave a press conference to announce their marriage. It was a field day for fiction. Josephine said she was born in St. Louis of a Spanish father and moved with her mother to Philadelphia at the age of two. Pepito said he was a lieutenant in a "crack regiment" of Italian cavalry. Josephine claimed to have verified Pepito's aristocratic lineage "way back to his great-uncle, who was the famous Cardinal Celesio." She said she wasn't going to let him work—"the Count don't know how to do anything but wear that monocle. Don't you think he looks cute?"—and radiated delight at being married and titled: "Oh, isn't it all wonderful to be a countess?" As for Pepito, he announced with some truth: "I am going to devote the rest of my life to making a great artist of her."

When the press checked into the story some more, it became clear that Pepito's title was spurious and the marriage itself nonexistent. The couple claimed it had taken place at the Italian consulate, at the American consulate, and at a town hall in one of the arrondissements but they couldn't remember which. There was no titled Abatino or Albertini family in Italy, and at the register of foreigners in the Paris Prefecture of Police, Pepito's occupation was listed as plasterer. Baker laughed it off. When asked where she was married, she said with an infectious laugh, "That's not important." When asked if she was really a countess, she said, "Yes, at least in Maurice Dekobra's film in which my manager, Pepito Abatino, also has a part. You know him, don't you? A guy with a dark mustache who looks like Adolphe Menjou? That's him, my husband. My husband in the film, right? Well, since it was amusing to be married, I let it out around town that I was. My, how quickly false news spreads! What I told a few friends as a joke, everyone took seriously. It was nice. It's fun to be called 'madame' and to get telegrams from everywhere on earth congratulating me."

It was all amusing and inconsequential—except with some of the folks back home. The black press in America had played up the story of Baker's marriage to a count. Pepito's father had been quoted extensively as approving the match: "Count's Father Glad His Son Chose Josephine as Bride; Is Proud of Her." He made a point the black newspapers wanted to see made. "We don't have any racial feeling over here or in Sicily. Besides, my daughter-in-law is no darker than many Southern European women." According to *The Defender* in Chicago and *The Amsterdam News* in New York, there had been nothing in the Italian press but praise of the bride's talent, beauty, and success. Only American newspapers published in Paris commented on the issue of color. So when the reports started coming out suggesting the whole marriage was a publicity stunt and Pepito's title a fraud, the skepticism seemed to some members of the black press a racially motivated slur.

Baker quietly dropped the title. She said she hadn't married him for it anyway. "If that boy sticks with me, he's got to bring home some bacon and buckwheat, too."

Better publicity came from the publication, three weeks after the marriage fiasco, of her memoirs written with the help of Marcel Sauvage. The two co-authors had a book-signing party at the Acacias, for which Baker dressed as a *femme de lettres* in a dark, sober silk dress. She took her role seriously, behaved with reserve and discretion, and seemed even a little intimidated by the event. She signed her name in people's books slowly and laboriously, like a schoolgirl. Critics and poets stood around drinking champagne. If she was scared, she took refuge in her cordiality, greeting each journalist with a gentle smile and seeming to have heard of nothing but him for a long time.

The book is really an extended interview, yet it's done with love and intelligence and ends up being a more convincing portrait of her than later more elaborate and studied versions of her life. Her beauty advice is to dance a lot and sweat a lot. That makes you sleep. Sleep is good for the eyes. Her favorite dish is spaghetti. She gives a recipe for corned beef hash. She loves animals and thinks we have a lot to learn from them. She has no idea about the future of women or even their present, but she hates lace and loves liberty. As for the future, well, there's plenty of time to think about it, but she hopes when it comes we will live naked, despite the fact that there are few women and very few men who could stand the exposure. She prays before she goes onstage and before she goes to bed. She makes up a prayer and sings it to a tune. She loves the cinema but not the telephone: what a pain, to hear a person's voice and not see him! Better to see him and not hear his voice! She'd love to have a seven-volume dictionary, just to feel its weight. She listed her pets: seven dogs, three cats, two parrots, one parakeet, a snake, a pig, a goat. She listed the presents she'd received: a pair of earrings that belonged to a duchess, six Chinese lacquered chairs, an automobile, electric toys, carved ivory elephants from Russia, stuffed bear, duck, rabbit, cat, and living animals as well, a pair of gold shoes, perfume in a crystal horse, furs, bracelets, peaches, strawberries.

"There's my childhood: I had no stockings. I was cold and danced to get warm." "I'm not intimidated by anyone. Everyone is made with two arms, two legs, a stomach, and a head. Just think about that." She hates ballet dancing and can't abide Pavlova (who couldn't abide her). She swims daily because land animals are never as elegant as fish. "People have done me the honor of believing I'm an animal." She confesses the secret of her success: a rabbit's foot given her by an old black man when she was still in New York. Without that, she says, she'd be no better off than any of those thousands of girls who have their hour onstage and disappear without ever being a star. Finally, she says she wants to dance her whole life through and die breathless, wiped out, at the end of a dance—but not in a music hall.

"I am tired of that artificial life. The work of being a star disgusts me now. All the intrigues which surround the star disgust me. . . . I want to work three or four more years and then quit the stage. I'll go live in Italy or the South of France. I will get married, as simply as possible. I will have children, and many animals. I love them. I want to live in peace surrounded by children and animals. But if one of my children wanted to go onstage in the music hall, I would strangle it with my own two hands."

The reviews were all excellent, and with reason. It's a charming book, not so much a narrative as a prose poem, conveying her humor and genial realism. She seems direct, without affectation, warmhearted, funny. Maurice de Vlaminck was so impressed that he sought her out in Paris. He had another of those Big Questions, her offhand answers to which were so striking in the book. "Are you a feminist?" he asked. "Do you think it's reasonable and useful for women to have the right to vote?" She didn't let him down by her response, at least as he relates it. First she looked at him bewildered. Then she smiled and handed him a rabbit's foot.

One of her offhand comments got her into trouble. "I've heard a lot of talk about the war. What a funny story! I swear I don't understood it at all, but it disgusts me. I have such a horror of men with only one arm, one leg, one eye. I sympathize with them with all my

heart, but I have a physical repulsion from everything unhealthy."
Wounded war veterans took offense and demonstrated outside her
cabaret. They were upset both by her saying she was disgusted by
mutilation and by her calling the war "a funny story." Her response
was to blame Sauvage, threatening to sue him if he didn't see to it
that the offensive lines—which she claimed she never uttered—were
dropped from the book. Sauvage replied that if she proceeded with
the suit, he would tell what their conversations had really been like.
"Believe me, it would be pretty picturesque." He was so ungenerous
as to suggest that Baker ought not try to think. He had not shown
the proofs to her, for that would have done no good, she being incapable
of understanding them; rather he had shown them to her French
entourage, including her manager, Pepito Abatino.

For all that, she remained on good enough terms with Sauvage to
work with him again in the future. As penance to her public, she
danced a benefit on behalf of crippled war veterans. It was, as far as
she was concerned, all publicity. To live, to thrive, a performer had
to stay in the newspapers, and no one knew better than Baker how
to do that. In an age of publicity stunts, hers were perhaps no more
outrageous than others but, particularly once she hooked up with
Pepito, they were more relentless.

She had been filmed a couple of times, doing dances from the 1926
Folies-Bergère show and then dances from the 1927 show. These had
not been pleasant experiences. She knew nothing about lighting or
makeup for film. Her eyelids, without oil on them, burned under the
hot lights, which also blinded her. But now she was to have the lead
in a feature film for which Maurice Dekobra, a well-known novelist,
did the screenplay, with suggestions from Pepito. *La Sirène des Tropiques* was produced and directed by Mario Nalpas, and its assistant
director was a young Spaniard named Luis Buñuel. The silent film
was shot in the summer of 1927 in the forest of Fontainebleau outside
of Paris, a fact all too obvious in the film, which is supposed to take
place largely in the Antilles.

It tells the basic Cinderella story with which it would be Josephine

Baker's cinematic lot to be associated: an innocent girl from the tropics goes to Paris, where she dances and is transformed into an elegant woman by beautiful clothes. There is more, almost all of it silly. Baker, as a native girl, is pursued by a leering white trader. She falls into a flour bin and turns white. He follows her to the pond when she bathes and he almost rapes her, but she is saved by Pierre Batcheff, the handsome romantic lead, who resembles Leslie Howard. The bad guy lures Batcheff onto a rope ladder which breaks and Batcheff falls into a ravine. Baker rescues him. They fall in love. Suddenly she is in a circle, surrounded by natives. They break into a Charleston—apparently, their native dance. Next she is in Paris, doing a Charleston at a party with a jungle theme. Continuity has not been perfected, so she gets up to dance wearing one dress, with rhinestones, and sits down after her dance in another, with beads. Pepito Abatino sits at the same table, playing her husband. Pierre Batcheff turns up again and fights a duel. Baker climbs a tree and shoots Batcheff's opponent. They are still in love, but she renounces him for the sake of his fiancée, who gives her a Bible in thanks. Inside the Bible is a message which is flashed on the screen: "Sacrifice is the purest form of joy on earth."

Much of this film has been lost, and what's left is scrappy and hard to follow. Still, it's fair to say it was never a good movie. Pierre Batcheff and Buñuel thought it was a joke. For Baker, it was worse than a joke. She was humiliated by it. She had no dignity in this part, and it isn't just the result of silly "bits" like the flour. She herself overdoes it, trying frenetically to please, always rolling her eyes and flapping her arms. In the scene with Batcheff's fiancée, she overacts horrendously. As she reaches for the Bible, her hand trembles. Film exaggerates all movement, and her animation, which served her so well onstage, served her ill on the screen. Knowing she was not doing well, Baker was difficult on the set. According to Pierre Batcheff's wife, she demanded a fur coat before letting the filming proceed and in general behaved like a spoiled brat. "The finished film brought tears to my eyes. Was that ugly, silly person me?"

It was clear to both Josephine and Pepito that a change was in order, not just publicity tricks but something fundamental. Pepito had a good idea of what it should be, and since his idea echoed her childhood dreams of glamour, Josephine was happy to go along with it. Simply, Pepito realized she could no longer trade on her spontaneity and freshness. If she was to succeed in Europe in a permanent way, she would have to transform herself into a European. Her performing would have to become more studied and less instinctive. She would have to train her voice, discipline her dancing, learn to speak French. All this education would take time. She would have to stop performing on a regular basis, go away from Paris, as though for an illicit pregnancy, and present her new self upon her return. Accordingly, he arranged a worldwide tour to begin in March 1928. But first they had to wind up business in Paris.

She quit Chez Joséphine, having performed there for a little over a year. Prieur, who had bought her the place, offered it to several other dancers, but eventually gave up and closed the place down. Not much later, he would be sent to prison for fraud, and Baker would prove loyal to him. Returning from her tour in Germany, she would pose for photographers hugging Prieur to show her support; she would tell the press that he was a charming gentleman and a good dancer. He had helped her and she wouldn't let him down when he was in distress, although she felt no compunction about leaving him flat when she wanted to get away from Paris.

After finishing out the 1927 Folies season and before a three-week skiing vacation at St. Moritz with Pepito, she formally said her good-byes to Paris. It was the start of what would turn out to become a habit of farewell performances.

The highly orchestrated event took place at the end of January 1928. The enormous Salle Pleyel was packed. The audience consisted of all the fashionable people in Paris, not just the kind who went to openings but also the weightier kind who subscribed to the opera. Most of the Americans in Paris were there. The evening was intended to give a hint of things to come—to suggest that a new Josephine Baker was in the making. She appeared at first in her old ragamuffin costume dancing like a doll whose elastic had come unstrung. The audience was, as I suspect Pepito intended them to be, bored. It had become an old story. She had been doing the same thing for a year and a half. Then came the surprise. She went offstage and reappeared in—a dress! A well-cut, elegant dress, such as she wore for her night-club performances but not onstage. Her tight-fitting cloche of rhine-stones shone in the spotlight. She sang a song in French. Everyone understood. Look how much progress she has made, they said. Look how assimilated she has become, how domesticated, how civilized.

Next she made a pretty little speech, very hesitantly, but in French. "Je voulais ... remercier le public ... qui a été si gentil ... j'étais une pauvre toute petite fille ... et il a fait de moi une grande ... grande ... chose." This was the theme of the evening—I was a poor little girl, and it was you, the people of Paris, who made me this great ... thing. The flattery worked. There was great enthusiasm for this speech. But then, as though she were at an awards ceremony, Baker went on to thank all the people who had helped make her a star: Monsieur Perugia, who made her shoes, Madame Agnès who did her hair, her couturier, her furrier, her lingerie maker. The list went on and on, and no one found it either funny or interesting. Worse followed. To benefit charity, she auctioned off some programs for the evening, signed by her and by the celebrated jazz pianists Wiener and Doucet, who were the other half of the program. The audience was good-natured enough during the first auction, which produced three hundred francs, but began to get restless during the second, and positively irritated by the third. She kept up a patter in something like French. Finally, there were catcalls. With great presence of mind, but ironically recalling the reaction of the Countess of Pourtalès to *The Rite of Spring* and of some of her audience to the Revue Nègre, she said, "Remember you're still in France." Her aplomb won the audience back. But it must have been a traumatic evening for her, reinforcing her belief that the public, especially the Parisian public, could turn against you in a second.

She had set out a year and a half before to seduce Paris as though it were a lover. Now Paris was behaving according to one classic scenario of the Frenchman with a foreign mistress. He is attracted to her because she is different, but after a while the differences seem irritating deficiencies and he wants her to shape up, Parisianize herself, buy her lingerie, for example, at the same place his mother does. The usual sad ending of this scenario is that when the foreign mistress has transformed herself into a Parisian, the Frenchman loses interest. She is now no different from the others. Pepito understood the situation and saw the solution. The public is indeed like a man, he told her. It is happy to go on loving the same woman—as long as she is never the same.

Leaving France in 1928 for a year-long tour of the rest of Europe, Josephine Baker became controversial. Hitler would not come to power until 1933, but *Mein Kampf* had recently been published and was selling thousands of copies. It left no doubt about how Hitler viewed blacks: they were "half-apes" on whom it was a "criminal absurdity" to waste any money or time. While they could now and then be trained to perform as lawyers, teachers, opera singers, or even clergymen, it was like training dogs to do tricks. "It is a sin against the will of the eternal Creator to let hundreds and hundreds of thousands of His most talented beings degenerate in the proletarian swamp of today, while Hottentots and Zulu Kafirs are trained for intellectual vocations." Applied to Jews, the combination of racism and economic resentment was at the heart of National Socialism. About blacks, Hitler did not have to work so hard to make his point, relying on entrenched fear and contempt.

It was barely five years since the conclusion of a postwar international uproar involving France's use of African troops in the occupation of the west bank of the Rhine. During the war, the French Army, which had allowed American blacks to fight under its colors, placed into combat many regiments of troops from its own colonies, Senegal, Tunisia, Algeria, Morocco. The use of Senegalese troops in battle was fiercely resented by the Germans, whose Colonial Office complained that the French were thereby endangering European civilization. But when the French used African troops to occupy the Rhineland, the outcry was even greater—and not restricted to Germany. One of the chief leaders of protest against "the black horror on the Rhine" was an English radical, E. D. Morel, who spoke and wrote against the imposition of "barbarians . . . with tremendous sexual instincts—into the heart of Europe." In Sweden, fifty thousand women signed a petition supporting his opinions, and there was organized support also in Italy, Norway, and the United States, where a rally at Madison Square Garden in 1921 attracted twelve thousand people. Pamphlets against the "black horror" were translated—often paid for by the German government, sometimes printed in Berlin—into Spanish, French, Italian, Dutch, and Portuguese. The furor died down by 1923 but many Germans did not forget the threat, the insult, the humiliation, the profanation, as they saw it, of having black troops on German soil. It was still a gnawing irritation to Hitler when he wrote *Mein Kampf* that, as he put it, "the main artery of the German people flows through the playground of black African hordes." It was clear to him that Jews were behind it. The French Army was being used by international Jewish bankers to destroy the white race by bringing black rapists among the Aryan maidens of the Rhineland.

If Wagner's operas provided the appropriate background music for this kind of apocalyptic fantasy, jazz definitely did not. It didn't encourage military sacrifice and ecstatic death, didn't evoke nationalistic river spirits, or swan boats, mountaintops, Valkyries, Valhallas, or twilights of the gods. Jazz represented the opposing voice: down-to-earth and everyday. It spoke to the forces that made for cultural vitality in Weimar Germany, for an avant-garde art show in Berlin in 1925 had touted the *Neue Sachlichkeit*, "the new matter-of-factness," but it did not speak to the forces that would gain political power.

The fact that black jazz musicians could make good livings in the cities of Austria and Germany amidst postwar poverty was particularly galling to many natives and helped contribute to their dislike of everything that was not local and nationalistic. In the hostility which Baker provoked as she toured Europe in 1928–29, economic frustration, moral indignation, resistance to cultural innovation, xenophobia, all mixed with racism. Once again, as she had in Paris, but now playing to stronger passions, she embodied the jazz age and people reacted to her not so much as an individual but as a cultural symbol.

The French had been the first to pick up on jazz and French composers had been the first Europeans to use jazz elements in "serious" art music, but in the serious music circles of Germany and Central Europe the impact of jazz was more substantial; it was more widely discussed than in France and also more controversial. Radio, a new institution, helped popularize it in Germany. The commercial radio system began broadcasting in 1923 and played jazz along with symphonic music, dance music, live concerts and operas. The Berlin radio stations were famous for their jazz programming, with many live broadcasts from Berlin night spots. In 1927, the weekly program guide ran instructions on how to dance the tango, the Charleston, the Black Bottom, and the fox-trot.

Berlin had another jazz resource in *The Chocolate Kiddies Revue*, which ran between 1925 and 1927, with music by Duke Ellington. The band leader was Sam Wooding, another World War I Army band veteran, who had been playing New York's popular Club Alabam. Wooding and his group, the Chocolate Dandies, became very popular in Germany and recorded some of the revue's songs for the German Vox label. It was not a bad introduction to live jazz for the Germans. *The Chocolate Kiddies Revue* ran for two years whereas the Revue Nègre ran for three months, a measure of the difference in attention span for jazz between the German and French capitals.

Of the German composers whose work was deeply affected by jazz, Kurt Weill is probably the best-known today, and *The Threepenny Opera*, his collaboration with Brecht, best serves to epitomize the multimedia cultural vitality of Germany in the late twenties, inspired by jazz, popular culture, and the populist ideal of utilitarian art. That the Bauhaus had its own jazz band from 1923 to 1933 suggests how important jazz was considered as a source of cultural renewal in all the arts. Visual artists were attracted to jazz personnel, especially saxophone players and Charleston dancers, as subjects, often portraying them in a new visual style—jagged, fragmented, energetic—derived from jazz.

It made a lot of Germans very unhappy, and the unhappiness started to focus in the fall of 1927, not long before Baker's Central European appearances, when the Hoch Conservatory in Frankfurt announced that it would offer instruction in jazz beginning with the new year. There would be classes—the first anywhere—in jazz instrumental techniques and, if there was enough demand, in jazz vocal performance. The director of the conservatory, announcing the new courses, claimed they would provide a "transfusion of fresh Negro blood."

The conservative music press howled in response. Jazz was pernicious, destructive of idealism, allied to the hated *Gebrauchsmusik* ("workaday music"), simple music meant to be played by amateurs, such as Weill had written for populist reasons. Jazz was anti-German and led to pacifism and internationalism. Was such barbarism really to be fostered in a German school? Why not import Negroes directly if a transfusion of Negro blood was needed?

It was true that a keen response to jazz tended to go along with an enthusiasm for America and all things American which swept German art in the twenties, producing such diverse symptoms as a fascination with boxing and with the faster pace at which life was thought to be lived in America. This infatuation with America had political consequences in Germany it never had in France. Vienneseborn Ernst Křenek went to Berlin to begin his career and there was introduced to American jazz by Artur Schnabel, the pianist and composer who had toured in America and brought back sheet music and records of American jazz songs. Křenek's opera *Jonny spielt auf (Jonny Strikes Up the Band)* opened in Leipzig in 1925 when Křenek was twenty-five and became a worldwide success. It is not a jazz opera but uses jazz as a tag for its important character, Jonny, a black jazz musician. Years later, Křenek explained that his hero, a composer, represented the "ponderous, inhibited Central European intellectual." In opposition to him, Křenek placed Jonny, "a child of nature, totally free of inhibitions, acting on impulse at the spur of the moment." At the end of the opera, the composer takes the train West, toward America and freedom, prefiguring what Křenek himself would be forced to do in 1937. Like so many other German artists and intellectuals, he resettled in the States.

People who thought of jazz as vital and America as the land of freedom were likely to find themselves before long living in America. Whether or not they were Jewish, they would have to act on the strength of what in France remained largely a metaphor, the association of jazz and freedom. Naturally, many of their actions in turn appeared metaphoric, symbolically charged. A German Jewish music publisher who began life over again in New York in the late thirties recalled the feeling of freedom he had the first time he put on an American shirt, which buttoned all the way down the front, instead of a German one, which you had to put on over your head. "You put on a shirt with your eyes open, your head erect, in the proud posture of a free man in a free country."

When the National Socialists came to power in 1933, the conservative music critics' distaste for jazz took on the force of law. The Nazis saw jazz as the collaborative product of two despised groups, blacks and Jews—thus acknowledging the contribution to jazz of Jewish songwriters like Irving Berlin, George Gershwin, and Harold Arlen, whose melodies black jazz musicians often used as a basis for improvisation. Jazz was banned from German radio in 1935. Three years later, the Degenerate Music exhibit in Düsseldorf, a follow-up to the previous year's Munich exhibit of Degenerate Art, singled out for disapproval jazz records and scores by Křenek, Stravinsky, Hindemith, and Weill. The cover of the catalogue shows a black saxophonist in a top hat on whose lapel is a Jewish star, hinting at the alliance of Jews and blacks in the "invasion by brutal jazz rhythms of the Germanic world of music." The Nazis went to great lengths to expel jazz from Germany—which shows how well it had rooted there.

The first stop on Josephine Baker's European tour was Vienna, and before she even arrived in the city, there was organized opposition to her performances. If she expected her reception in conservative Vienna to be like her triumph in Berlin in the Revue Nègre three years earlier, she received a nasty surprise. According to *The New York Times*, which covered these remote but politically important events in some detail, "she aroused an anti-negro feeling that Vienna never knew existed." A right-wing student group, which had previously targeted only socialists and Jews, demonstrated against her and declared their intention of "preventing colored artists from playing in Vienna." The students' anger had been stimulated in part because Jonny, the black jazz musician in *Jonny spielt auf*, boasts about his sexual power over white women. They got angry, too, when they thought of all the money Baker was being paid, money which might better have gone to an Austrian. There was also the matter of morality. They had heard that she performed virtually naked and that her dances were obscene.

On this ground—that she was degenerate herself and would be the cause of degeneracy in others—the students were supported by the Catholic Church. Together these right-wing forces sought to stop Baker from performing in Vienna. There was the usual irony of censorship: they had not seen what they were so anxious to stop and were so sure would prove harmful. However, posters for her show were all around the city, a provocation in themselves, for they showed Baker with nothing on but her bananas, and Vienna was less accustomed to such sights than Paris—or Berlin. Schoolchildren then who are old people now remember staring at the revealing poster four times a day, on the way to and from school.

All the fuss made Baker's appearance in Vienna quite an event. The bells of St. Paul's Church started ringing at the moment of her arrival, warning people to stay off the streets lest they be contaminated by the sight of her. Other churches sounded their bells, too, so it must have been inadvertently quite festive. Some students promised to demonstrate, but an equally aggressive group of enthusiasts showed up at the railroad station to greet her. Moreover, there was a police guard. The protective police and the enthusiastic admirers escorted her to the hotel, where the conservative students held their demonstration. Pepito, who saw it all as welcome publicity, was happy.

The conservative groups were powerful enough to get the Vienna City Council to deny her permission to perform at the Ronacher Theater, into which she'd been booked. The council invoked some technicality—a stage concession the manager of the theater had failed to obtain—but they did not rule on the larger issue of whether she would corrupt the city by performing, and Baker found another, smaller theater to play in—the Johann Strauss.

The forces of opposition then went higher and petitioned the Austrian Parliament to prevent the "pornographic exhibition." The deputies spent an afternoon discussing her "perverse acting" and commenting, mostly unfavorably, upon her body and color. However, Dr.

Jerzabek, leader of the Clerical Party, made a point of saying it was her nudity and not her color that he objected to. He was particularly upset by the posters, which showed her in nothing but feathers and pearls, "like a Congo savage."

In Parliament, Baker had a defender: Count Adelbert Sternberg, whose title could be traced, as his visiting card boasted, back to Charlemagne. He gave a lecture on Josephine Baker which articulated the views of the liberal opposition, a panegyric in favor of freedom, jazz dance, Africa, and nudity, with particular emphasis on the female nude as the embodiment of humanist ideals. "Who fights nudity blasphemes God who created people nude."

In general, it was felt to be a shame that the Viennese, so short of money, should spend $15,000 a month to see Baker dance. But there was no way of stopping her. Nor would there be until Hitler put through a law banning blacks and Jews from the stage. They did, however, make sure she paid a substantial theater tax.

St. Paul's Church, which was next door to the Johann Strauss Theater, announced it would hold three days of service "in atonement for outrages on morality committed by Josephine Baker and other performers." On the night of her opening, the bells of St. Paul's rang again, hoping through one last exertion to lure back the audience at the nearby theater from sin to virtue. Father Frey, a Jesuit priest, preached a sermon against Josephine Baker and the Charleston, two faces of the same problem, symbols of a sinning age. He preached above all against "black whites"—Europeans who danced the Charleston or who went to see it danced at the Johann Strauss Theater.

As for Baker, the protests against her made a strong impression on her. The passions she aroused in Vienna, she said, were ones to which she had always wanted to be a stranger. They were close to the passions behind the East St. Louis race riot. She was aware that she had arrived in Vienna at a bad time, a time of crisis and unemployment. She could understand people's irritation at the high price of tickets to her show, and she could see how her fabulously expensive costumes (25,000 francs apiece) seemed to mock their poverty. Still, it was horrible to confront people who considered you the devil incarnate or a demon of immorality without ever having seen you.

With Pepito, she worked out her response. She made her entrance onto the stage of the Johann Strauss Theater wearing a long, demure dress, and she sang "Pretty Little Baby," an innocuous Tin Pan Alley dance tune which gave her an opportunity to show her geniality. Its simple lyrics could be understood by listeners with only a small amount of English.

> *What's the use of crying,*
> *When there's no denying,*
> *Pretty little baby,*
> *I'm in love with you.*

She had learned the lesson of the Folies-Bergère on how to put the audience at its ease: lead with your least threatening stuff. She sang the perky tune in a voice trembling with fear of various sorts and believed she had made her point: that she was a person, not a demon, with simple emotions and a desire to be loved.

If she didn't want to be seen as a demon of immorality, a symbol of decadence or luxury, she was equally uncomfortable being just a nude body and a rallying point for people who liked nude bodies. When Count Sternberg defended Baker in the Austrian Parliament with the argument that enemies of nudity blaspheme God, he was alluding to the *Nacktkultur* (nudist) movement, which had many followers, especially in Germany, from early in the twenties. The premise of this movement, radically compressed, was that nudity is natural, clothes artificial. Being cut off from nature (that is, compelled to wear clothes), people became mentally and sexually unhealthy.

Maurice Parmalee, who spent several years in German nudist camps in the twenties, introduced the *Nacktkultur* movement to English-speaking readers in a book called *Nudism in Modern Life: The New Gymnosophy*, published in London in 1927 and New York in 1931. (*Gymnos* is Greek for "nude.") With nutty utopian literalness, Parmalee assumed that all artificial distinctions between people would disappear when clothes did. Most bodies were beautiful, he said, if we could learn to see their particular beauty. He, for one, could see the beauty in the navel, always a welcome break in the broad oval expanse below the chest. As for race, Parmalee believed each race had a beauty of its own, and brown skin was especially pleasing to gymnosophists because they were accustomed to suntanned bodies. Nevertheless, race prejudice was the single greatest barrier to the existence of a gymnosophic utopia: people who do not like each other on little exposure, he said, are scarcely going to want to see more of each other!

According to Parmalee, "nationalism, militarism, race pride and prejudice" were innately at odds with nudism. And it may have been true in prudish, provincial Vienna at the time of Baker's performance. In that place at that time, the forces of nudism were allied with the liberal democratic internationalists. But in Germany the cult of the body needed only minor changes in order to become an important part of Nazi ideology. The naked or near-naked body had to be striving for some sort of ideal perfection, preferably some more than individual goal, it had to be seen in juxtaposition with the leader, it had to be asexual in employment. Then, even a black body, like that of Jesse Owens, the American athlete, could serve the purposes of fascist aesthetics—as Leni Riefenstahl makes him do in her film about the 1936 Olympics.

It was much harder to assimilate the irreverent gyrations of Josephine Baker to that strand of Nazi idealism, and her affiliation with jazz put her, as far as Nazis were concerned, in the camp of the urban, the intellectual, the Jewish. Her nudity was not that of the noble savage, uncorrupted by civilization, whom Nazis tended to admire, but the nudity of urban nightlife, sophistication, decadence. Even today, Germans take their nudity seriously. But Josephine's nudity was always playful. Moreover, she adored clothes. In addition to her passionate acquisition of the work of Paris designers, she bought the local costumes of every place she visited. Pepito once accused her of being the most overdressed nude dancer he'd ever known. If clothes were French and nudity was German, the long dress she wore for her opening in Vienna was as much of a rebuke to her supporters as to her attackers.

The opening itself passed without incident. She was warmly received. Yet so polarized in general was Baker's reception in Vienna that one could predict her fans would include psychoanalysts, who tended to be Jewish, progressive, and international in outlook. Like the nudists, they distrusted concealment and believed society had created neurosis by inhibiting instinctual behavior. Josephine Baker was the impudent, transgressing id in a particularly seductive form.

Throughout her European tour, she repeated her Paris practice of doing late-night cabaret performances, sometimes rechristening the place Chez Joséphine for the length of her visit. One night a group of psychoanalysts went to see her perform at a chic nightclub, the Wolf Pavilion, after a meeting at which a paper of Sándor Ferenczi's had been presented and discussed. After her dance, she came down to chat with the audience. She picked out Ferenczi himself to tease. She sat on his lap as though it were the most natural thing in the world. Her hair, as usual, was tightly plastered down on her head with a thick pomade. Ferenczi was bald. She stroked herself on the head and then ran her hand over Ferenczi's hairless pate. "There," she said. "Now it will grow."

When she left Vienna and continued her tour in Hungary, Yugoslavia, Denmark, Rumania, Czechoslovakia, and Germany, Baker continued to provoke controversy. Her second stop was Budapest, where her performance was cleared in advance. She did a sample Charleston for the Minister of the Interior and a committee of censors. Nonetheless, angry students went so far as to attack her audience with ammonia bombs. As the Austrians had been angry that she wasn't Austrian, the Hungarians were angry that she wasn't Hungarian. They, too, resented seeing so many blacks on their stages and in their restaurants. In Zagreb, students of the Clerical Party rioted. They also threw things inside the theater, shouting, "Long live Croatian culture! Down with vulgarity!" In Prague, at the start of a ten-day run at a cabaret, Baker was forced to take refuge on the roof of her limousine because of the uproar that marked her arrival. Even in Denmark there was discussion about whether she should be allowed to dance bare-breasted, but, predictably, it was more temperate and fair-minded than elsewhere. Miss Dagmar, a sculptress and representative of the Danish Women's Temperance League, held that Baker's performance should be prohibited, although it was "probably no worse than others." Assistant Inspector Heiberg, representing the police, said he'd never seen

Baker dance and so could not prohibit something which, for all he knew, was extremely attractive.

With a few demure additions, she was doing the same act that had begun to cause yawns in Paris. But her act itself was no longer the issue in some cases. In the winter of 1929, the Munich police prohibited her performance on the grounds that she might cause disorders and corrupt public morals. Their decision was supported by the ultranationalist newspaper: "It would have been evidently disagreeable to the police of Munich to have to protect from the public fury this Negress who has already been booed everywhere."

One French journalist said of Baker's reception in Munich, "Since the occupation of the Rhineland by the Senegalese, certain Germans detest the black race; this coldness is surely addressed more to the race than to the dancer." By and large, however, the French newspapers reported on these events in a tone of lighthearted irony. Before the war, said one, the restaurants of Europe were filled with Hungarian violinists. "It certainly must be irritating for them to be replaced by blacks." Another said that the protests against Baker in Central Europe were a stage of the fight between the saxophone and the violin, the Charleston and the waltz. The sax was certain to win. The old order was merely protesting its own passing. The services of expiation in Vienna struck some French reporters as particularly hilarious. This sort of thing would never, they said, happen in Paris. In retrospect, with a clear view of the political dimension of these cultural battles, the French underestimation of them seems ominous.

When Baker crossed the ocean to perform in Argentina and found herself as controversial there as she had been in Austria, Germany, and Hungary, she was stunned and horrified. Again, liberals and conservatives split on the issue of her performance. Again, she was a lost soul, a femme fatale, an object of scandal, a demon of immorality. President Hipólito Irigoyen opposed her. Her supporters shouted "Down with Irigoyen" before her performance. She concluded that it all had very little to do with her, and she was losing patience with being a symbol.

From Buenos Aires, she sent an uncharacteristically angry letter back to newspapers in Paris, saying that she was going to give up dancing, "which practiced by a white woman is moral and by a black one transgresses." Before her European tour, she had thought of racism as American. Now she saw the problem as global.

A certain bitterness was born in the experience of touring and an irony about morality. "The old Catholic parties hounded me with a Christian hatred from station to station, city to city, one stage to another," she said in her book about her travels. But in the experience of touring, of reaching across language barriers to touch the hearts of audiences of all nations, was also born that cabaret internationalism which was her response to provincial hatreds.

During the long rides by train, plane, and boat between cities and countries and continents, she talked with Pepito about hatred and about love, on the international level. Pepito, who was nothing if not encouraging, urged Josephine to express her ideas in a book. Together they worked out a story which expressed her ideas, and after they got back to France, Pepito, with the writer Félix de la Camara, wrote the book which they had sketched out together. *Mon Sang dans tes veines* (*My Blood in Your Veins*) represents Josephine Baker's reply to what she saw in Central and Eastern Europe in the late twenties.

In the novel, Mr. Ira Cushman Barclay, who has made a fortune in chewing gum, builds an estate for himself, called the Oaks, an hour west of Boston. He soon dies of cerebral overwork, the leading cause of death among chewing gum manufacturers, leaving his wife and son Fred, eight months old. When Fred is ten, Mrs. Barclay's black maid has a daughter, Joan. She and Fred grow up together, the best of friends. Time goes by. There is an inserted riff on how the ancients valued dark skin more than light. Fred fights in World War I and returns to occupy himself with chewing gum. He no longer has time for Joan, who misses him deeply. Wandering through the woods, she stumbles on a cobweb-covered chapel and is stunned to find inside a black madonna. Fred explains it is a copy of a Polish icon in Krakow, and Joan thinks how nice Europeans must be to worship a black madonna.

For pages, Joan ponders the injustice of race discrimination. Why, Topsy and Pat, the dogs, are black and white and eat from the same bowl. But not the people at the Oaks! Like Cinderella, Joan watches while others luckier than herself enjoy themselves. Fred brings his friends home to cavort around the swimming pool. His friends have all increased the fortunes made by their parents, the kind of audacious immigrants who make America great and prove that fresh blood regenerates a country, giving new vigor to anemic, decadent civilizations.

Of these young people, Clarence Clifton is Fred's favorite. She comes from New Orleans and consequently hates black people. She is also a flapper, that is, concerned with nothing but her own pleasure. While Mrs. Barclay sits knitting sweaters for poor children, Clarence sits smoking. In various episodes, Clarence displays her hatred of Joan and contempt for black people. She doesn't even like to see old family photos in which Fred appears with the little black girl.

Then one day Fred is run over by his own Rolls-Royce. He is brought to a doctor who lives in a hut in the forest. Fred needs an immediate blood transfusion, and the blood has to come from someone young, so the doctor himself is out. Radiant and smiling, Joan offers her blood. A black giving blood to a white? "Scientifically," the doctor says, "there's no reason not to." The novel now erupts into a fugue, a cadenza on blood, how the blood of various races mixed on the battlefields of France, how Isis cried over the bloody body of Osiris, how Christ through his blood redeemed mankind—an effusion on transfusion which the whole book exists to justify.

The tubes are set up between them and the blood flows directly from Joan's veins into the unconscious Fred's. She makes the doctor promise not to tell Fred when he awakes who saved him. Fred, however, is bent on discovering just that. He burgles the doctor's files. Can it be? "I now have black blood in my veins?" He tells Clarence he can't marry her now and she agrees: "You've become a black white man." Joan, happy to have repaid her debt to the Barclays, rejoins Nature.

My Blood in Your Veins is little more than a curiosity in the history of fiction. As a publishing event it was of no importance at all. Few copies were printed, and it was badly reviewed. Many reviewers could not resist jokes about Josephine's ghostwriters, for which the French word is *nègres*. But the book has interest. Celebrities, however given to writing memoirs and autobiographies, more or less crafted public statements, rarely offer the direct access to their fantasy life that a high-minded trashy novel like this one provides. *My Blood in Your Veins* allows us to see into Josephine Baker's inner being when she was in her early twenties. Adolescent female fantasies of rescuing the man one loves are combined with extraordinary racial fervor and didacticism and expressed in an imagery of blood transfusion which is very much of the time.

Blood was important to racists. They located in the blood those mysterious substances that made a race a race, that gave it strength and vigor, or doomed it to inferiority. It was "the somatic determinant of whatever one wished to explain." According to Gobineau, a civilization declines because "it no longer has the same blood in its veins, continual adulterations having gradually affected the quality of that blood." The horror of mixing blood went back to Gobineau. Although, in his view, it initially produced vigor, in the long run it led to disaster and degeneration.

Dracula captures a fascination with blood—and with the myth of blood degenerating and being capable of regeneration—which has certainly proved enduring but which dates back to the turn of the century. Vampires and bloodsuckers became important metaphors. "Mingling blood" was a euphemism for sex, with the result that blood and sexual fluids were not clearly distinguished: blood came to seem sexy.

A best-selling novel in Germany after World War I was called *Die Sünde wieder das Blut* (*Sins Against the Blood*). It told the story of an Aryan woman, once married to a Jew, who married an Aryan the second time around. But the child of these two Aryans looked distinctly Jewish. That was because her blood had been permanently tainted by the Jewish liaison. This was possible according to a phenomenon known as "telegony," or long-range generation. To atone for her "sin against the blood," the woman kills herself and her child. Her Aryan husband is shot through the heart in defense of the Fatherland on Christmas Day, 1914. He had been acquitted of guilt for his murder of his wife's first husband because he'd convinced the jury that the German people would be destroyed if it didn't get rid of "the Jewish vampire." Originally published in 1918, this tissue of myths about blood and doom had sold 200,000 copies by 1922, and a sequel appeared in 1921 which sold 100,000 copies immediately.

It must have been a shock for racists like Arthur Dinter, author of *Sins Against the Blood*, to face scientific research of the early twenties about blood. Karl Landsteiner, an Austrian who emigrated to America in 1922, discovered that there were four types of blood—he called them A, B, AB, and O—based on the presence or absence of certain sugar molecules (mucopolysaccharides) and that blood within these groups could be safely exchanged. His research enabled blood transfusions to be performed—a clinical possibility which seemed as miraculous in the twenties as artificial heart transplants do now. One bon vivant keeping tabs on what was fashionable in Paris in 1926 noted that, along with cocktails and nervous breakdowns, blood transfusions were new on the scene and already becoming routine. There was, then, no mysterious pigment or racial character in the blood. There were merely these mucopolysaccarides, neutral as all get-out, A, B, AB, and O, which did not reflect race in any way. There was no scientific reason why the blood of races couldn't mix, provided the transfusion occurred between people of the same blood type.

Blood transfusion caught the popular imagination. People who donated blood to other people were seen as being significantly connected to them, and newspapers featured the stories of many such gifts. Schoolteacher gives blood to save pupil, father gives blood to save son, father dies despite blood given by his two sons, wife submits to transfusion to save husband's life, high school baseball team offers blood to save pitcher, police band offers blood to save patrolman, man offers blood to district attorney who caused his arrest. In New York, the stories begin in a trickle in 1919, start to swell in 1921, and continue in a flood until 1930, when it is still considered news that Mayor Walker's nephews gave blood to a dying priest. But in that year the first bills were introduced in New York to regulate blood donors. The romance was over. It was in that year, too, that Karl Landsteiner was given the Nobel Prize for his work on blood tests. And the following year,

an exotic dancer would produce a transfusion novel, which, however
inept as fiction, attempted to turn the tradition of racist "blood novels"
on its head.

After Budapest, Josephine Baker performed in Copenhagen, Prague
(a big city for jazz before World War II), Bucharest, Oslo, Stockholm,
and Berlin, where she was reunited onstage with Louis Douglas, the
principal dancer of the Revue Nègre, who had settled in Germany.
She was not traveling with her own show and her own musicians, so
the quality of the work around her was not always the best. In each
city shows were patched together quickly. Pepito felt more and more
that this was inappropriate for a great star like Baker and that the
next time she should bring her own show with her. As it was, too
much depended on her. An American journalist who caught her in
Copenhagen, where she was backed by a chorus from Vienna and
some Tiller Girls, said "she carries the whole show on her shoulders
—and hips." Her weight was down from 137 pounds in Paris to 115.

She turned twenty-two in the spring of her first year of touring,
and her energy was immense. The point of the tour had been to create
a new Josephine before returning to Paris. Pepito didn't forget. He
encouraged her to try new things before these foreign audiences. Vienna was the first place she sang in public. In Budapest, she acted for
the first time, performing in a little skit—in Hungarian.

For two and a half years, Josephine and Pepito stayed out of Paris
except for short visits. They went to Austria, Hungary, Rumania,
Italy, Spain, Germany, Denmark, Sweden, Norway, Holland, Hungary again, Germany again, then to South America—Argentina, Chile,
Uruguay, Brazil. They visited twenty-four countries and many more
cities. In Spain, they stopped in Seville, Pamplona, Valencia, Grenada,
Córdoba, Madrid, Valladolid, Málaga, and Barcelona. At Seville during Holy Week a parade of penitents in high, pointed cowls carrying
smoking torches reminded her of the Ku Klux Klan. Pepito made the
bookings and travel arrangements and handled her publicity. He taught
her to introduce herself at the major newspaper offices when she arrived
in a new city and to leave her calling card at embassies.

"Every new country is a new dance I want to do," she said. She
collected local costumes and names: Josephina, Giuseppina, La Bake-

rova, Phifine. She liked traveling by plane, which she described as a cradle with wings. The frenetic pace of touring suited her. So did the many opportunities travel affords for wisecracks. Of Scandinavia: "It's crazy how clean everything is in those countries. You can lean anywhere." In Oslo, she was escorted through the streets by two policemen on horses and, to show she hadn't been arrested, she kept up a stream of jokes. When she entered Sweden, she needed special permission to bring in her dogs, of which she then had two. But one was pregnant and gave birth to two more in Sweden. An official, checking on the dogs, asked if they had been declared. Yes. Admitted? Yes. How many? Two. "And those?" he said, pointing to the puppies. "Aren't they dogs?" "No," said Baker. "They're just samples. And you wouldn't want me to put them back where they came from, would you?"

Whereas 1927 had been the year of Lindbergh's great fame in Europe, 1928 was the year that Italians, Scandinavians, and Central Europeans talked about Josephine Baker. People who didn't see her personal appearances could hardly avoid her posters. There were also magazine and newspaper photos and her films—*La Sirène des Tropiques* and the various shorts made of her dancing. She had recorded some jazzy American tunes for the Odéon label in Paris in 1927, including "Breezing Along with the Breeze," "Bye Bye Blackbird," and "After I Say I'm Sorry," and these, too, were making their way around Europe. Her memoirs had been translated into German, Spanish, and Italian. Readers in Czechoslovakia, who knew from the memoirs that Josephine believed a rabbit's foot brought her luck, showered the stage with rabbit's feet at the end of her performance.

A trouper, she loved rising to occasions, and this kind of touring gave her many opportunities to do so. She performed in Bucharest in an open-air theater on a hot day with rain threatening. If rain put a stop to the performance before the halfway point, the manager had to refund the audience's money. An audience of 3,000 was packed into a theater meant to hold 1,700. The first drops of rain fell when the music began. The musicians were soon missing half the notes, and one act was pushing another offstage. By the time Baker came on, it was pouring. She danced with an umbrella. The musicians and people in the audience opened umbrellas, too. Some women put their skirts over their heads to keep off the rain. Many people left, but others came in to take their places. After a while, Baker gave up on the umbrella and danced in the drenching rain. Her bananas got soggy and dropped off. Her makeup ran down her cheeks. Finally the manager said they had reached the halfway point, needn't reimburse the audience, and could stop. Baker continued to dance. "What an audience. What enthusiasm. What a storm. What a bath. So much for Rumania!"

The controversy she aroused during her long European tour scared her and made her appreciate France even more than before. It was in Central Europe, missing France, that she began seriously to learn to speak French. On a trip back to Paris in April 1929, she stopped by a couple of newspaper offices to demonstrate her new command of the language and to sound her new theme.

"I don't want to live without Paris. It's my country. The Charleston, the bananas, finished. Understand? I have to be worthy of Paris. I want to become an artist."

Pepito amplified: "I want to show a wholly new Josephine Baker. She's no longer a curiosity. She's an artist now. She sings beautifully and she's a good comic actress. She'll be a great French star."

"But I *am* French," Josephine protested. "I'm black, but I'm French. And I love Paris. I *adore* Paris. I will have that written on the roof of the house I just bought. Yours is the only country where a person can live in peace."

She returned with new determination and self-confidence. It no longer bothered her if people said she was ugly. "I have no pretension to being pretty," she said. "I have pointed knees and the breasts of a seventeen-year-old boy. But even if my face is ugly and my teeth stick out, my eyes are beautiful and my body is intelligent."

As a nineteen-year-old in 1925, she had courted frenzy. Her stage performances were scheduled explosions. Offstage she did anything to attract attention. There was something frantic about her efforts to please. At twenty-four, after two years of training, she was no longer at the mercy of her own talent. Her performances were more disciplined. She had learned to measure her activity, how to be quiet. The diamond in the rough of 1925 had been polished and placed in a 1930 Cartier setting.

A journalist they talked to noted that Josephine had lost weight and calmed down during her travels. It was touching, he said, to see her trying to be worthy of the love she had inspired in her French audience. She reminded him of a little girl trying to tame her caprices in order to please her parents.

"The *danse sauvage* is finished," she said. "I was sixteen when I danced the Charleston almost nude." (She had been nineteen.) "Now I am a woman. You have to grow and change all the time. When you no longer have something new to do or say you disappear."

She packed her banana skirt away, firmly but respectfully, in a trunk. One day, Pepito, in a playful mood, took it out and put it on. Josephine was indignant. "You shouldn't make fun of the tools of a person's trade."

To welcome her back to Paris, André Rivollet, her next literary collaborator, arranged a luncheon for her on the Champs-Élysées. Her closest friends were there: Pepito, of course, who was always with her, and Monsieur and Madame Dalliez, the couple at whose home she and Pepito stayed for the past couple of years whenever they were in Paris, and Joe Alex, her dance partner from the Revue Nègre. The other guests were a glittering collection of artists, writers, and fashionable Parisians, whose presence served to underline the fact that Josephine, in coming back to Paris, had made herself into one of the city's monuments. Marie Laurencin, the Countess de la Rochefoucauld, the Baron and Baronne de Rothschild, the Countess de Noailles, never before intimates of Josephine, all were there, because the best way to make yourself seem a familiar and long-standing part of the scene is to go away for a while and return.

CHAPTER 5
QUEEN OF THE
COLONIES

In the thirties, the most respectable of the Paris music halls was the Casino de Paris. Its audience tended less toward foreigners than that of the Folies-Bergère and it emphasized singing and dancing more than displays of flesh. It was possible for a visiting American to mistake the Casino de Paris for a regular theater, take his wife and daughter there, be shocked by the skimpiness of the costumes, and have to escort them off at the intermission. Such an embarrassment occurred to Nancy Reagan's father, allowing Mrs. Reagan, when she was a very young girl, a quick glimpse of Josephine Baker in her prime.

The Casino de Paris was run by Henri Varna, a producer who knew how to do things right. He hired Josephine Baker to star in the 1930–31 show and immediately bought her a leopard. It was purchased at the famous German animal farm, Hagenbrecht's, and flown to Le Bourget. The star and the leopard, Chiquita, wearing a diamond collar which was sold years later for $20,000, became inseparable. Accompanied by Chiquita to Deauville that summer, Josephine was a sensation in the gambling rooms and on the boardwalk. Back in Paris, when the couple went to the theater and the leopard got loose, terrifying the audience, the incident made newspapers as far away as America, as it was surely intended to. Sometimes Chiquita, a male despite the name, took a taxi alone to a rendezvous with Josephine, because he hated Pepito's erratic style of driving. Variously cited in the press as a panther, a tiger, and a jaguar, Chiquita made great copy, providing an objective correlative for Josephine's jungle elegance. When they walked together on the streets of Paris, people cheered. This was the kind of style the city loved.

Varna knew—and taught Josephine—that a star owed it to her public to behave like royalty. At the end of the first performance at the Casino, Josephine was overwhelmed by the applause and took her bows with timid awe, thanking the audience for their kindness. "Thank you, thank you so much, ladies and gentlemen." Varna rebuked her. Was she a street singer? No, she was a star! The applause was her due. The proper response was to nod now and then to acknowledge it.

The show at the Casino de Paris was called *Paris qui remue*. That translates literally as *Paris Which Bustles* but better, perhaps, as *Swinging Paris*. The theater had recently been bought by Varna and Oscar Dufrenne, who would soon own many of the most famous entertainment spots in Paris. Their previous show, their first at the Casino de Paris, had starred Mistinguett, the famous, imperious "Miss," who was the pet of the French music-hall audience in the way Fannie Brice was of the American. The show had been called *Paris Miss* in her honor. She would star again in the show following Baker's at the Casino de Paris, *Paris qui brille* (*Glittering Paris*), but in the middle there was Baker.

Mistinguett was not happy that her place at the Casino was being taken by Baker, and she did not keep her objections to herself. Word reached Baker that Mistinguett did not want "that little black girl" in her dressing room and so she refused to use it, changing, until she had made her point, behind a kind of tent thrown up in the hall. Mistinguett's dance partner, an American named Earl Leslie, was hired to help choreograph the show, and about that, too, Miss let her resentment be known. Leslie himself felt he had to choose sides. Did Henri Varna really intend to let Baker walk down the onstage staircase that Mistinguett had made her own? Apparently, he did.

The same illustrator, Zig, did posters and program covers for both Mistinguett's and Josephine Baker's Casino de Paris shows, very much in the same style. They are dressed in bathing suits, trailing feathers, draped in jewels. Each is recognizably herself, yet registers primarily as an icon of glamour. In marked contrast to the caricatured negritude of Paul Colin's 1925 poster for the Revue Nègre, the only allusion to Baker's race in Zig's poster for the 1930–31 Casino de Paris show is a slight caramelizing of the skin. This image of Baker and the matching one of her on the cover of the program—in which the leopard stands on its hind legs offering a beribboned bouquet—represent her complete transformation from a black novelty act into a Parisian music-hall star.

Nevertheless, her race had something to do with Dufrenne and Varna's decision to hire her for the 1930–31 season, for 1931 was the year of the Colonial Exposition in Paris, and this enormous celebration of France's colonial empire provided the theme for *Paris qui remue*, which, despite its title, had very little to do with Paris, swinging or otherwise. If the French do not know geography, said one critic after seeing this show, it's because they do not go to the music hall. It invoked Martinique, Algeria, Indochina, Equatorial Africa, and Madagascar. When the sketches were not directly about the colonies, they alluded to the Colonial Exposition in other ways. "Noblesse d'auto," for example, with sets by Paul Colin, showed all the aristocrats of the automotive world—a Voisin, a Bugatti, a Mercedes, a Delage (Josephine's new car), a Rolls, and a Chrysler—heading off to carry people of fashion out to the grounds of the Colonial Exposition.

The exposition was built on about two hundred and fifty acres around Lake Daumesnil in and near the Bois de Vincennes. The No. 8 line of the Métro had been extended to the Porte Dorée to bring to the suburbs those Parisians who did not have Bugattis or Voisins. The main building, the Musée des Colonies, designed to remain after the exposition closed, was a clean-lined Art Moderne structure with an immense bas-relief on its façade, executed between 1928 and 1931 by the sculptor Janniot. This, and the murals in the ground-floor salons, had the same theme: the contribution of the overseas territories to France and to civilization.

Laid out neatly and geometrically in front of the Musée des Colonies, now the Museum of African and Oceanic Art, were pavilions and buildings representing all the variety of the empire. Indochina, the jewel of the empire, had the largest pavilion, which included a reconstruction of a temple at Angkor Wat. French West Africa and French Equatorial Africa also had imposing buildings. The former contained a model African village in which Africans went about their daily life, occasionally interrupting their labors for a "native" dance.

The colonies of North Africa, among others, reproduced their distinctive architecture in buildings which held displays of textiles, costumes, ceramics, and metalwork. Many of the pavilions had restaurants around the lake serving regional food. Regional music was played. Featured also were dioramas of the principal towns and large photographs showing close-up views of the architecture and the people in their native habitats. Other colonial powers besides France were represented. The Dutch pavilion displayed reliefs from the Buddhist shrine of Borobudur. There was a scaled-down version of a Mogul tomb in Agra.

The amount of information about France's overseas territories generated by the exposition was enormous. The government printing press deluged the public with pamphlets: the textiles of Indochina, hunting in the Cameroons. The biweekly *Revue des Deux Mondes* covered the exposition in issue after issue, with one series of articles on individual pavilions and another on the art. There was a notable tenderness in much of the writing. One former colonial administrator went so far as to say that France had been lucky to have the least evolved and the most loyal of colonial subjects: they would never use against the French the weapons the French had taught them to use. It was in many minds that colonial troops had fought for France in the Great War. Thirty-five thousand men from French West Africa alone had died.

In the summer and fall of 1931, between May and December, the Colonial Exposition was a favorite place for Parisians to go. Former colonial administrators may have wandered the grounds of the exposition daydreaming about the world they had ruled, congratulating themselves on the empire they had built for France in the face of the public's indifference or even hostility. But the purpose of the show was to educate a public which had never seen the nonmetropolitan parts of France—one can say in retrospect: to whip up public enthusiasm for an empire that France was just about to lose. The exposition's theme was that colonialism was a two-way street: France had given much to its colonies, but the colonies had given much—and not just raw materials—to France.

While the Colonial Exposition showed the colonies as natural and cultural resources, the Casino de Paris showed the colonies as sexual resources. The Colonial Exposition said, "We gave our colonies medicine, literacy, industrialization. They gave us textiles, jewelry, ceramics."

"And sex," the Casino de Paris seemed to add.

In the revue of 1930–31, Josephine Baker's first song—set in a sketch ostensibly about music in the colonies (Madagascan drums, Indian bells, Algerian tambourines)—was "La Petite Tonkinoise." She was "the little girl from Tonkin," the Vietnamese mistress of a French colonist, who loved him more than all the rest.

> C'est moi qui suis sa petite,
> Son Annana—, son Annana—, son Annamite,
> Je suis vive, je suis charmante,
> Comme un petit oiseau qui chante.
> Il m'appelle sa petite bourgeoise.
> Sa Tonkiki—, sa Tonkiki—, sa Tonkinoise.
> D'autres lui font les beaux yeux,
> Mais, c'est moi qui l'aime le mieux.

I'm his little girl. I am charming. I am lively. I am like a little bird. I am his Annamite, his Tonkinese. I am (above all) *his*. The song was not new. Vincent Scotto had written it in 1905 for the music-hall artist Polin. But it was too appropriate not to use in the year of the Colonial Exposition.

Vincent Scotto wrote a song especially for Josephine Baker to sing in *Paris qui remue*, and it seemed so right for her it became her theme song. By the time the show had run for a year, 481 performances, Josephine figured she had sung "J'ai deux amours" a thousand times. There is no calculating how many times she had sung it by the time of her death forty-five years later. A hundred thousand? The song let her claim to have two loves—her country and Paris.

> *J'ai deux amours,*
> *Mon pays et Paris.*
> *Par eux toujours*
> *Mon coeur est ravi.*

It was a graceful reminder to her audience of her exotic status as a foreigner but also of her dedication to her adopted city. Over her many years of singing the song, Baker found it capable of some flexibility, and as her attachment to her native land weakened, she would sometimes at the end of the song say "Mon pays c'est Paris" (my country is Paris) instead of "Mon pays et Paris" (my country and Paris).

In its original setting, however, "J'ai deux amours" was not the song of an American girl who has made it in Paris and yearns for home. It was part of an elaborate sketch called "Ounawa," for which the leopard Chiquita had been purchased, set in the equatorial jungle. It is the song of an African girl in love with a French colonist. He invites her to return with him to Paris and she wants to go, but the people of her tribe won't allow this betrayal. She is torn: "j'ai deux amours." On the one hand racial and national identity, on the other romance, sex, and swinging Paris.

Another of Baker's numbers from the Casino de Paris show, while not overtly colonial, touched on the rape fantasy so closely allied to the sexual fantasy of French colonialism. It featured her own favorite costume in the show, designed—as were the sets—by Georges Barbier, and it consisted of an enormous pair of diaphanous wings, shaped somewhat like those of a dragonfly. She entered from the top, down a steep ramp, and arrived onto the forest floor, where she was pursued by savage hunters who tried to rip off her wings. She protested, begged, fled. They surrounded her and tore off her plumage, leaving her wretched.

Comparisons of French and British colonialism almost always make the point that France offered her colonial peoples fuller assimilation. They could be French. They merely had to learn to speak French and adopt French culture. In return they had the blessings of French culture—including good food, cheerful clothing, and a certain Latin *douceur de vie*. Anyone who has traveled in the Caribbean between islands with a British colonial past and those with a French colonial past can feel the difference. But former colonials had long since started to resent the very seductions of French culture. Frantz Fanon would complain on their behalf at being put in the position of rebelling against the colonizers in the colonizers' own language.

There is another way of characterizing the difference between English colonialism and French. It is visible in the fantasy productions of the Paris music halls. The French were publicly willing to imagine themselves making love with colonial women. If their colonies were harems, they regarded them with the greater affection one has for a harem than for a bauxite mine, an ebony grove, or a rubber plantation. An important colonial administrator put it tellingly in his book about governing West Africa: "The territory is not just raw material for finance, commerce, army and administration to work with; nor is it something to be made an idol of. It is a living body, and we must enter into relations with it if we are to govern it with full knowledge of what we are doing."

Josephine Baker was chosen to be queen of the Colonial Exposition in March 1931, but almost immediately there were protests, which focused on a couple of issues: that Josephine Baker was a native of the United States and that the United States was not a French colony, that she was not a native speaker of French or any of the African dialects, and that she had oiled her hair smooth, like any white flapper's.

"Queen, Where Is Yo' Kink?" read the headline in one American newspaper's account of this affair. So she lost out on being queen, but she toured the exposition in state, escorted by Henri Varna. She loved it all and told Varna that he had never produced better backdrops for her.

One merchant made her a gift of a necklace. "Are you Tunisian? Syrian?" she asked. "I am a Syrian from Belleville," he said, naming the seedy quarter on the edge of Paris where many Arabs lived. Varna translated into music-hall: "Belleville—that is the native island of Maurice Chevalier."

Baker was singing now. In July 1930, she recorded for Columbia Records in Paris the six songs she would do in the Casino de Paris revue: "La Petite Tonkinoise," "J'ai deux amours," "Voulez-vous de la canne à sucre," "Dis-nous, Joséphine," "Pretty Little Baby," and "Suppose." She did not like recording very much, needing the response of a live audience to feel secure. The equipment—the microphones, wires, and cables—seemed predatory, as though they were drinking up her vitality and giving nothing back. If the technicians got so absorbed in their work that they could not react to her, she froze. Although she never got stage fright onstage, she got it in recording sessions. To continue to feel comfortable, she had to get people laughing. Sometimes she would giggle uncontrollably until the musicians joined in and Pepito had to bring them to order—which he would do with the air of a father asking that his *enfant terrible* not be encouraged.

This was not the first time she had recorded. For Odéon, in the middle of 1927, she had recorded "Bye Bye Blackbird," "I'm Leaving for Alabamy" (which reached the label as "I'm Leaving for Albany"), "I Love Dancing," "Lonesome Homesick Blues," "After I Say I'm Sorry," "Then I'll Be Happy," "Hello, Bluebird," and "I'm Just Breezing Along with the Breeze." The labels identify Baker as "the black star of the Folies-Bergère," but her repertoire was entirely American and her pronunciation, as captured on these records, was American as well: "bird" was "boyd" and "first" was "foyst," as in the Brooklynesque accent of New Orleans. In many sides, she had a good Dix-ieland backup group called Jacob's Jazz. She was peppy, bouncy, upbeat, and made up in energy and attack what she lacked in finesse. Sometimes, as in "Then I'll Be Happy," she scat-sang, imitating a trumpet, to good effect. But she could not sustain a note, and the singing was not impressive.

In the 1930 recordings, she can hold a note, and while her voice is not as rich and interesting as it would become later in her life, she can be listened to without a wince. "Pretty Little Baby" and "Suppose," the two songs in English, are the only cuts at all resembling her early repertoire, but even they are closer to music-hall songs than to jazz. "Suppose," in particular, is half spoken, half quavered in the manner of Jolson and vaudeville. The spoken introduction leading into song was something she would do well throughout her career. She does it in "Voulez-vous de la canne à sucre," which she sang on the stage of the Casino de Paris as a woman from Martinique offering the audience sugarcane.

Singing, she opened herself up to new rejection. The music critics had never had a chance at her before. But they loved her. In fact, everybody loved her, and the show at the Casino de Paris was a success with critics and audience alike, with Baker attracting larger audiences than Mistinguett had.

At her most glamorous, in a simple but tight-fitting dress, escorted by a gaggle of young men in tuxedos, Baker was now completely at home. With her male backup chorus, she sang "Dis-nous, Joséphine," the first in what would be a long series of songs mythologizing her own career. The young men sing of her return from her voyages and ask if Paris seems changed to her. She, in the sung equivalent of a diplomatic press conference, declares herself charmed with all the cities of the world but "there's only one Paris."

A tone of happy surprise greeted the new Josephine's performance: "We said goodbye to a perky and amusing but primitive little black girl. An artist, a great artist comes back to us. She is sensitive, moving, still beautiful, but now her beauty is even more striking because it's set off by her talent. . . . Josephine has reconquered the most fickle and difficult public in the world. She has taken up her scepter again, sweetly, with the timid self-mockery that wins everyone's sympathies." Critics loved Baker's voice, her French, her new elegance. Fréjaville himself called her "a very great artist," which was like a spaniel winning the Westminster Kennel Club show. He adored her voice—"as pure as a child's voice, that accent, that sincerity, that confidence, that wildness, that musical virtuosity which seems so natural, and the pretty melancholy of Scotto's tune 'J'ai deux amours.' "

When people compared her, as many did, to Mistinguett, they generally found Baker the French star's equal. "Mademoiselle Josephine Baker descended the traditional staircase with as much ease and *abatage* as the Other and accomplished with smiling good grace all the requisite exploits." The reviews seem like reports of a sporting event. Mistinguett and Baker are scrutinized like rival athletes who perform difficult compulsory figures with more or less skill and *abatage*, a word which means, roughly, stage presence but carries the untranslatable connotation of knocking them dead. Many of the critics still remembered and mentioned Robert de Flers's attack on Baker as a threat to French taste. Some remembered it with satisfaction, because in the meantime de Flers had died and Josephine Baker had been assimilated. Clearly in *that* face-off, she had come out ahead.

But from an American perspective, there was some cause for regret. A French music-hall star had been born, but an American jazz performer seemed to have died. Janet Flanner, for example, loved the show, with its ridiculous delights—the surfeit of staircases (enough, she said, for a Freudian dream), its British dancing choruses, its Russian ballet, its live cheetah (Chiquita the leopard?), its trained pigeons, and the "four best cancan dancers in captivity," but she deplored the fact that Baker "has, alas, almost become a little lady."

> Her caramel-colored body, which overnight became a legend in Europe, is still magnificent, but it has become thinned, trained, almost civilized. Her voice, especially in the voo-deo-do's, is still a magic flute that hasn't yet heard of Mozart—though even that, one fears, will come with time. There is a rumor that she wants to sing refined ballads; one is surprised

that she doesn't want to play Othello. On that lovely animal visage lies now a sad look, not of captivity, but of dawning intelligence.

Flanner wanted the little animal to stay an animal, whereas the animal wanted to prove precisely that she could be a lady.

When Noble Sissle, the co-author of *Shuffle Along*, came to visit and invited her to return to the States for an all-black show, a new version of *Shuffle Along*, she was ever so slightly defensive. She wanted him to understand she felt she "could be more useful in the white man's world." But she didn't have the nerve to say it, and she let him draw his own conclusions about why she wanted to stay in Paris. He drew the reasonable enough conclusion that she wanted to stay because of love for Pepito and because she was such a success there. Still, he made her feel guilty. "Didn't being a *black* star in a *white* show prove something too?" Admittedly, when her dresser brought in her feathers and coolie hat for the Tonkinese number and complained that there were rhinestones missing in the White Bird's ankle bracelet, she had to wonder if she was fooling herself.

After years of moving around between rented places, she and Pepito had bought a house in 1929, a châteaulike, large, but ultimately suburban house, called Beau-Chêne.

Adolf Loos, the distinguished Viennese architect, who spent 1922 to 1928 in Paris, had designed a daring house for Baker in 1927. With a flat, boxlike exterior striped in alternating bands of black and white marble, it presented an impassive face to the world, but the inside contained surprises and delights. The house focused on a swimming pool, hidden from the street by an enormous wall with high windows for light. But this exciting house was never built because Josephine left Paris on her two-year world tour.

Another distinguished modernist architect became an admirer, perhaps a lover of hers, on that tour. Le Corbusier was traveling on the same ship back from South America as Josephine and Pepito. He and Josephine became great pals, and he went to the ship's costume ball dressed as Josephine Baker, with darkened skin and a waistband of feathers.

But when push came to shove Baker did not want to live in a hard-edged modern house. Although so many avant-garde artists adored her, her own tastes were not avant-garde. She thought the reputation of Picasso was a case of the emperor's new clothes. "Just a few lines, and not even straight!" For herself she preferred traditional upper-middle-class comforts and charm.

Beau-Chêne, a large, gracious stone house built in a neo-Renaissance style with dormers and turrets in the suburb of Le Vésinet, was surrounded by acres of land—plenty of room for all the animals she had acquired: dogs, cats, monkeys, parakeets, rabbits, turtles, ducks, chickens, geese, pigeons, pheasants, and turkeys. It had goldfish and lily ponds, a long gravel driveway, statues of Greek maidens in formal gardens, old oak trees, high gates, and "Joséphine Baker" spelled out in red and yellow coleus plants across the terrace. Inside, the place was a hodgepodge of styles that took Baker's fancy: a Louis XVI room with lots of gilt, an East Indian room with temple bells, a chrome and baby blue office. Although she could drive to the Casino de Paris in under an hour, it was far enough away for her to feel that she was in the country.

At home she dressed simply in skirts and blouses. She seemed much younger, almost like a little girl. She loved nature—even the circumscribed and domesticated bit of nature at her disposal in Le Vésinet. The most cynical interviewers who saw her in this setting were charmed. She walked around the grounds admiring how the plants grew, feeding things to her rabbits and turtles, followed by her dogs. She had thirteen dogs now, of different breeds and nationalities. She emphasized this as she would emphasize the variegated backgrounds of the children she adopted decades later. Many of the dogs had been abandoned. She took them in because she couldn't bear to see them suffer. She convinced these complicated Parisian journalists of the sincerity of the simple truths she lived by—a love of animals and a desire to ease suffering—so that not infrequently they ended up seeing her as a kind of St. Francis of Assisi or St. Vincent de Paul.

"She is the most likable, the least pretentious, the freest and at the same time the most timid of women."

The reverse of Circe, who turned suitors into swine, she turned journalists into poets. These jaded men waxed lyrical about childlike charms they would have ridiculed in many another. She was exempt, by race and by nationality, from the withering sophistication which Parisians and journalists can impose upon themselves. So they loved her. Now almost no one who saw her at Beau-Chêne or backstage disliked her.

She walked offstage one night and into her dressing room to find one tough journalist interviewing Pepito. Josephine announced she had eaten lamb with garlic for dinner. The meal had been exquisite, she said, but she was sure she had poisoned the entire audience with her breath. "How can I convey," he wrote, "the spontaneity, the vitality, the gentleness, the simplicity of Josephine Baker?" He couldn't even capture, he complained, the charm of her accent, with its childlike and exotic musicality. She had performed the verbal equivalent of burping and he was hers. If she left an ironing board in her drawing room at home, journalists loved her lack of pretension. The hodge-podge of styles at Beau-Chêne was refreshingly "unselfconscious."

Sometimes the backstage interviews must have been hard on her. She complained about having to mouth stock phrases or—but this was sometimes a relief—about the way these people answered their own questions. By and large she seemed to keep her cheerfulness intact and, more often than she thought, managed to express her own irreverence.

"Oh, how nice of you to come and see me. But you know I have nothing interesting to tell," she said one night.

She was wearing a white peignoir. She made the reporter turn around while she rearranged it, but he could see her body in a mirror and the robe, like two white wings, at her side.

"How come you have such white teeth?" he asked.

"*I* don't know."

"Do you prefer white men or black to make love with?"

She pulled him over to the sofa, sat him down, and said, "Really!

How can you ask such banal questions?" He said she spoke the word "banal" so caressingly, it almost seemed a compliment.

Then, since he wouldn't let his question go, she patiently told him that skin color had nothing to do with love. "*La peau*! Pfftt! Nothing."

The only time she got really exasperated was when another reporter asked her, "What is art?"

"Pepito! This gentleman wants to know what art is. Pepito, what is art? Eh?"

Always obliging, Pepito commenced a lecture on the nature of art, but Josephine, who had suddenly gotten an idea, interrupted him.

"Art is an elastic sort of love," she said. "Maybe even a little too elastic."

That she had gotten from there to here, from St. Louis to Paris, was as astonishing to her as to others. That she had gone virtually from black to white was no doubt even more troubling. One way to get control of the process was to see herself as having been made by various people. A story not of her own choice and will but of work and education imposed on her by others.

In a harsh mood of reminiscence in later years, Baker said, "I had no talent when I started, and I still have none. What I did onstage, the music told me to do. My personality was created by press agents. They gave me their brains." At various times, she credited Caroline Dudley, André Daven, Pepito, and Henri Varna for making her what she was onstage. And of course, the French public. She never forgot to credit the kindness of the public for having made her what she was. More than a species of politeness, this was part of an effort to shift responsibility for a new identity about which she felt more than a little guilt. The most extreme form this impulse takes is to say there's really nothing there and I didn't do it anyway.

At the time of her success at the Casino de Paris, there was a telling incident. She heard from her old friend Mrs. Jones who had taught her to play the trombone back in St. Louis. Along with her congratulations, Mrs. Jones sent, as a remembrance, a spike wound around with some of her hair. Josephine sent the spike on to Henri Varna as an emblem of her life: she was the spike which had had to be pounded into shape, she said, and Varna had done the pounding. What Mrs. Jones sent as a good-luck charm, a piece of folk superstition, Baker turned into a symbol of the rational processes—discipline and hard work—that had made her what she was.

It is true that in these years—the early thirties—she was borrowing heavily from other people to create a self. She was a semi-willing Galatea to Pepito's Pygmalion: he arranged for the acting, singing, and dancing lessons; she, somewhat resentfully, put in the time. Henri Varna loaded books on her head as she walked down the steep staircase of the Casino de Paris until she could do it as regally as Mistinguett. (When Baker reached the bottom of the staircase, characteristically she winked, mocking the trick she'd just pulled off.) For her next Casino de Paris show, which opened in December 1932, Pepito had to contrive even more astonishing transformations. He put her in the hands of a ballet master and made her learn to dance in toe shoes, a facility which is not acquired without much anguished effort. In rare footage of *La Joie de Paris*, her 1932–33 show, she may be seen, a strange cultural hybrid, doing some of her old jazz moves on her toes—as Sally Banes, the dance critic, puts it, "trucking on point."

The training of her stage self was matched by a stupefying amount of quasi- or para-literary effort. In 1931 Marcel Sauvage updated his earlier *Mémoires* of Baker with a book about her European tour called *Voyages et aventures de Joséphine Baker*. In the same year, the novel she had planned with Pepito, *My Blood in Your Veins*, appeared, written by Pepito and Félix de la Camara. André Rivollet was at work on another and slightly different volume of memoirs which would appear in 1935, *Une Vie de toutes les couleurs (A Many-Colored Life)*. Finally, also in 1931 Pepito published a little book he had put together from Baker's press clippings called *Joséphine Baker vue par la presse française*.

This curious volume, illustrated with caricatures of herself which Baker had been collecting and which were shown at a Paris gallery in 1931, is a cross between a press package and an autograph album. Pepito included passages from a few of the best reviews of the Revue Nègre, then page after page of praise for her performance in the 1930

Casino de Paris show, underscoring her transformation into a finished artist. The autographs, inscriptions in presentation copies of books or in her guest book, include ones from Colette ("to the most beautiful panther, the most charming woman, with my friendship"), Erich Maria Remarque ("to Josephine Baker, who brought a blast of jungle air, elemental power and beauty, onto the tired stages of Western civilization"), and Pirandello ("to the great actress with all my admiration").

Baker herself contributed an autobiographical prose poem:

At the age of eight I was already working to calm the hunger of my family.
I have suffered: hunger, cold—
I have a family
They said I was homely
That I danced like an ape
Then I was less homely—Cosmetics
I was hooted
Then I was applauded—The crowd
I continued to dance—I loved jazz
I continued to sing—I loved sadness; my soul is sick
I had an opportunity—Destiny
I had a mascot—a panther—Ancestral superstition—
I made a tour of the world—In third class and in Pullman
I am moral
They said I was the reverse
I do not smoke—I have white teeth
I do not drink—I am an American
I have a religion
I adore children
I love flowers
I aid the poor—I have suffered much
I love the animals—they are the sincerest
I sing and dance still—Perseverance
I earn much money—I do not love money
I save my money—for the time when I am no longer an attraction.

She wants us to know that the glittering Josephine of today hides a self formed by misfortune, as though we should not hold her good luck against her. The fierceness of her desire to account for herself is touching, but at least one thing she said was untrue: she was not saving money.

There was Josephine of the Casino de Paris, and there was Josephine of Le Vésinet. Josephine of the Casino appeared at openings, signed autographs, modeled expensive dresses, rode a horse in the Bois de Boulogne, drove a car, flew a plane. Josephine of Le Vésinet walked her dogs, played with her cats, fed her rabbits, napped with her leopard, and ate large plates of pasta. The daytime world, in which she worked, exercised, ate modestly, and napped, was genuine. The nighttime world in which she reigned as queen was an artificial illusion that might one day come unmade. Vésinet was solid; the other was a world of phantoms where things changed overnight. Since the money, the jewels, and the expensive clothes were unreal, there was no need to save.

She polarized her life, locating the real Josephine in Le Vésinet and the false or public Josephine at the Casino de Paris. But what made Josephine onstage so unforgettable was that the sweetness, simplicity, vivacity, and directness she thought of as part of her country-and-animal self made themselves felt when she was all gussied up in front of an audience. She was more at home as a creature of glamour than she liked to admit. Just as she sang about being torn between her country and Paris, but wasn't really, Paris having all her love, she presented herself as torn between being a simple child of nature and a glamorous creature of the boulevards. But she wasn't really torn that way either. In her greatest performances, the child was radiantly present in lamé and feathers, and with all the artifice of her packaging, her spontaneity and earthiness were never lost. Although she seemed to have become completely French, completely a music-hall star, it was the jazz spirit that made her performances great.

By 1933 she and Pepito had been together for seven years. That seemed to Josephine a long time—longer than she had been with any man—and their relationship was becoming complicated. She wanted to get married, but not to Pepito. It wasn't that he was exploiting her, as so many people said. Of course he was making money off her. He deserved it. He was the best manager in Paris. He had done a brilliant job of handling her career. The house at Le Vésinet and another on the avenue Bugeaud were in his name. But she had plenty of money and could always make more. In show business, they called every man who was good at managing a woman's affairs her pimp. She got a kick out of calling him that. "Mon maquereau." But that wasn't why she wouldn't marry him.

There is a kind of woman whose greatest power over a man lies in her ability to turn away from him. Cleopatra tormented and captivated Antony this way, according to Shakespeare. Baker repeatedly got involved with other men, hurt Pepito with her infidelity, then resented how upset he got. In the contradictory fashion with which the mind is so comfortable, she knew both that she was tied to Pepito in some way she was not tied to the others, which meant that these transient attractions did not matter, and that she was justified in looking for someone more appropriate to marry, someone who was not her man of business, who was not a fake count, who was not seventeen years older than she was, someone French.

As she saw it, the problem was not her infidelity but his jealousy. If he wouldn't get so upset, everything would be okay. She could have her flings and would probably always come back to him. As it was, they had fights over every male dancer at the Folies-Bergère, every rich businessman she slept with. Furthermore, these fights, however much she complained about them and dreaded them, were emotionally satisfying to her. A woman who has doubted her attractiveness in childhood likes extravagant signs of attraction later in life, and what more authentic sign of attraction than violent jealousy? Thus, "Pepito's jealousy," which she gave as a reason for refusing to marry him, signaled a whole complex of behavior which kept them a passionate if volatile couple, and—she was right—not a good bet for marriage.

Pepito's way of trying to win her—a battle all the more intriguing to him because it could never finally be won—was to do his best for her career. He began to use her career as a kind of stick to keep her in line. She was a great artist. She must work and work. Not for her the pleasures of family life, children. Nor of Jacques Pills, the young entertainer Josephine was involved with in the early thirties, who would later marry Edith Piaf. He demanded sacrifice of Josephine as though she were Pavlova. He identified himself wholly with the professional side of her life, setting up deal after deal, booking after booking, each one a love gift. With every professional success, he felt he was tying her closer to him. But his lectures on work came to seem like nagging. And in retrospect, it seems inevitable that when she encountered at last some failure in her career, she would take it out on him.

Pepito's strategy was imperialist: she must conquer new territory, expand, make her name in new ways, or she would fade like so many other beautiful women who had once been famous. As it turned out, her growth was more subtle: her voice got better and better, her contact with an audience ever more electric. She continued to be a music-hall star for fifty years, but she never became, as Pepito hoped, a film star, or a musical-comedy star, or a star in America. To a great extent, her failure to expand had to do with race: there were few roles she could play in a film or on a stage and the persona she had developed in France did not yet work for a black woman in America, as she found out when she returned in 1936. But if the problem was race, it was Pepito who paid the price.

The French film industry in the early thirties operated more anarchically than Hollywood. Instead of a few major studios which concentrated money and therefore power, hundreds of production companies existed, making one or two films apiece. Because of a lack of capital, filmmakers in France could not afford—as those in Germany and America could—to experiment with new techniques, so they were stuck with the old ones and improvised films, as a film historian puts it, with joyous mediocrity.

Furthermore, without powerful studios to discipline them, stars tended to get out of hand. Their eccentricities flourished, and films became personal showcases. Hollywood tended to generate the opposite problem: actors virtually indentured to a studio, their creativity stifled by businessmen. "We may wonder," says Raymond Borde, "in seeing the French example, where the actor kept almost total liberty, if the American discipline was not better."

Both of Josephine Baker's major films of the thirties, *Zou-Zou* (1934) and *Princesse Tam-Tam* (1935), were created as vehicles for her. They were produced by Arys Nissotti, a Tunisian casino owner whom she and Pepito had met in 1928. Pepito wrote the scenario and was "artistic director" for *Princesse Tam-Tam*, and his brother provided the idea on which Carlo Rim's screenplay for *Zou-Zou* was based. It is likely that Pepito and Josephine put some of their own money into the films as well. The two films, under their close personal control, reflected what they thought she should do on screen.

Zou-Zou, a light romantic comedy, continues to have a certain life. In part, this is because Baker's co-star is the young Jean Gabin, the French Spencer Tracy. The two men on screen share the rare quality of sweetness housed inside unambiguous masculinity, and, like Tracy, Gabin seems never to be acting. This made him a particularly poor choice as a partner for Baker in *Zou-Zou*, because she overdid almost every move.

The film's premise was that Gabin and Baker had been raised together like brother and sister. Gabin grows up to become a sailor, and Baker, devotedly in love with him, leaves Toulon, their childhood home, moves to Paris, and becomes a laundress. Gabin, on leave, visits her and falls in love with one of her fellow laundresses, Yvette Leban. Among the lingerie they iron is that of a music-hall star imperiously played by Edith Méra. This brings Baker to the music hall and gives her an opportunity to clown around on the stage, improvising a dance in which her elastic, ectoplasmic shadow is projected, enormous, on the backdrop.

One keeps waiting for the *42nd Street* plot twist by which Edith Méra is incapacitated and Baker is called on to fill in for her, but it seems endlessly postponed. At long last, Gabin is mistakenly arrested, and to earn money to pay for his defense, Baker consents to replace Méra, who has finally eloped with a lover. She is, of course, a sensation. We have a couple of scenes of her onstage which are, along with the shadow dance, the best things in the movie: in a birdcage, almost nude, she sings about the island home she misses, and, ravishing in an evening gown, she sings a torch song, "C'est lui." The movie ends with Baker, dressed fashionably with fur hat and fur wristlets, going to meet Gabin when he is released from prison. She arrives in time to see him tenderly kissing Yvette Leban.

In an American version, her transformation into a star would probably have taken place earlier in the film and the second half would have shown her, alcoholic and miserable, paying for her success. Here, her transformation isn't resented. In fact, the whole movie leads up to it, teasingly withholds it. Once again the point of Baker's story is seen to be that Parisianization is possible. Serious barriers to advancement do not exist. Careers are open to talent, as Napoleon had proved to the French long before and as they never tired of hearing, perhaps because they wished it were true.

Compared to what happens to women in American versions of this story, notably *A Star Is Born*, Zou-Zou doesn't suffer much. Still, why can't she have the man? It had been the same in *La Sirène des Tropiques*: she had had to give up Pierre Batcheff. Josephine herself really wanted to get Gabin and asked Pepito why she could not. Would the public object because of her color? Pepito insisted that wasn't it. "Zou-Zou is a star. She lives for her work. Like you," he said. Pepito liked the story of the female star who has to give up the emotional side of her life as the price of stardom. Josephine did not. Her failure to understand why she couldn't have both would be increasingly the issue between them as Josephine wanted to expand emotionally and Pepito, in a desperate effort to hold on to her, wanted her to expand professionally.

Striking in *Zou-Zou* is the difference between Baker's performance as a poor little laundress and her performance as a glamorous star. As laundress, she is stagey and exaggerated, asking us to love her cuteness. At best one responds to her nervous energy and a physical appeal very close to that of Fannie Brice. But her exaggerated haplessness is not cute, and it raises the question of why Marc Allégret, a respected director and man of taste, did not rein her in. Was it because he could not? Or because he liked her that way? My guess is, he liked her. There is a flutey, sparkling, vivacious female type the French loved to see on film—Simone Simon, Annabella—which is likely to make an American gag and think about how cuteness can change its face from culture to culture.

As a glamorous star, Baker is simple, direct, without mannerisms. She does not ask us to love her; she knows we will, and part of her charm is that she is sure of exactly how charming she is. She can even play against that certainty, mocking her own effect. Dressed beautifully, given a song or a dance, she generates tremendous excitement, whereas dressed in a cotton frock, rescuing puppies and freeing birds from cages, she generates disbelief if not worse.

Baker had hated *La Sirène des Tropiques*, but she loved this film, identifying it closely with the story of her own life. "The film enchants me," she said while it was being shot. "Everyone seems so happy with what I do that even I am getting optimistic about it. Everything seems easy, because I feel the story very strongly. It all seems so real, so true, that I sometimes think it's my own life being played out on the sets."

Over and over, in different forms, she allows herself to be cast in this transformation story. In her films, she is an unsophisticated "native" who becomes a glamorous creature of the city. In her nightclub acts, she emerges from an egg or appears as a fledgling creature with wings. To put it another way, her glamour is concealed inside her humble, unpolished, and invariably colonial shell. The shell splits to reveal the ravishing creature hidden inside. The question is: Why can't she just show the ravishing creature? Why does she need to keep dragging her shell along with her?

Someone cannot accept the ravishing black creature without a reminder of the pickaninny she started from. But who? The French audience? Pepito? Baker herself? Or all of them? For the audience, the insistence on the poor little girl she had been was a way of desexualizing her glamour. Her reward was not marriage, the heroine's usual reward, but Parisianization, a reward without a man attached. For Baker, compulsively displaying the poor little girl she no longer was constituted a way of holding on to her racial identity while enjoying a glamour that transcended color. But for her, too—and for Pepito, although for different reasons—the diluting of her erotic impact may have been welcome.

In *Princesse Tam-Tam*, the transformation story in North African dress, a jaded French novelist dreams of making a Tunisian goat girl into a glamorous woman he can bring to Paris and flaunt as an exotic princess, in order to unsettle his wife, who is carrying on with a maharajah. Predictably, the film's best moments are the dance sequences, especially one in which, imitating a chicken, Baker dances on the steps of a ruined Roman amphitheater. (The film was shot on location in Tunisia.) A conga scene is also lively. But the musical numbers stand out from the dramatic background, whose narrative subtlety may be suggested by the film's last shot: a copy of a book called *Civilization* lies on the floor of the abandoned hut where the novelist had lived in Tunisia. A donkey munches a page. At the end of the film, the North African girl, back from her fantastic voyage and in her own country, marries the novelist's servant, and the novelist is reunited with his wife. This ending, too, disappointed Baker. By the rules of the cheap romance, she said, she should at least have gotten to marry the maharajah. It seemed nasty of Pepito to make her marry the servant.

If, in real life, it all began with desire, in the film versions of her transformation all traces of desire are erased. Neither Zou-Zou nor Aouina, the heroine of *Princesse Tam-Tam*, is responsible for her own change. Each is the passive object of others' activity. *Princesse Tam-Tam* is as much a tribute to Pygmalion, the transformer, as to Galatea, the transformed. If Josephine had created her own screenplays, you could say that she was covering the traces of her own activity, as women tend to do. But since Pepito played such a large part in shaping her screen roles, the passivity of the transformed woman may show his desire to play up his own part, *his* creativity, and to give himself the starring role in her transformation.

In between the two films, in the fall of 1934, she had a successful run in the starring role of Offenbach's operetta *La Créole*. This was a new departure. She had never performed in a Paris theater, as opposed to a music hall, and she had never sung light opera. Anxious as she was to shed her rhinestones and feathers and to play to family audiences, at first she was skeptical of the music. "Ça ne jazze pas," she said. She was worried, too, that Monsieur Offenbach might not like her for the part. But it was explained to her that Monsieur Offenbach had been dead for many years, and gradually she got to like his melodies, which, according to Janet Flanner, seemed to have been written for Baker's "high, airy voice, half child's, half thrush's."

She threw herself into the enterprise with her usual onstage energy, dancing, romping, clowning, singing. She had the fun of working with a chorus of children, who had been added to spice up the slight production and who thronged Baker's dressing room at every chance. Her part was that of a Jamaican girl, daughter of an English father and native mother, who is seduced and abandoned by a French sailor and follows him back to France in a comic, happy-ending version of *Madame Butterfly*. The book was improved by Albert Willemetz, the scriptwriter for *Zou-Zou*, whose idea the whole thing had been, and considerable liberties were taken with the music. Most critics agreed that the operetta was fluff and only worth seeing for Josephine Baker's performance, but that was so good that the Théâtre Marigny off the Champs-Élysées was filled for months. She herself was extremely proud of the fact that ten years after arriving in France, she was onstage speaking French, acting in French, surrounded by "strictly French actors." The heroine's voyage from Jamaica to La Rochelle also seemed to her to allude to her "personal adventure, from the outskirts of St. Louis to the suburbs of Paris." That pleased her. "Who doesn't have his vanity? I admit mine. In all the shows I've done, films included, I've insisted that the different stages of my life be represented. Each time . . . there is just a hint of a reminder of the past, for the sake of contrast."

Having conquered Paris over and over, having proved herself on stage and screen, Baker, after ten years in France, wanted to return home and dazzle on Broadway as she'd done on the Champs-Élysées. Pepito arranged what seemed the perfect opportunity: she would perform in the Ziegfeld Follies of 1936.

The Ziegfeld Follies was the closest thing in America to the revues of Paris. In fact, Ziegfeld had taken from France the idea of beautiful women in lavish costumes embedded in an evening of singing, dancing, and comedy acts. The Follies had been "glorifying the American girl" since 1907, having beaten out its major competition in the annual spectacle game, George White's *Scandals*, but Florenz Ziegfeld himself had died in 1932, leaving his wife, Billie Burke (the Good Witch of *The Wizard of Oz*), one of the major producers, along with the Shuberts.

Ziegfeld had had a special instinct for spotting comic talent. Will Rogers had been merely a cowboy act until Ziegfeld encouraged him to say out loud the things he was muttering under his breath as he lassoed and roped. Some of the greatest comedians in America— W. C. Fields, Bert Williams, Ed Wynn, and Eddie Cantor—were developed at the Follies. Ziegfeld found Fannie Brice in vaudeville and put her on the Broadway stage, where she had been enchanting audiences since 1910.

A singer as well as a comedian, Fannie Brice occupied a special place in the Follies and in the hearts of her fans. She could make people both laugh and cry. Lacking a beautiful face, she had a good figure and beautiful chestnut-golden hair and could seem beautiful if she wanted to. She dressed expensively offstage and commanded considerable glamour. But onstage, Ziegfeld restrained the glamour. Her greatest hit was the French torch song "Mon Homme," whose lyrics were by two men whose paths Josephine Baker had crossed, Albert Willemetz, the writer of *Zou-Zou* and *La Créole*, and Jacques Charles, who had doctored the Revue Nègre. The song crossed the Atlantic and became "My Man," and the first time Fannie Brice sang it, she wore an evening gown and did the thing with polish and sophistication. Ziegfeld didn't like it. "This goes," he said, ripping her gown at the shoulder. "And this," disheveling her coiffure. Eventually she sang her most famous song in a tattered costume which underlined her pathos. There would be no Parisianizing of the onstage Fannie Brice.

Baker's color may have stacked the odds against her success in America, but it is also true that Brice, with a nervous energy and funny-girl appeal so similar to Baker's, was already doing the act with which Baker could best have pleased an American audience. And Fannie Brice was the star and principal draw of the 1936 Follies.

. . .

Accompanied by Pepito, Josephine arrived on the new and elegant French liner *Normandie* in September 1935, almost ten years to the day after her departure on the *Berengaria*. She was apprehensive yet confident of success. Everything she had done for ten years had turned out splendidly. It was hard to imagine failure anymore. She would make a name in New York to match her renown in Paris. Perhaps after that she would move back to America.

Extensive rehearsals had been scheduled for this most lavish of Follies shows. It was supposed to open in mid-fall, but illness, casting problems, and production delays postponed everything by two months. Rehearsals began in October. Baker said she had never rehearsed so hard and had so little fun doing it. Because the show had such a big cast and so many scenes, rehearsals were split among four theaters, so she hardly got to see anything but her own scenes or have anyone see her. "In Paris rehearsing is a pleasure. In New York it is a matter of discipline." She was comparing the two cities constantly—and always to the advantage of Paris. She rehearsed for weeks from 2 to 6 P.M. and again from nine to midnight. In the morning, she worked with a dance coach and also had daily voice lessons. During lunch, she had sessions with the costume designer, Vincente Minnelli, then twenty-eight.

The production had gathered a great deal of talent. Vernon Duke, the composer of "April in Paris," wrote the music and Ira Gershwin the lyrics. Minnelli did sets as well as costumes. The ballet master was George Balanchine. The show had one hit song, which was sung neither by Fannie Brice nor by Josephine Baker but by Bob Hope, to Eve Arden, known to 1950s TV fans as Our Miss Brooks: "I Can't Get Started with You."

The director of this extravaganza was John Murray Anderson, known for his work with revues. A famous eccentric, he never started work before noon and never put ideas for his shows into writing but planned the day's work in an hour-long bath each morning. He wore the same suit for the entire rehearsal period, and then, before opening night, burned it. Anderson went a little wild on the 1936 Follies, generating too much material by far. When it opened on Christmas night in Boston, it was clear that a lot had to go. Among the acts cut were the comic Ken Murray and ventriloquist Edgar Bergen with Charlie McCarthy.

According to Baker, it was Anderson's idea to present her as a sophisticated Parisian songstress. The numbers originally planned for her were the kind of thing black performers had been doing in New York for the past few years, but when Anderson saw her in rehearsal, he changed his mind, realizing that Baker was different now from what she'd been before. "You are from Paris," he said. "It's stupid to let you sing Harlem songs."

Her opening number was a strenuous conga-like dance whose line of descent can be imagined. Her costume was also a lineal descendant of the earlier costume: a stylization of the famous bananas with a matching top added in which the bananas were changed to tusks. In silhouette and from a distance, they looked like spikes. What had been wittily, mockingly phallic was turned into something ugly and aggressive. But at least she got to move in this scene. In her other two, she was completely beglamored, first as a maharanee, a stately creature from India, her face partly covered by a veil, at the races in Paris, and then, in a scene called "5 A.M.," in which her movements were choreographed by Balanchine, as a lady weary of nightlife.

Her out-of-town reviews were mixed. Covering the Boston opening, the *New York World-Telegram* reported that in all her numbers she won the large audience, but the *Boston Traveler* critic, while liking her dancing, found her two songs barely audible. From Boston the show went to Philadelphia in the middle of January. The *Philadelphia Ledger*'s critic acknowledged her talent as "sophisticated songstress and extravagant dancer," but said the material didn't give her much of a chance to do anything but present her legend. Her "impersonation of a French songstress" was so convincing that he wished she could be given some good songs. There was the same note of skepticism about her sophistication in the *Evening Bulletin*, which said that her "long residence in Paris has resulted in almost transforming her into a French cabaret performer."

Finally, after four months of preparation, the show opened in New

York on January 31, and here Baker's reviews were devastating. She alone among the principals was singled out for sarcasm and disdain. In the enormous Winter Garden Theater, where the Follies played in New York, her voice could hardly be heard. "She sings prettily, if more or less to herself," said one member of the audience. "Miss Baker has refined her art until there is nothing left in it," said Brooks Atkinson, the *Times*'s drama critic. That he was expecting something rather more boisterous from a black woman is clear from his next comment, that the Nicholas Brothers, who follow her with some excellent tap dancing, "restore your faith in dusky revelry."

Time was even harsher: "Josephine Baker is a St. Louis washerwoman's daughter who stepped out of a Negro burlesque show into a life of adulation and luxury in Paris during the booming 1920's. In sex appeal to jaded Europeans of the jazz-loving type, a Negro wench always has a head start. The particular tawny hue of tall and stringy Josephine Baker's bare skin stirred French pulses. But to Manhattan theatregoers last week she was just a slightly buck-toothed young Negro woman whose figure might be matched in any night-club show, and whose dancing and singing might be topped practically anywhere outside of Paris." *The Defender*, the black Chicago newspaper, ran an editorial protesting *Time*'s use of the word "wench," a "vile word" it held to be associated with sadism and diseased imaginings, but the *Time* review is also notable for its resentment of Baker's French popularity. What is more irritating to American audiences than a foreign success?

Brooks Atkinson spoke for most people when he said, "If the 1936 edition [of the Follies] offered nothing but Fannie Brice, most of us would feel sufficiently grateful." She was in top form, according to Atkinson, "stretching her mobile mouth a hundred different ways" and "rolling those eloquent eyes." She mocked English accents in Ira Gershwin's "Fancy Fancy." She mocked artistic modern dancing in "Modernistic Moe." As the wife of a man who has given away a winning lottery ticket, she sang "He Hasn't a Thing Except Me" in the same mock-ballad style as "My Man." And as her best-loved character, Baby Snooks, she went to Hollywood and played the Cinderella chorus girl in a send-up of motion-picture musical comedies and Cinderella chorus girls. With Fannie Brice crossing her eyes and mugging, and making fun of Baker's favorite role, what was there for Baker to do?

Her failure in the Follies was a bitter disappointment, but she could at least take some comfort in what she had escaped by leaving America. What she had escaped was being Ethel Waters. Americans did not see Baker as being in competition with Fannie Brice. The person interviewers asked her about repeatedly was Ethel Waters, white Broadway's only black female star.

After years of singing in nightclubs, Waters, who was not then the matronly figure she became in the 1940s and that most people remember, made a sensation in the 1933 Irving Berlin revue *As Thousands Cheer* by playing—of all people—Josephine Baker. Love curl and all, she sang the song which Baker's success had inspired Berlin to write, "Harlem on My Mind," popularizing an image of her dripping diamonds, the darling of Paris society, but homesick for Harlem, with a "longing to be low-down."

In the fall of 1935, when Baker arrived to be in the Follies, Ethel Waters was appearing in *At Home Abroad*. For Baker, the comparison between herself and the woman she had once understudied was a sore subject, and she disclaimed the competition a little sniffily. "Any artist must develop a technique of his own, and I have tried to avoid singing 'colored mammy, back to Alabammy' songs. Not all Negroes have to jump around as though they were monkeys or African savages. Besides, I sing soprano, and that would hardly adapt itself to the traditional blues and other Beale Street ballads." *Porgy and Bess*, she said, was another matter, and she would have loved to sing the lead in that. It had just opened on Broadway that fall.

What she meant by her snide remarks about Ethel Waters was that she was glad she hadn't had to make a career of being black. She was not the person called in when the white theater needed a maid or a mammy or a novelty act. She could simply sing, a "soprano," not a black singer. It was the difference between "J'ai deux amours," which anyone torn between two homes could sing, and "Harlem on My

Mind," which you had to be black to sing. *As Thousands Cheer* was a triumph for Waters, because she had star billing in a white show. But all her material was ethnically tagged. In addition to the Josephine Baker imitation in "Harlem on My Mind," she did "Heat Wave" in a Latin costume and "Supper Time," about a woman preparing dinner for a husband who will never come home because he has been lynched.

It was as a performer, not as a black performer, that Baker wanted to succeed in her 1935–36 American appearance. But that was impossible. She might have forgotten her race, but no one else did. At the St. Moritz, where she and Pepito were staying, she was asked to use the service entrance. When she arrived at a party for George Gershwin one night and let her white mink coat slip to the floor, revealing her yellow satin dress, Beatrice Lillie took one look at her and said, "Who dat?" And one evening, with a group of socialites including Mrs. Potter Palmer of Chicago, she was refused admission to an East Side nightclub.

Every snub registered deeply. She had two responses: One was to say, in effect, I am not black, I am French. The other was to say, I am black and I will take refuge from these insults with my people. In the first mood, she insisted on speaking French at a dinner party at Lorenz Hart's, provoking Hart's black maid to rebuke her: "Honey, you is full of shit. Talk the way yo' mouth was born." In the second mood, she left Pepito behind at the St. Moritz, tracked down one of her French lovers who was in New York on business, and took him with her to Harlem for a few days in a furnished apartment. She told him (what was not exactly true) that she couldn't get into any hotel in midtown.

She had made it abundantly clear to Pepito that she blamed him for the Follies debacle. If he had gotten better terms from the Shuberts, she would have had better material, better billing, a more prominent place in the show. He knew how to do things right in Paris, but he did not know New York. Her scooping up the Frenchman and taking him off to Harlem was another way of punishing Pepito for his failure. For him, it was the last straw. He left her and went back to Paris alone.

In Harlem, for a while, she relaxed and had some fun. Although her triumphs in France had been extensively covered by the black press, she seems to have been able to move around in Harlem without being recognized. Incognito, under the name Gracie Walker, she appeared in one of the Apollo Theater's amateur hours, in which new talent is subjected to the toughest of tests. If the audience does not like an act, it drowns the performer with jeers in a matter of seconds, and a man standing backstage with a blank-loaded pistol fires to signify that he or she is dead. Before going onstage, Josephine, like everyone else, knocked on a piece of good-luck wood. She sang another version of her life. "Time was when I lived in a cabin, / Where I had not a rag to my name; / Time was when I was happy." The pistol didn't fire.

She may have enjoyed her few days in Harlem, but she did not spend much time there on this trip. Much more often, she socialized with white theater people and celebrities downtown. This caused resentment in Harlem, and a columnist for *The Amsterdam News* devoted some space to justifying her behavior, noting the pleasure the community seemed to take from reports that Baker had been snubbed or discriminated against or kept out of hotels and nightclubs. "It serves her right," he reports some people as thinking. "She had no business trying to be white." But the columnist, Roi Ottley, didn't blame her. There were, as always, two schools of thought. The first held that "the Negro should know his place and stay in it and avoid the ofay as a plague." The second held that the doors of jim crowism and discrimination should be knocked down. Baker was in that group. "She is our wedge and we should force her in." She didn't flatter herself on her contacts with whites, he said. She was just trying to live ignoring color. "Harlem, instead of taking up the cudgel of prejudiced whites, should rally to the side of this courageous Negro woman. We should make her insults our insults."

The issue raised by Baker's stay in New York in 1936 was a touchy one—the issue of race loyalty. What Roi Ottley and Baker herself saw as a courageous effort to enforce integration, many members of the black community saw as turning her back on her race. She was close to a common American stereotype, that of the Tragic Mulatto who denies her people for the sake of personal advancement and a wider sphere for herself but finally fits neither in the white world nor in the black. Although the stereotype was old, the issue had been addressed recently in a film called *Imitation of Life*, in which ravishing Fredi Washington, who had been in the *Shuffle Along* chorus with Baker, played the role of Peola, a light-skinned black woman who passes for white and has to warn her own mother not to appear to know her. Apparently, the role aroused such resentment in black audiences that much hostility was directed personally against Fredi Washington, confused with the person she played.

As had been her habit when touring in Europe, Baker opened a nightclub at which she performed after she worked at the Follies. She called it Chez Josephine Baker, and it was on East Fifty-fourth Street, continuing to operate before 10:30 P.M. as the chic restaurant, Le Mirage. As in Paris, her dancing partners were white men, but in New York she was felt to be making an interracial point. She also hired President Roosevelt's cousin, Alice Delano Weekes, to dance with the black doorman. The provocations were noted by *Variety*, which called Baker's nightclub a place where you were more likely to see older women with good-looking young men than older men with pretty girls. I suppose they were saying it appealed to kinky tastes. Nevertheless, the club was a success, and Baker, chatting with the audience, handing people balloons, sitting on laps just like always, held on to the power of her personality in a small setting even when—because of Anderson's unskillful direction, because of her own anxiety about performing in America—she had momentarily lost it onstage.

To black reporters, Baker elaborated on the story of being refused a room at a midtown hotel. "That is enough for me. I get up and nearly run out of the hotel. Paris! I had lived there for years without experiencing such humiliation and without knowing how happy one is when he does not feel the weight of this horrible prejudice. After two hours I am in a nightmare. We go from one hotel to another, always the same courtesy, the same cold smile, the same shrugging of the shoulders. I let my manager continue this humiliating search alone. I will find him later. Here I am alone in the streets of New York."

It was her way of saying that if she had failed in New York, it was not her fault. The deck was stacked against her. It was solace she would allow to herself, but not to Pepito.

She took Pepito so much for granted that she did not worry about how hard she had been on him. He would get over his anger at her anger and come back to her eventually. Whatever she did, she knew he would always be there for her. They would always get back together.

Then word came from Paris that Pepito was dead. When he left New York, he had been suffering from something he thought was hepatitis. It turned out to be cancer. He died in the spring of 1936 without seeing her again. He left her everything he owned, telling a friend that she would need it.

She grieved for Pepito. She really had loved him, and she was left with the bitter regret of having her last words to him be angry ones. Nonetheless, she was sustained by her perennial optimism. She was only thirty, and there would be other men. She could get onstage and charm an audience. She could sit on a man's lap in her cabaret, wind him completely around her finger, then cross her eyes and make fun of him. She would miss Pepito, but life lay before her.

She herself did not stay much longer in America than Pepito had. After all the preparation, the Follies only ran until May 9 after opening in New York at the end of January. The show was forced to close because Fannie Brice was suffering from arthritis and problems with her teeth. The principals were all offered the chance to rejoin the show when it opened again in the fall, but neither Bob Hope nor Eve Arden nor Josephine Baker took up the offer.

Baker learned two things from her 1936 trip to America, both unpleasant, perhaps interconnected. America would not welcome her as France did, and no one in America could look at her without thinking about her race. Any plans she had for coming back to the States were destroyed. The only concrete step forward she made on this visit was to go to Philadelphia and obtain a divorce from Willie Baker, so she was free to marry again. Willie, who had risen no higher in life since Josephine had left him, sweetly said he was willing to take her back, and she, gentle with the powerless, explained to him with equal sweetness that it was impossible for her to come back.

. . .

France rescued her from America as it had before. While she was still playing in the Follies, Paul Derval, the director of the Folies-Bergère, came to offer her the lead in a new show. There was to be another exposition in 1937, and this edition of the Folies could expect to cash in on the crowds it drew to Paris. It would open in the fall of 1936.

It was a step backward, back to nude revues, and the actual show was run-of-the-mill Folies silliness. Baker, in only a few gold spangles, did a dance of tropical passion by the end of which three men, including Frédéric Rey, one of her lovers, lay face-down on the stage with her on top of them. Playing the mother of a two-year-old kidnapped by gypsies, she stole into the gypsy camp, rescued her child, and set the camp on fire. As Queen of the Far North, wearing a ten-foot-long ermine cape, she greeted a polar expedition in a sleigh drawn by Canadian huskies. It was routine stuff for the star of *La Créole* and *Zou-Zou*, back to what she'd been doing five years before. But it was a job. It was stability. Pepito was dead, and the Folies-Bergère was reassuringly like family.

More than ever she wanted to get married, but she was finding a husband much harder to come by than a lover. While the French haut monde liked having her around, it never really accepted her. Apart from members of the troupe, she had few friends. Her lovers were often wealthy men who were happy to sleep with her but nothing more. According to one Parisian whose mistress she was in the mid-thirties (it would reverse the expected French priorities too distressingly to describe him as her lover rather than her as his mistress), it was not her color that disqualified her for marriage so much as her profession. What French family would want a son to marry a naked dancer?

Josephine understood only in part what she was up against. She understood the power of French respectability, which regarded marriage as a chance for dynastic improvement, but she thought she could overcome it by personal sweetness and charm. One afternoon, she bought three dozen white roses and paid a call on this man's mother, who lived on the respectable but slightly dowdy, upper-middle-class Boulevard Lannes. Josephine presented Madame with the flowers and formally asked if she would allow her son to marry her. Madame chose to treat this as a joke and laughed delightedly.

"Mademoiselle," she said. "It is true that there have been some scapegraces in our family but not for two generations, and nothing like this. No, no, what you want is quite impossible."

Baker continued to see the man, a wealthy businessman who soon after married a more suitable woman, but her request had not been a joke and she did not abandon her search. When she found what she wanted, a Frenchman willing to marry her, and got engaged, her earlier lover—with the egotism born of a loving mother on the Boulevard Lannes—was convinced she did it just to irritate him ("pour m'emmerder").

Jean Lion was a sugar broker, rich, good-looking, worldly, Jewish. He and Josephine met in a suitably glamorous way, after riding in the Bois de Boulogne. He courted her stylishly, flying in airplanes, fox hunting in the Vendée. His family was furious that he was marrying Josephine Baker; nor could his friends understand why he would bother. He was a man who liked flamboyant gestures, liked to live in a way no one else dared to, and marrying Baker was certainly a flamboyant gesture no one else dared to make.

They were married on November 30, 1937, at Crèvecoeur-le-Grand, the little town his parents lived in. He was twenty-seven; she was thirty-one. Paul Derval of the Folies-Bergère was the witness. By the marriage, Baker acquired what she had wanted for so many years, French citizenship, but otherwise her life changed very little. They lived at Le Vésinet. She did not have a baby, as she hoped she would. She had already had a couple of operations to help her conceive, but they were not successful. She went on performing in the Folies-Bergère, while her husband went on—at totally different hours—working and playing. She routinely got home, after her evening performances, at five or six in the morning. He got up an hour or so later to go to the office. She slept through to the afternoon and ate in a hurry in order to get to the theater, frequently gone before he came home. A playboy, a narcissist, Lion was not willing to give up anything to be with her, and she countered by refusing to give up anything for him.

Fourteen months after their marriage, she filed for divorce. The judge who eventually granted the divorce in 1942 said that they had never had a chance to get to know each other. She retained the French citizenship and a great affection for his mother. On the eve of the Nazi occupation of France, she was still technically married to a Jew, thus allied to not one but two groups of people the Nazis would try to purge from Europe.

PART III
REACHING BACK

1939-75

Enduring, with feathers, 1959.

Keystone, Paris.

CHAPTER 6
VENUS IN JEEPS

World War II was not one of France's glorious moments. The Germans overcame French defenses and moved into Paris with embarrassing speed. In June 1940, an armistice was signed between France and Germany ending hostilities. From then on, France was occupied by Germans in the North and controlled in the South by Marshal Henri Pétain's government, which sought to fulfill the terms of the surrender and to avoid further fighting with the Germans at any cost. A very small percentage of the French population—one historian puts it at 2 percent—took part in the resistance which was called for by General Charles de Gaulle, who, in

London, proclaimed himself head of Free France. At the time, de Gaulle's proclamation did not seem the historic inevitability it does in retrospect. For many French people, who had already seen a generation wiped out by war in their lifetime, Pétain was right: it was worth any compromise to avoid all-out fighting. De Gaulle, who had never been elected to office, who was one general among others, had no large constituency.

Josephine Baker joined the resistance at the start and remained unwaveringly faithful to de Gaulle. The story of her wartime activity was made public in 1949 in an account, *The Secret War of Josephine Baker*, by her partner, Jacques Abtey, with a prefatory letter by de Gaulle, and again in 1961 in a novelized account by a writer who specialized in secret service activities. Her story was useful to the Gaullists in their postwar effort to rewrite history, making France look as though it had been united behind de Gaulle in active resistance, and in their political struggle to hold on to the colonies in North Africa and the Middle East. But even if Baker was used to support the Gaullist myth of a heroic resistance—and the enthusiasm for it of people of color—her heroism was nonetheless real and her Croix de Guerre well deserved.

This was the moment at which history supported and justified the ardent simplicities of Baker's worldview. She had insisted all along that race was the crucial issue, that all men must learn to live as brothers, that differences of "blood" should be ignored. Her enthusiastic adoption of French citizenship was tied in her mind to French racial tolerance. For her, the Nazis were not actors on a geopolitical stage but racists, and it was easy for her to tell the good guys from the bad. With a vision of France as not being true to itself when it accommodated the Nazis, she could rise above that concern for the continuity of daily life, the pleasures of routine, the solace of property, which led almost the entire population to collaborate. This was the war in which she was happy to be a soldier. She had been waiting for it a long time.

· · ·

In September 1939, when France declared war on Germany in response to the invasion of Poland, Baker had been recruited by the Deuxième Bureau, French military intelligence. They were looking for people who had cause and means to move around freely, might pick up information, and were willing to work without pay. Such people were called "honorable correspondents." The man who proposed Baker to the Deuxième Bureau was Daniel Marouani, a theatrical agent of Tunisian birth and her own agent's older brother. The man he suggested her to was Jacques Abtey, a thirty-three-year-old Alsatian, the head of military counterintelligence in Paris.

Initially, Abtey was not enthusiastic about working with Baker. He remembered—as who in the intelligence business did not?—the story of Mata Hari, the Dutch-born woman recruited by the French during World War I whom they ended up shooting as a double agent. Mata Hari, like Baker, was a dancer and leading light of the demimonde whose fame gave her access to powerful men. She was supposed to pass what she learned from them to the French. But the traffic, according to the French, went more importantly in the other direction. Mata Hari had no particular love for France and positively disliked England, so she had no qualms about working for the Germans.

Marouani arranged a meeting between Abtey and Baker at her house in Le Vésinet. When the two men drove up, Baker, wearing a crumpled felt hat, was walking around the grounds picking up snails and putting them in a jam jar. Abtey was surprised by her informality, her warmth, and her frank interest in what he wanted. She, for her part, was surprised that he was so good-looking. Blue-eyed, blond, and handsome, Abtey had the kind of looks Baker particularly liked to set off her own, whereas she had expected him to be short, fat, dark, with an unattractive mustache and clothes that smelled of tobacco—like Simenon's Inspector Maigret.

In front of a fire in the drawing room, drinking champagne, she talked about herself and her feeling for France with the unselfconscious eloquence of an actress who knows she is playing an important role.

"France made me what I am," she told him. "I will be grateful forever. The people of Paris have given me everything. They have given me their hearts, and I have given them mine. I am ready, Captain, to give them my life. You can use me as you wish."

She convinced Abtey that the similarities between her and Mata Hari were superficial and the difference essential: whereas Mata Hari had been an adventuress drifting around the world without a home, interested above all in her own comfort, Baker was fiercely and to the point of self-sacrifice devoted to France.

During the period the French called the phony war, the "drôle de guerre"—between September 1939, when France declared war on Germany, expecting to be invaded any day, and May 1940, when the Germans actually invaded—Baker collected what information she could about German troop locations from officials she met at parties. She specialized in gatherings at embassies and ministries, charming people as she had always done, but at the same time trying to remember interesting items to transmit to Abtey. She had a particularly good source of information at the Italian embassy, because, in one of her frequent bad political judgments—she had a soft spot for the dramatic style of dictators—she took a liking to Mussolini during a 1935 tour in Italy and supported his invasion of Ethiopia. She went so far as to claim she would help recruit blacks around the world to fight with Mussolini against the forces of Haile Selassie. She never did it, but the Italians loved her, and she now made use of the contact.

Every day she worked at a reception center for Belgian refugees who, after the Germans invaded Belgium, started streaming into Paris, distraught, bereft, and sick from their enforced journey. In a building that had once been a refuge for homeless men, Baker helped cheer up the despairing and care for the feeble. She was so pleased to be an intelligence agent that she saw spies where there were none, calling Abtey to look at suspicious characters who turned out merely to be blond Belgians fleeing from the Nazis.

By day an angel of mercy, by night she starred at the Casino de Paris. Henri Varna had canceled his scheduled 1940–41 show—an extravaganza on the theme of Brazil—as inappropriate for wartime, yet he felt some production was needed to sustain morale. What he devised was a back-to-back performance by Baker and Maurice Chevalier. The show opened at the front for the soldiers at the Maginot Line, who sat week after week, bored and scared, waiting for the German attack.

On opening night, Chevalier insisted on performing last, traditionally the star's spot. It was not gallant of him, but Baker conceded and went first. As it turned out, the soldiers would not let her go, demanded encore after encore, and since the show could not go on beyond the curfew, Chevalier was left with only a truncated time for performance. In his irritation, he threatened not to do another show, and she reminded him that they were performing for the sake of the soldiers—not for personal gratification. From that time, she had nothing but scorn for him, and he disliked her cordially in return. "You are too young to know," he said, "that rivals can be dangerous."

They never finished the season. In the second week of June, after the Nazis overran the Maginot Line and as they moved quickly toward Paris, Henri Varna gathered the troupe, told them the show was closing, and wished them luck. Paris—for all they knew, all of France—would be occupied by the Germans.

Some entertainers remained in Paris and performed throughout the German occupation, but from the moment the Germans entered Paris, the professional life of Jews and blacks in all fields, including entertainment, was finished. Those who could got out. Those who couldn't made themselves invisible. One Jewish director reportedly spent the whole war in the basement of his theater—not an avant-garde intellectual such as François Truffaut portrayed in *The Last Metro*, but the director of the Folies-Bergère, Michel Gyarmathy. Those who could neither get out nor hide were eventually rounded up by the Nazis and sent off, first to detention centers, then to the death camps.

Baker left by car for Les Milandes, the château in the Dordogne which she had bought in 1936. The roads were jammed with people fleeing Paris. With her were her maid, Paulette, a Belgian refugee couple, and her dogs. Thoughtfully, she took along gasoline, which she knew she would be unable to get en route. Like a Folies star, she stored the gasoline in champagne bottles.

With the Germans in Paris, it seemed to many French people that the war was already lost. It was not at all obvious what response to make. On June 18, Charles de Gaulle, speaking on the radio from London, outlined one possibility and gave it a name, "resistance." "Whatever happens, the flame of the French resistance must not go out and will not go out." De Gaulle had declared himself the head of what he called the Forces Françaises Libres, which he eventually got the British to subsidize. In June 1940, it became the goal of some few anti-Nazi Frenchmen to join de Gaulle and the forces of the Free French in London.

When the government headed by Pétain left Paris on June 15 to relocate in Bordeaux, Jacques Abtey, Josephine's partner, left with it, shepherding documents to safety. Eventually the government would have to move again, to Vichy, since Bordeaux was in the occupied zone, but before that, Abtey decided to try to join de Gaulle and establish liaison between resistance networks in France and those in England. He did not know how he could get to England, but he thought Baker might be able to help somehow. So he went from Bordeaux to Castelnaud-Fayrac, the little town where her property was located. A natural actor and a master of accents, he had disguised himself as the British Mr. Fox until Germany was officially at war with Britain. Now, to join Baker, he changed his identity again, becoming the American—and therefore neutral—Jack Sanders. When he arrived at Les Milandes, Baker, delighted to see again the man she had been working with for close to a year, took him by the arm. "Foxy," she said. "When are we going to join de Gaulle?"

That summer, the summer of 1940, an odd group of people inhabited Les Milandes: Jack Sanders, Josephine Baker, a Mexican-born French naval officer, a Breton aviator, the Belgian refugee couple, and three others who joined them to listen to de Gaulle's broadcasts on the radio. While he thought about how to reach England, Abtey went kayaking, hunting, and fishing. Then he made contact with Colonel Paillole, who directed military counterintelligence from Marseille, under the cover of an office of rural works.

Paillole was initially as skeptical about Baker as Abtey had been, because of Mata Hari and also because he thought show business personalities too fragile. But Abtey convinced him of Baker's strength and they agreed on a plan. Abtey would become Jacques-François Hébert, former music-hall performer and now secretary and assistant to Josephine Baker. She would go on tour in Portugal and South America, and Abtey would accompany her, carrying information from Paillole to Portugal, for transmission to England, about airfields, harbors, and German troop concentrations in the West of France. It would be written in invisible ink on Josephine's sheet music. All Abtey needed was a false passport, making him, among other things, older than he was. No man under forty was allowed to leave France. Through Baker, they could get the visas they had to have.

So much of wartime drama involved permits. The intelligence work that Abtey and Baker did together at the start of the war involved moving around, which in turn depended on getting the right papers. There was, of course, the possibility of clandestine movement, sneaking across borders, but that was much more dangerous and, ultimately, even more time-consuming. Baker was an excellent cover. Everyone knew her. Everyone wanted to see her close up. She was like Poe's purloined letter, so obvious as to be invisible.

Abtey's false passport came through, but visas for Portugal were more difficult. Baker got the idea of setting up an engagement in Brazil, whose ambassador she knew, and through him arranging for transit visas for Spain and Portugal and exit visas for France. By late November 1940, Baker and Abtey were on a train heading through Pau in the Pyrenees and across the border into Spain at Canfranc, along one of the classic, tragic refugee routes. Baker was wrapped in an immense fur, enjoying her part and not in the least nervous.

At the frontier, the ruse worked perfectly. Official and refugee, everyone wanted to see the famous Josephine Baker and no one paid attention to her companion, Jacques-François Hébert. For his part, Abtey was impressed that his partner had seen to it that the words "Accompanies Madame Josephine Baker" were on his visa. It meant she would be implicated if his real identity were discovered.

From Madrid, they took a plane to Lisbon, where Baker checked into the Aviz and Abtey into a less expensive hotel. The journalists descended on her. Yes, she said, she was just stopping over on her way to Rio, where she was booked to perform. Yes, she had sung at the front. Yes, she had seen some horrible things. No, she had not been to Paris since the Occupation. Yes, she did not like the Germans.

To go from France to Lisbon in November 1940 was to go from a nightmare to something more like an amusement park. With its good connections by air and sea to America, England, and Germany, neutral Lisbon was crowded and lively, filled with people on war business as well as people who wanted to get out of Europe entirely. Above all, it was a center for intelligence activities, a pool of spies, with agents for both sides busily keeping tabs on each other. Abtey saw the English air attaché to transmit his information to England and also outlined to him his plan to join de Gaulle and to establish ties between the resistance forces in England and France. In a few days, word came from London: his liaison work was approved but was to be conducted in France. He was instructed to wait in Portugal for further orders but to send Baker back to France immediately to make contact with Paillole.

She went to Marseille and installed herself at the grandest hotel in town, the Hotel de Noailles. She met Paillole, who liked her both for the solidity Abtey had promised him was there and for her un-French optimism: she was certain that the Americans would eventually enter the war and that the war would be won. Not many people in 1940 shared her hopefulness.

In Marseille, she crossed paths with someone else she knew, Frédéric Rey, a dancer who had been her lover. Rey had been discovered as a very young man in his native Austria by Mistinguett, who smuggled him into France in one of her costume baskets. He had partnered her onstage until Baker took him away to dance with her. Now Rey, whose papers were definitely not in order because of his illegal entry into France, was trying desperately to get out, and Baker vowed to help him. "*Il faut!*" she said, jabbing her fist at the air in front of her nose, with what Rey said was her characteristic gesture and her favorite expression. "*Il faut que tu quittes la France.* You must!"

Marseille, France's great port on the Mediterranean, was, like Lisbon, a center for people trying to escape the Nazis, only more frenzied and bleak. Although the city was in the Free Zone and so not technically under Nazi control, the French police were officers of the armistice—

that is, sworn to keep peace with the Germans and thus, in the harsher language of after the war, collaborators. Moreover, everyone knew it was only a matter of time before the Nazis crossed the Line of Demarcation, which restricted them to the North, and occupied the whole of France to the Mediterranean. Marseille had always been a tough city. One local gangster was known to have ways of getting people out of the country for large sums of money. In desperation, people turned to him for help. But his way of getting them out of the country was to turn them immediately over to the Gestapo.

Baker's situation was not so desperate as Frédéric Rey's, but she did have problems—no money and no visible reason for being where she was—and he came up with the solution to both by suggesting she resurrect *La Créole*, the Offenbach operetta she had performed in Paris in 1934. Until now she had rejected the idea of performing in France, saying, "As long as there's a German in France, Josephine won't sing." But under the pressure of circumstance she prudently redefined her prohibitions: she would not perform in Paris, but the unoccupied zone was okay. Thus she agreed to appear at the Théâtre de l'Opéra de Marseille in the Offenbach revival. It had been six years since she had played the part and she had to dig back into her mind to remember it, but she prepared it, and coached all the other parts, in a lightning ten days.

While Baker was in rehearsals in Marseille, Abtey spent his days on the beach at Estoril. He said that he was headed for South America to prepare Baker's appearances there, but he was simply waiting for instructions from London. Eventually word came. A route had been worked out. When he met with his contact, an Englishman named Bacon, Abtey specified the terms of his work. He was a member of the Free French military force, not a spy; Baker had the same status; she would receive no money but he was entitled to regular military pay. The terms were important, because he did not want to be seen as an information peddler but as a military intelligence officer. He would be funneling information that Paillole and his resistance network collected in France to de Gaulle and his British allies in London. He and Baker were to base themselves in Morocco, where Paillole would feed them the information that Abtey in turn would bring to Portugal, making use of a small boat the service would buy. From Portugal direct contact could be made with London.

Abtey rejoined Baker in Marseille just in time for the opening of *La Créole* on Christmas Eve of 1940. Daniel Marouani and his brother Félix were there, too, because they were treating this as a regular theatrical engagement and Josephine was an important client. When Abtey told her that they would be bound for Morocco, Josephine sent someone to Les Milandes to pick up her pets, including three monkeys, two white mice, and a Great Dane named Bonzo. She couldn't leave without them, she said. She knew that if positions were reversed, they wouldn't leave without her.

One of the many people trying to get out of France via Marseille was a German-born movie producer named Rodolphe Solmsen, who had left Germany in 1933 when Hitler came to power and promulgated his racial laws—including one which would have forbidden Solmsen, a Jew, to marry his non-Jewish fiancée. He began life again in France, his fiancée joined him, they married and had a daughter in 1938. Then in September 1939, with France's declaration of war on Germany, all German-born people living in Paris were asked to report to the Co-lombe Stadium, ostensibly to separate the bona fide refugees from Germans who were possibly spies. In fact, they were uniformly sent back to Germany, where the many Jews among them were sent to concentration camps.

Solmsen, who had already sent his wife and child to South America, realized that no one who went to the stadium would come back. He slipped away from Paris and took advantage of a French law which allowed him to stay in France if he joined the Foreign Legion. Frédéric Rey had done the same thing for the same reason. For almost a year, Solmsen, a child of privilege, who drove to his point of embarkation in his own car, did the notoriously hard service of the Foreign Legion, only to have the Legion disband after the French-German armistice. Like Rey in a similar situation, he made his way to Marseille and was trying without any success to get out of France when, in December 1940, his path crossed that of Josephine Baker.

He had no passport, no exit visa, no transit visas for Spain and Portugal, no entry visa for Peru, his destination. In order to get the transit visas, he first had to have the entry visa for his destination. The paperwork nightmares of World War II lay in the possibility of obtaining a visa only to have it expire before one came to the end of the immense lines at the consulates in order to secure the complementary visas. But Solmsen, despite the fact that his wife, daughter, mother, and sister were already in Peru, and his sister's husband was doing his utmost to obtain his entry visa, did not even have that. Other things, too, went unaccountably wrong.

At one point, Solmsen obtained a special interview with the American consul to request a visa for the States. Introduced by the head of Western Electric for Europe, Solmsen was received cordially and told there would be no problem getting a visa to the States if he could prove he had capital there. He wired his brother-in-law to make sure that the family account at Chase Manhattan still existed and contained the substantial deposits he thought it had. Word came back that all was in order. But when he returned to the consulate, he was received coldly. Chase Manhattan had wired that there was no such account as Solmsen claimed to have. Solmsen was bewildered. The explanation was unthinkable: his brother-in-law was working against him, trying to seal him in Europe to prevent the discovery of an embezzlement of family funds.

He returned to the Hotel de Noailles, where his main occupation was buying drinks for the Peruvian, Spanish, and Portuguese consuls. He was on excellent terms with them, but to no end. At this point Josephine Baker turned up with Daniel Marouani and, not long afterward, Jacques Abtey. Marouani, Baker, and Solmsen had known each other slightly in Paris, where they had all been part of the entertainment world, but now they were part of a circle of friends who became inseparable: Baker, Abtey, Solmsen and a friend of his named Fritz, and Frédéric Rey, whom Abtey recruited and who would continue to work with them in North Africa. They became such good friends that when Baker went to Nice to perform *La Créole* for a week at the start of January, she insisted they all come along, saying that whatever happened, they would be safe with her and Jacques.

Finally Mrs. Solmsen, in despair about her brother-in-law's inability to get a Peruvian entry visa for her husband, tried to get one herself and was successful. She wired the good news to Solmsen. At the same time, the Germans were expected to cross the Line of Demarcation any day. The last moment seemed to be arriving. Baker and Abtey were ordered to leave France immediately—not even waiting for Baker to finish her scheduled tour of *La Créole* to other cities in the South —because Paillole doubted they would be able to leave at all if they waited any longer.

On Baker's behalf, Abtey went to the management of the Théâtre de l'Opéra de Marseille and asked that she be released from her contract because of her urgent need to leave France. He explained that she had worked for the Deuxième Bureau in the past, and therefore was at particular risk when the Nazis took over. He did not tell them that she was still under quasi-military orders. They were sympathetic and suggested that to do it with no danger to anyone she should have a doctor certify that she was sick and had to cancel her engagement for reasons of health. This was done. It required no lying on the doctor's part, as Baker had been coughing all winter and X rays showed shadows on both her lungs. The doctor testified that she needed to find a warmer climate immediately.

Everything was clear for Abtey and Baker to leave France. Arrangements were made for them to fly to Algiers and for Rey to follow by boat with the monkeys and the Great Dane. From Algiers, they would all go to Morocco. But just as she had refused to leave without her animals, Baker now announced that she would not leave unless Solmsen and his friend Fritz could leave, too. At her insistence, Abtey contacted friends in the Deuxième Bureau to request passports and visas for the two men. He was told it would take time. Baker and Abtey then took Solmsen to see the commander of the port and put his name and that of his friend on a list of people who could embark immediately on a special boat if the Nazis invaded the Free Zone.

Solmsen, while he appreciated these gestures, did not believe in the passport and visa, and he did not think the Nazis would allow the special boat, filled with such interesting people, to leave so easily. One day, returning to his hotel, he received the alarming news that a man was waiting for him. Although he knew that the police usually came for people in the morning and in a group, he approached his visitor with a certain amount of fear and said, "You're waiting for me?" The man took two passports from his pocket and handed them over. "For you and the other friend of Madame Baker," he said. Later Solmsen wrote: "Josephine and Jacques had kept their word. When I almost did not believe in it anymore, they had opened the door to liberty and life. I do not know if I could have managed this escape by some other means and I do not even want to know. For me it was Josephine and Jacques who saved my life."

They all met at the Hotel Aletti, the first-class hotel on the waterfront in Algiers, and breathed a small sigh of relief to have a body of water between them and the Nazis—a small sigh only, because even in North Africa they were in Vichy France. Baker and Abtey continued to look out for Solmsen and Fritz, arranging Moroccan visas when they moved on to Casablanca. They became part of Baker's wartime family, and she was determined to care for them.

Algiers had seemed a European city. The streets and the architecture were indistinguishable from those of cities in the South of France. But Casablanca was African. They felt in another world entirely, a world Baker immediately liked. In one of those pockets of Arab life that were virtually unchanged since the Middle Ages, Baker and Abtey settled, waiting for something to happen.

Nothing happened. Abtey's line of communication with Lisbon was not working. No sailboat materialized, and unable to obtain a Portuguese visa, he could not carry information from Paillole to Lisbon, where it could be transmitted to England. Even Baker, whose charm with consuls had never failed before, could not get him a visa, only one for herself.

She went alone, with Paillole's information written again on her sheet music in invisible ink. In Tangier, before crossing over to Portugal, she was entertained by well-placed Arabs and Spaniards who loaded her with gifts, including a permanent transit visa for Spain. In Portugal, she delivered her messages, gave performances, and, wherever she went, made friends and attended parties, picking up scraps of information. She did everything she could to get Abtey a visa— without success. Apparently, his identity was known.

Back together in Morocco, the striking couple—the blond Abtey and Baker, who could be mistaken for an Arab—were inactive but happy, except that she was still coughing. Hoping its climate would help Baker's lungs, they moved to Marrakesh, more remote and even less European than Casablanca. At first they stayed at the luxurious Mamounia Hotel, then moved to a house in the medina, the ancient walled city within the city. The house was a magical place that presented a blank face to the world but to those who entered revealed itself to be a lush little paradise. In a garden planted with orange trees, there was room for her animals to run. Since her marriage to Jean Lion, she considered herself Jewish, praying from a Hebrew-French prayer book. But her affinity for Arab life seemed no contradiction. She loved it for a minimalism which seemed to her, after the vulgarities of the music hall, deeply spiritual. She admired the elegant simplicity of Arab houses and of certain Arab gestures, like the placing of mint leaves into boiling water to brew mint tea. She even took to wearing a djellabah at home.

Baker and Abtey had important friends in Morocco: the Sultan's cousin, Moulay Larbi el Alaoui, and his brother-in-law, Si Mohammed Menebhi, the former Grand Vizier's son, who lived in his father's palace in Marrakesh. Through them, Baker and her entourage got to know Si Thami el Glaoui, the powerful and charismatic Pasha of Marrakesh, whose hospitality made anything Europe had to offer seem puny. He entertained with enormous feasts at which one would not have been surprised to see Salome dancing for the head of John the Baptist; this despite the fact that el Glaoui had been educated in Paris and supported de Gaulle over Vichy.

One day, Abtey admitted to Solmsen that he had no precise idea of the future. He was stymied by the lack of a visa to Portugal. The projected information network had not worked out. He was out of money, and his English contact in Portugal, Bacon, told him there would be no more until there was more information, which infuriated

Abtey, because he thought Bacon had agreed that he was a military officer, entitled to regular military pay, not an information peddler.

Even doing nothing, life in Marrakesh was so agreeable that Solmsen might have stayed with them there. He found a friend from Paris staying at the Mamounia, and they played golf on el Glaoui's private course. But because of his wife and child, he decided to leave. Abtey helped him get an exit visa, and with his papers in order to Peru, he had no trouble getting a transit visa for the United States. He left Rabat on a banana boat bound for Martinique, and after further close calls and adventures, he was reunited with his family in that summer of 1941.

Somewhat later, when the distinction between foreign-born Jews and French Jews had broken down and it was dangerous for any Jew to remain in France, another man sought Josephine out in North Africa and asked for her help in getting a visa to South America for himself and his family. It was her former husband, Jean Lion. He and Solmsen were among the lucky ones with money and connections; most Jews in France could not buy their way out and so went to the camps.

After a while in Marrakesh, with her health much improved, Baker decided to give a series of performances in Spain, taking advantage of the permanent visa she had been granted. It was early spring of 1941. In Madrid, Valencia, and Barcelona, Spanish audiences, who had not seen her in ten years, were surprised she was not still wearing her bananas. She said she had had to eat them because of the war. She had become very good at ad-libbing jokes onstage, and audiences loved it. Her performances were sold out everywhere she went. To a newspaper reporter, she said that the French people (she meant, above all, herself and Abtey) were bitter toward actors who had returned to Paris and were collaborating with the Germans, and that she would not return until the Nazis left. The reporter asked her if she planned to remarry, and she said she had just received an offer but "this is not the time to get hitched up again."

As usual, she took advantage of all opportunities—and there were many—to go to parties, especially at embassies. She had only to announce she was in town and invitations started flooding into her hotel. Since the German presence in Spain was large, valuable information was plentifully available if one was clever. Baker made notes of what she heard on small pieces of paper and pinned them inside her underwear with safety pins.

She returned without problems to Marrakesh, stopping briefly in Casablanca for some X rays, which confirmed that her lungs had cleared. While she was gone, Abtey had opened a new avenue of communication, to Washington, through the American vice-consul in Casablanca, and it was to him that he passed the information Baker had gathered at her embassy parties. They were pleased that their partnership was back in action and were having a pleasant walk around the old city, when suddenly Baker had excruciating pains in her abdomen.

She developed a high fever and lay packed in ice for three days. Abtey, unable to find an ambulance, stretched her out in the back of a big car and drove her the two hundred fifty miles to Casablanca, where she could be treated. He installed her in the Mers Sultan clinic in June 1941. She did not leave it until December 1942, nineteen months later. Not only was her career as a military intelligence agent over; her life almost ended three times.

According to her own account, when she first stopped in Casablanca to be X-rayed, she was so intrigued by the process that she asked the doctor to X-ray something else. Regarding the procedure as a kind of higher fortune-telling, she particularly wanted to know if there was any reason why she could not have children. The doctor, going along with her whim, injected some fluid to outline her uterus. He reported no obstruction, which made her happy, but his unclean hypodermic, she said, produced an infection in her abdominal lining that developed into peritonitis, which in turn caused a general infection of her blood, septicemia. So she said. But the uterus cannot be X-rayed.

Lynn Haney, a recent biographer, found a woman who nursed Baker in the Casablanca clinic and who gave a different account of the origins of her illness. Baker, she said, was pregnant when she entered the clinic and gave birth to a stillborn baby. (The father, Haney suggests, might have been el Glaoui.) The stillbirth was followed by an infection so severe that it required a hysterectomy. But the infection was not contained. She developed peritonitis and then septicemia.

Before penicillin, septicemia was almost always fatal, but somehow Baker managed to survive. Again and again, she recovered to the point of getting up, only to suffer a worse relapse. She was so weak that she could hardly talk, hardly raise her hand. The repeated inflammations of her abdominal lining built up scars, and she developed blockages that had to be operated on; however, she was too weak to endure the operation until a year after entering the clinic. By 1946, she would have been operated on five times, and she joked that they should have put a zipper in her stomach, they opened it up so often.

While she was sick, Maurice Chevalier came to Casablanca to perform and, hearing she was there, tried to pay a call on her. She refused to see him. In addition to her old dislike of him, she knew he had been performing in Paris and regarded him as a collaborator. She probably did not know that he had also performed in Germany, something which proved hard for him to live down after the war, when he made a filmed statement trying to exonerate himself by claiming he had entertained only French prisoners of war. At any rate, she would not see him, and he gave out the story that she was dying, penniless, in a Casablanca hospital. "Don't leave me, Maurice," he told reporters she had said. "I am so unhappy." Eventually the story spread and before long newspapers as far away as America were carrying the report that she had died in North Africa. One of Langston Hughes's first assignments for *The Defender* was to write an obituary for Josephine Baker.

Whenever he could, Abtey stayed in her room on a cot. He helped the nurse change Josephine's sheets. He was devoted to her, distressed to see her wasted body and splotched skin. His own work was now going well. A new American vice-consul had replaced the old one, and Abtey, acting as intermediary between him and Colonel Paillole, met with him in Baker's room at the clinic. Since she was in some sense an American, it was considered normal for the American vice-consul to pay her repeated visits. The information was important. On a special trip he had made to Marseille to see Paillole, Abtey had picked up details of the German defenses at Bordeaux.

There was also liaison work to do before the Allied invasion of North Africa, which was to take place in November 1942. Ties had to be developed between the local governments and the representatives of the United States. Baker's Arab friends, especially el Glaoui, were among the most powerful people in Morocco, and the Pasha was notably friendly to the Americans, who in turn liked his sense of humor and enjoyed his lavish parties. A great deal of visiting and exchanging of gifts went on between his retinue and American headquarters staff in Casablanca, and at least some of these contacts took place in Baker's hospital room.

Despite Abtey's liaison efforts, communication between the Allied forces and their friends in North Africa was feeble, in large part because Roosevelt did not trust de Gaulle and did everything possible to avoid recognizing him as France's representative. There were two French armies in North Africa at the time, those fighting under the Croix de Lorraine, the sign of de Gaulle and the resistance, and those fighting under the authority of the Vichy armistice with the Germans. The Free French had hoped to hand over North Africa to the debarking Americans, but misled as to exact landing times and places, they were unable to. Americans were killed by Frenchmen fighting on behalf of Germans, and that made Abtey angry, because with good intelligence work it should not have happened. Soon after, a truce was signed with the Vichy French, and Abtey was even more furious that the Americans had thus legitimized the collaborationists and not the Résistants as the representatives of France.

When the American troops entered Casablanca, Baker wanted to go outside to see them. Abtey tried to make her stay put, not only for fear of disturbing her internal wounds but also because there was still shooting in the streets.

"Let me go," she said. "Nothing more can happen to me. Who can stay in bed at a moment like this?" Against blow after blow, she had found the strength to keep going, and this was the first good thing that had happened in over a year. Now she managed to get to her balcony to see the troops before Abtey pulled her back. In fact, the battle of Casablanca went on for three days and three nights, and Baker watched from the roof. She had always been certain that the Americans would come and tip the balance of the war, and again her inspired naïveté proved truer than more complex and perhaps better-informed readings of the situation.

A month after the landings, nineteen months after entering the clinic, Baker left it and went to recuperate in Marrakesh. But soon after she arrived—she was staying at the Mamounia—she fell sick again, from paratyphoid. Ollie Stewart, a black war correspondent also staying at the Mamounia, was sick from the local food. A waiter who came to take care of him said, "I hope you will not be as sick as the woman who sings, Mademoiselle Baker." Rallying his own energy, the journalist located Baker's room at the Mamounia, saw her being cared for by a nurse, and sent back word to America that she was alive. The day before *Time* ran her obituary, the *Times* clarified: "Negro Dancer Reported Dead Is Living in Morocco."

Living, but barely. The bout of paratyphoid discouraged her profoundly. She thought she would never get well, would have one sickness after another for the rest of her life. Even if she got better, she did not see how she could ever go back onstage. Her legs were like sticks; her expressive little rear end had melted away in her fevers.

When she could leave the Mamounia, she moved to Si Menebhi's fairy-tale palace in the Marrakesh medina to complete her recuperation. Her friend hired a crowd of beggars to sit under her window and pray, in loud, soothing chants, for her recovery.

Sidney Williams, director of Red Cross activities for black American soldiers in England and North Africa, sought her out there when she was feeling better. "It was strictly out of Arabian Nights," said Williams. "I have never seen such a place. I knew enough to take my shoes off and enjoy the hospitality." He asked her to perform at the opening of a Red Cross club for black American soldiers in Casablanca. Hesitantly, scared to go back onstage because she could hardly stand up, she agreed and in March 1943 was in front of an audience, singing, for the first time in two years. Her knees were shaking, she was afraid the stitches in her abdomen would open up, but she wowed her audience.

Afterward, she drank American coffee and ate apple pie with a journalist named Kenneth Crawford, giggling over reports of her death. She told him just that she had been staying with the Kaifa of Marrakesh, recovering her health after a long illness. "I couldn't leave French territory," she said. "It would have been like leaving a sinking ship, and I'm no rat." Crawford noted that she seemed as young and vivacious as she had been in her heyday, but she said she was feeling every one of her thirty-six years. Moreover, she joked, she needed a new dress. She had been wearing the same polka-dot number for years now.

As she got back her strength, she started performing regularly for British, French, and American soldiers in North Africa. Abtey's friend Zimmer accompanied her as producer, arranging for stage and speakers to be set up, and Frédéric Rey went along as dancer. They traveled by jeep and truck and did four or five shows a day. The Free French had no organized entertainment network for their troops, like the American USO or the British ENSA, so Baker and her friends managed for the most part on their own. Even the cynical Noël Coward, also in North Africa, was impressed by the terms Baker had set for her own service—no civilians and no admission charge. To this day, veterans gratefully remember her performances, in which the polka-dot dress became a standing joke.

Lawrence Pool, a doctor with a mobile surgical unit in North Africa, saw her in Algiers. The show took place in a large theater with a roof that let in sunlight through an enormous dome of leaded glass. The theater was packed with French, British, and American soldiers, and Baker was in the middle of her act, singing, dancing, and cracking jokes, when air-raid sirens went off. According to Army regulations, the soldiers were not supposed to move an inch, in order to prevent stampedes, so they stayed seated as the antiaircraft guns on their ships in the harbor a block away boomed and bombs started falling nearby. A hospital four blocks away was demolished. They expected the glass dome to fall in on them at any moment. As soon

as the sirens went off, the musicians stopped playing, but Baker, taking
off her shoes, came to the edge of the stage, sat with feet dangling
into the orchestra pit, and steadied the soldiers' nerves by keeping up
a steady stream of funny patter in English and French.

Another American saw her perform one night in Casablanca after
the Germans crossed the Line of Demarcation and occupied the whole
of France. That night the audience consisted mostly of Free French
soldiers and they were wearing black armbands. She sang "J'ai deux
amours," and virtually everyone in the audience began to cry. The
prewar music-hall song, with its bittersweet sophistication, quintessentially French, provoked almost painful nostalgia. It had become a song
of longing for a homeland and capital city from which she and her
audience were exiled. "J'ai deux amours, mon pays et Paris, / Par eux
toujours, mon coeur est ravi." Baker singing this *was* Paris, as she had
been on the stage of the Casino, but now, in North Africa, in her
polka-dot dress, Paris *in extremis*, a Paris many of these men had not
seen for years and were not sure they would ever see again.

The biggest effort of the Free French forces outside France was
propaganda—bringing the existence and the work of the Forces Françaises Libres (after 1943, France Combattante) to the attention of the
rest of the world and fighting to be recognized as the official representatives of France. This was the work that Baker now did. Abtey
trained her to understand the political situation in North Africa as he
did and to think in terms of global political changes after the war.
Who would lead France? What would become of her empire? All the
Arab countries of North Africa and the Middle East were starting to
generate vigorous nationalist movements and to want independence.
If colonialism was finished, what relationship would France have to
her former colonies? With whom would the Arabs align themselves
during the war and after?

He told her that while the French were fighting among themselves
for ascendancy in North Africa—Pétainistes against Résistants, Résistants who were followers of de Gaulle against those who were
followers of General Henri Giraud, the man the Americans

preferred—the Americans and British were working to detach North Africa from France entirely. As part of this effort, they tried to implicate the French in Germany's racial policies. This got Baker particularly angry. How could the American Army present itself as the champion of racial tolerance when it continued to draw color lines? For example, there were the separate clubs for black soldiers and white soldiers, with blacks forbidden in the white club but whites allowed to go to the black club—which many did, the food and drink being better there, because of better ties to the North Africans. At a party Josephine gave at Si Menebhi's palace to celebrate her departure on tour, a drunken white officer, seated at a table with Sidney Williams and some other black Americans, said he had never sat with niggers before, and a fight was barely averted.

The job she took on from now on was more than keeping up the soldiers' morale, although she certainly did that. She "worked" North Africa, the way a politician works a state, to generate respect for and commitment to France Libre, which is to say, for Charles de Gaulle. At the end of every performance, she unfurled an enormous flag with the Cross of Lorraine, the symbol of de Gaulle and the Fighting French, across the back of the stage. When de Gaulle arrived in the spring of 1943 to set up his headquarters in Algiers, he gave her a little Cross of Lorraine in gold in thanks for her services. She was his ambassador, his propaganda arm in North Africa.

She was also a mobile demonstration of Free France's respect for people of color and as such an important part of the campaign to hold on to the African colonies. On an extensive tour she made with Abtey, under military orders, they were accompanied by Si Mohammed Menebhi himself, disguised as an interpreter. He wore a uniform while they traveled, but when they came to a major city he put on his native dress and was received as a visiting dignitary by the local Arab rulers. On his djellabah he wore a Cross of Lorraine, and he described himself as an envoy of General de Gaulle who wanted to demonstrate Moroccan-French solidarity.

The three of them traveled by jeep across the whole width of North Africa, some three thousand miles, from Marrakesh to Cairo. They slept on the ground by the side of the roads, never able to go far from the jeep because of the danger of mines. They suffered terrible heat during the day and terrible cold at night. For long stretches, they ate only what they could carry along with them, such as tuna fish in tins.

Josephine loved this life and maintained, for most of the trip, a good-natured, uncomplaining willingness to rise to the occasion. Improvisation mobilized her best energies in life as it did in her art. When, at the start of her touring, she realized that she had no money left and had to make do from day to day, she said, "Isn't it wonderful?"

"Isn't it wonderful?" was a recurring refrain. Once she was asked to star in a show ENSA organized for some troops marooned in the desert, their leaves canceled and with orders to go into battle. The truck with their equipment broke down en route, and when the entertainers reached the camp, they found three thousand men who had been in the desert for three years but no stage and a temperamental generator. The soldiers arranged themselves on the sand in a natural basin, a few boards were laid down for a stage, and Baker, with the lights and her mike fading and surging, began her act. "O la la! A floor show! Just like Paris. Isn't it wonderful?"

From Cairo they flew to Beirut, to begin a tour of the Middle East. In Syria and Palestine as well as Lebanon, they did benefits for the resistance, and Baker auctioned off her gold Cross of Lorraine for 350,000 old francs. The whole tour brought in 3,143,000 francs, but the public recognition of de Gaulle was even more important than the money.

In Cairo one night, Baker and King Farouk were both at the elegant Shepheard's Hotel, and the king asked her to sing. Very politely, she refused. Egypt was officially neutral and had not regularized its relations with Free France. She would not let herself be linked in any way with a government whose position toward de Gaulle was ambiguous. However, through intermediaries, she offered to sing in Cairo at a celebration in honor of ties between Free France and Egypt and asked Farouk to preside. When he agreed, thus shifting slightly Egypt's public allegiance, it was a small diplomatic coup. That was the kind of work she did, and the kind of work she was good at. Not as dramatic as military information in invisible ink on sheet music, but perhaps as important.

They returned to Cairo from Palestine by air and recrossed the whole of North Africa the way they had come, by jeep. Baker's good nature was finally wearing thin. She and Abtey fought and she insisted on riding for a while in a separate jeep. As they neared Marrakesh, she was so impatient to be home she would not let them stop. They got to Casablanca after nightfall, and both Abtey and Si Menebhi wanted to stay over and continue on to Marrakesh next morning. They were already exhausted and did not have much gas. But Baker insisted, and rather than put her in a funk—her funks were impressive and men went to great lengths to avoid them—they left that night for Marrakesh and arrived in the small hours of the morning, Si Menebhi clasping two little palm trees which Baker wanted to bring back for her garden.

Largely as an expression of thanks for the propaganda services she had rendered on this enormous tour of the Middle East, she was made a sublieutenant in the Women's Auxiliary of the French Air Force. She would remain in North Africa until the fall of 1944, her life alternating between the fantasy luxury of Si Menebhi's palace and the hard soldier's life she led on tour, as it had done since she left the clinic in December 1942. Once, flying to Corsica to perform for troops there, her plane crashed into the sea. In the few seconds they had to prepare, the huge flag with the Cross of Lorraine was stuffed between Baker and the front wall of the cabin to protect her from the impact. They were rescued at sea, and the show, as it must, went on.

Paris was liberated in August 1944. Baker returned to France with the other women in the Air Force, by train from Algiers to Oran and then by ship back to France, landing in Marseille in October 1944. She did not travel exactly like any other member of the military, however. Bonzo and the rest of the animals she had brought from France had disappeared one by one in the difficult times, but under her coat she had hidden another little dog. His name was Mitraillette, which sounds coquettish but means submachine gun. She named him for the way he peed: rat-tat-tat, six little bursts in a row.

She performed now all over France for Army posts and hospitals, recruiting as her orchestra leader Jo Bouillon, who would be her next husband, and putting herself—and him—in debt by her refusal to accept money for her services. To some of the Frenchmen she met now, she seemed to combine high-minded and courageous self-sacrifice with a naïveté that in the circumstances was almost surreal. Sharing a victory dinner with a resistance unit whose men felt lucky to have emerged from the desperate fighting alive, she berated the commander for being so unkind to animals as to serve a suckling pig.

During the next year her health continued to be poor, and she was in a clinic in Neuilly in October 1946 for yet another stomach operation when she was decorated with the treasured Medal of the Resistance. The ceremony took place in her room. She was in bed, wearing a red-and-white gown, beautifully coiffed and made up, surrounded by flowers. Colonel de Boissoudy pinned the medal on her gown with General de Gaulle's daughter, Madame de Boissieu, looking on. General de Gaulle himself sent a letter in which he said he greatly "appreciated the services she had rendered during the war" and was "touched by the enthusiasm with which she had dedicated her talent to the cause of the resistance."

It was possible for an American in France to get honorably through the war in a different style from Josephine Baker's. Gertrude Stein, by sheer bullheaded pretending that nothing unusual was happening, managed to live rather openly at Biligny, protected by her neighbors, going about her daily life. Stein, who was Jewish, took a risk. She stayed because one of the deepest needs of her soul was for continuity, and France, to her, meant continuity, the steady repetition of daily life against which she could play the innovations of her art. Baker's deepest psychic requirements seem to have been exactly the reverse, for new situations in which to invent new personas.

Strangely, for a woman who had owned so much, who so much loved the beautiful clothes in which her profession decked her out, the idea of starting over from nothing excited her. Seizing the stage history offered, she enacted the rescue fantasies that increasingly became her response to the unresolved miseries of her childhood. No one had saved her, but she would save everybody—Belgian refugees, soldiers, Jews, the entire French nation if she could. Her war work was a way of taking her place at the center of an extended family which would revise and amend the unsatisfactory family of her childhood, and the war which gave her her finest hours marked a change in the way she thought of herself, from the one who needed saving to the one who would save.

CHAPTER 7
THE FAMILY
OF MAN

In the fall of 1949, when Paul Robeson was stirring up so much passion in America with his civil rights work and his sympathy for Communism that one of his concerts led to a riot, Josephine Baker was again starring in the Folies-Bergère. As Mary, Queen of Scots, she walked to her execution singing Schubert's "Ave Maria." When the ax fell, the stage was suddenly transformed, by backdrops of stained-glass windows, into a cathedral. The music swelled, and the dancers, costumed as stained-glass figures, detached themselves from the backdrops to form an honor guard for Baker, who, swathed in a cape so as to appear headless, continued to

sing "Ave Maria." She now represented Mary's soul, on its way to
heaven.

She loved the theater. She loved her work. But the war had raised
her life to a level at which more than her own comfort and success
had been at stake in whatever she did. It was hard to go back to being
a civilian. Others in that situation turned to alcohol. Lee Miller, celebrated model in the 1920s, had become a photographer and during
the war performed with daring and brilliance as a war correspondent.
When she returned to ordinary life, there was nothing to match the
intensity of the war or the importance of what she had done during
it, and she began to suffer from depression, eventually taking to drink.
"We cannot keep the world permanently at war to provide you with
excitement," her doctor said.

For Josephine Baker the war was not an interlude after which life
returned to disappointing normalcy. It was a turning point, the moment
when the search for individual satisfaction and identity dead-ended
and led to an identification of herself with a cause. In the American
struggle for civil rights she saw a continuation of the war which she
imagined had been fought to free the world from racism. When she
spoke at the 1963 March on Washington, she pointedly wore the
uniform of the Free French Air Force. Although her battlefield in the
1950s was America, she imagined she fought there as a soldier of
France, and for a brief time, her fantasies about her role on the stage
of history and her impact coincided.

Soon after she recovered from the cycle of inflammation and operation
which had begun in 1940 and tormented her through 1946, she turned
her energies to making Les Milandes, her country home in the Dordogne, into a combination tourist attraction and educational center.
She planned to adopt children of many races and nationalities to demonstrate the possibilities of world brotherhood and to build around
them a model community. Essential to these plans was Jo Bouillon,
the French orchestra leader she had married in 1947.

Unlike her previous husband, Jean Lion, Bouillon adored Baker
in a self-effacing way and was willing to devote himself to her service.

That was fine with her. She married him so they could work together—his orchestra could back her up—and because she wanted a family and thought he would be a good father. Bouillon, whose own father was a professor of music in Montpellier and whose brother, Gabriel, taught at the conservatory in Paris, came to show business from a route quite different from Baker's. He was no rich playboy, like Jean Lion. He was down-to-earth, responsible, practical, prudent, and Baker counted heavily on his stable bourgeois background to keep her daily life functioning smoothly.

Originally a run-down house on a hilltop in a beautiful part of France known for its rivers, its foie gras, and its cave paintings, Les Milandes became under the guidance of Bouillon and Baker one of the world's most improbable tourist attractions. They restored the fifteenth-century house, bringing in electricity, plumbing, and phones. In the surrounding village, which had been virtually abandoned, they installed sixty families to do the work of rebuilding, making sure that their houses, too, had the benefits of the twentieth century. The farm was stocked with six hundred chickens, with cows and pigs, dogs and peacocks. Why peacocks? "They're the only things around here that remind me of my music-hall days," Baker explained.

When the work was all finished, there would be two hotels, three restaurants, a miniature golf course, tennis, volleyball, and basketball courts, a wax museum of scenes from Josephine Baker's life, stables, a patisserie, a foie gras factory, a gas station, and a post office. Since getting tourists to this remote spot was difficult—the nearest major railroad station was an hour by car, and the drive from Paris could take as much as nine hours—a heliport was planned. All this took money, and Baker had spent during the war virtually everything she had. Nor could she, in her forties, generate income as easily as she could when she was in her twenties and thirties.

To finance Les Milandes, she tried again for success in America in 1948, but she did no better than she had in 1936. Her show flopped in Boston, and in New York she and Bouillon, who was white, were refused rooms by dozens of midtown hotels. She went to all-black Fisk University in Tennessee to make a speech and told her audience it was the first time she had felt at home since she arrived in America.

She advised them all to go to North Africa or France, to experience life without prejudice. Incognito, she traveled in the South to examine the racial situation, and her conclusion was that it was worse than ever. Her quick trip left her determined to do something about it, and she brought her resolve to bear on the next year she was in America, 1951.

That year, she started in Cuba and had such a success in Havana, still the Paris of the Caribbean, that word of it reached Miami. The management of the Copa City got the idea of booking her for a major appearance. In the negotiations, she began what became her standard practice with nightclubs, to insist on a nondiscrimination clause in her contract. She would not perform unless the management was prepared to guarantee that black patrons would be admitted. No entertainer before her had played to a nonsegregated audience in Miami, and the negotiations with the Copa City were long and difficult. At one point she was turning down ten thousand dollars a week because they refused to guarantee the integrated audience. Finally the management gave in, and she opened at the Copa City in January 1951.

Gorgeously dressed and trailing foreign languages, she sang, danced, mugged, joked, chattered, and reminisced in a celebration of her own warmth and cosmopolitanism. For opening night her manager, Ned Schuyler, flew in celebrities from New York, both black and white, to celebrate what he and Baker both considered a historic event. She told them, "This is the most important moment of my life. It's the first time I've been in my native land for twenty-six years . . . because the other times don't count."

In March, she played the Strand, a large New York movie theater which still had stage shows. She performed four times a day, as in vaudeville, before each showing of a film which, by odd coincidence, happened to be about the Ku Klux Klan. Her voice was good, her showmanship superb. Every move and phrase was timed for maximum effect. Art was making up for what she had, with the years, lost to nature. One night she saw a man close to the stage looking at her through binoculars. She stopped the show and brought down the house by saying, "Don't do that. You'll spoil the illusion."

She sang in French, Italian, Portuguese, Spanish, and English. She might have sung in Braille, said *Variety*, and the audience would have adored that, too, the way she handled them. She had become one of the elite, those who endure. "The showmanship that is Josephine Baker's, as currently demonstrated at the Strand, is something that doesn't happen synthetically or overnight. It's of the same tradition that accounts for the durability of almost every show biz standard still on top after many years." Most New York box offices had been hurt by the televising of the Kefauver Senate Crime Investigating Committee proceedings, but Baker's receipts were not affected, giving some people hope that vaudeville might be able to hold its own against the new entertainment upstart.

Her $250,000 Parisian wardrobe was an important part of her act, mentioned in most advertisements. She wore dresses by Dior, Balenciaga, Rochas, Griffe, and Balmain, among others—a total of thirteen different outfits. Designers from Seventh Avenue sat in the audience sketching her clothes. She had a French maid to help her and a special makeshift dressing room nearer the stage, in addition to her regular dressing room, for the quick costume changes that became her specialty—"changing the scenery" she called it. For a picture story in the *Daily News*, she demonstrated that she could, assisted by the maid, make ten costume changes in nineteen minutes, including shoes and stockings. One of her outfits had a cloak made of sixty-six feet of satin trimmed with fifty-five pounds of pink fox—the equivalent in weight of forty decent lobsters. A writer from *The New Yorker* who came to interview Baker at the Strand was introduced to her wardrobe instead.

She was making $7,500 per week at the Strand and signed to perform in Chicago at $11,000 per week. In Boston, she played the RKO. *Variety* said, "Vocalizing in foreign lingos, dancing with shoulders shaking and hips swinging, interwoven with chitchat and topped off with a fabulous wardrobe, she clicks with the less sophisticated audience as well." Once she called a dozen young people onto the stage for an impromptu dance contest, giving the winners candy bars and herself winning the audience. "I have no talent," she said around this time. "I have only friends. I like people. They like me. We become friends." It was her act.

In Hollywood, too, her two-week run was a hit, with the longest lines waiting for tickets since the advent of television. Her manager announced, "It isn't a question of whether the movies want Josephine but whether they want her enough to make the kind of movie consistent with her way of thinking on the matter of segregation." She would not be in another all-black musical like *Cabin in the Sky*.

Even in her nightclub acts, singing in French, Italian, Portuguese, Yiddish, she was proving something; her cabaret internationalism was another way of expressing a political position. More and more she concentrated on the international theme, expressing familiar sentiments in unfamiliar languages. If she wanted to be seen as a citizen of the world, it was at least partly to suggest that people could rise above narrow national ties and commit themselves to the human race, and her message was welcome in an America that had started to discover Europe during the war and was eager to see more of it—in unthreatening, charm-bracelet pieces. This was the decade that embraced the phrase "the family of man," the title of an epoch-making show at the Museum of Modern Art in New York of photographs of people from all over the world in universal attitudes of joy, love, grief, and anger.

Baker, who had represented a fantasy America to Europeans in the twenties, now represented a fantasy Europe to Americans of the fifties. Doing so underlined another point she was eager to make: that black people were not children of nature. With her sophistication and her couture wardrobe, her act now in every way called attention to artifice, the triumph of art over nature, symbolized by the foot-high, conical, Oriental-looking chignon into which her hair was shaped. At the age of forty-five, she started to have the success in America that she had always wanted, as a class performer and not a novelty.

She went on to combine performance with civil rights activism in many places, perhaps most notably in Las Vegas, where she was the first black headliner to succeed in getting her whole troupe housed at the hotel where they were working. Before that, black performers without clout had to commute across town for the night. She also demanded an integrated audience and, going even further than her usual nondiscrimination clause, reserved a table for six for every performance which the local NAACP filled with blacks. On the first night of her run, when the management seated that group but refused to seat other blacks waiting to get in, claiming they had fulfilled the contract by seating six, Baker insisted on the intent of her contract—to ensure an integrated audience—and forced them to come around. Next she arranged to fill tables with mixed groups, white members of the NAACP arriving with black friends. When the mixed groups first showed up, they were told they had no reservations, but again Baker persisted, occupying the table herself. *Variety* said, "This was the first manifestation of protest by a minority group that has achieved any semblance of success in Las Vegas." The breaking down of color lines in nightclubs, hotels, and restaurants became her specialty.

Since her goal was either to integrate or to publicize the failure to do so, she made news frequently. In June, she was scheduled to do a benefit performance at the NAACP convention in Atlanta on the understanding that the audience must not be segregated and that she and her troupe must be lodged at a leading hotel. When her requests for reservations were turned down by three hotels, she refused to go to Atlanta and publicized the situation there instead.

She also used her visibility to press for more jobs for blacks, descending in all her charm on selected businesses to congratulate, berate, or encourage. In Chicago, she visited the head of the Illinois Central Railroad to ask why black passengers were still segregated on trains going into the South. In San Francisco, accompanied by officials of the NAACP, she paid calls on the Chamber of Commerce, the City of Paris department store, and Oakland's Key System Transit Company, where an executive explained that their buses—to say nothing of their passengers—were too valuable to entrust to black drivers. Her answer was quick. "How come so many Negroes qualify to drive trucks in the Army but not to drive your buses?"

Especially after the New York branch of the NAACP honored her with a daylong testimonial, Josephine Baker Day, on May 20, 1951, she felt herself bound to use her special position—her fame combined with the invulnerability that came from being based outside America—to protest injustice wherever she saw it. Like a comic-book superwoman, one moment she was an innocuous celebrity eating a meal and then (quick moral change in invisible phone booth of the mind) an intrepid fighter for civil rights, leaping into the fray, clad in the uniform of the Free French Air Force Women's Auxiliary. In July, having dinner at the Biltmore Hotel after her final performance in Los Angeles, she heard a man at a nearby table say, "I won't stay in the same room with niggers." She called the police, who could do nothing because no policeman had heard the remark, but they suggested she make a citizen's arrest. The man was a forty-five-year-old salesman from Dallas, and Baker arrested him as the police suggested. He was sentenced by a municipal judge to ten days in jail or a hundred-dollar fine for disturbing the peace; he paid the fine. Shortly after that, Baker reinvented her history by telling an interviewer that her father had been a policeman.

For a person concerned about race relations, there was much cause for worry in 1951. In the Chicago suburb of Cicero, a young black bus driver, Harvey E. Clark, tried to move his family into an apartment in a previously all-white neighborhood. In response, white rioters wrecked the twenty-family apartment house. A Cook County grand jury returned indictments not against the white rioters but against the people who had helped Clark get the apartment. Although the indictments were subsequently dismissed, they were charged with "conspiracy to injure property . . . by causing a depreciation in the real estate market by renting to Negroes" and with causing and inciting a riot.

There was the case of the "Martinsville Seven," in which seven black men, of whom six were minors, accused of raping a white woman were eventually convicted and sentenced to death. Forty-five black men had been executed for rape since 1908, but no white man had ever been given the death penalty for that crime.

Executions of black men for rape were increasingly seen as a kind of legal lynching. Willie McGee, convicted of raping a white woman in Mississippi and sentenced to death, became the center of another storm of protest. A Save Willie McGee rally in Harlem, at the Golden Gate Ballroom, in March when Baker was appearing in New York at the Strand, listed her as one of the principal speakers, although at the last moment she learned that the event was being orchestrated by Communist groups and refused to appear, sending only a statement of support. As the time for McGee's execution grew close, Baker was in Detroit, where McGee's wife, Rosalee, lived. She spent a lot of time with her and paid for a round-trip air ticket so Mrs. McGee could see her husband before his execution. But executed he was. Before starting her show at the Fox Theater that night, Baker walked to the front of the stage and told the audience that she would go on but that her heart was not in it. "They have killed Willie McGee, one of my people." With tears on her face, she recited the facts of the case. She said that it wasn't just Willie McGee who was executed. "A part of every American Negro died a little with him." In subsequent days, she continued to spend time with Mrs. McGee and never lost a chance to speak out about the injustice she believed had been done. At a reception in her honor, when photographers refused to photograph her with Mrs. McGee, she walked out. She was becoming adept at a certain kind of quiet confrontation.

In New Jersey, in another celebrated case, six black men, known as the "Trenton Six," were on trial for killing an aged white furniture dealer. Arthur Garfield Hays, the noted civil rights lawyer, insisted that color was an important issue in the case, but the prosecutor disagreed. It might be proper to raise that issue in some of the southern states, he said, but "we never inject the racial element in any cases in New Jersey." Baker, performing in Philadelphia, took time off to go to Trenton to visit the accused men, one of whom, John MacKenzie, had served overseas, been wounded, and seen Baker perform at an American hospital in France. To see her again, in these different circumstances, made him weep.

In the spring of the year of her American tour, the *Philadelphia Inquirer* said of Baker, "Her appearances have been marked by perhaps the most outspoken opposition to racial discrimination and segregation ever shown by a Negro artist, except Robeson." Baker's activity came to a head in October at the Stork Club in New York, in an incident which made the NAACP's annual report of civil rights events along with the Trenton Six, the Martinsville Seven, Willie McGee, the Cicero riots, and protests against racial stereotypes in the radio shows *Beulah* and *Amos 'n' Andy*.

. . .

On Tuesday night, October 16, 1951, toward midnight, after her own show at the Roxy and the Broadway shows were over, Baker met some theater friends for a late supper and drinks at the Stork Club. The friends were Mr. and Mrs. Roger Rico. He was the French baritone who had replaced Ezio Pinza in the lead of *South Pacific*. Also with them was Bessie Buchanan, who had danced with Baker in the chorus of *Shuffle Along* and at the Plantation Club in 1925 and who, four years after this, would begin a political career as the first black woman elected to the New York Assembly.

The Stork Club on East Fifty-third Street, one of New York's most fashionable nightclubs at the time, was an exercise in carefully calibrated snobbery. Fine and not so fine variations in treatment separated the famous from the not famous, the more important celebrities from the less. The most important were seated in the Cub Room, the inner sanctum of the Stork Club, isolated from the rest by a red velvet rope and a vigilant headwaiter. Even inside the Cub Room distinctions persisted. If the Stork Club's owner and resident host, Sherman Billingsley, wanted to be nice to people, he sent them Arpège or French champagne, he came over and talked to them for varying lengths of time and with varying degrees of warmth, or he insisted on taking their check. In these early days of television, he had a weekly program filmed at the Stork Club in which he interviewed visiting celebrities about their busy and interesting lives, a kind of early avatar of *Lifestyles of the Rich and Famous*. His ruling conceit was that the Stork Club was his home and all these wonderful people were his personal guests. He had been a poor boy in Oklahoma, had made it to where he was by bootlegging, and liked to congratulate himself on the glamour of his life.

One of his best friends was Walter Winchell, the powerful newspaper and radio columnist, who had a permanent table in the Cub Room. The Stork Club served Winchell as a combination office and salon. He was there almost every night, picking up news, working on his columns, consulting with his assistants. Celebrities came to his table to say hello, for Winchell, who reached fifty million people by news-paper and radio, was the best publicity in America. Grace Kelly came over to tell Winchell about her engagement to Prince Rainier, and when Ernest Hemingway heard a good line at dinner from Spencer Tracy ("Sometimes I think life's a terminal illness"), he popped right over to Winchell's table to pass it on. In return for everything he got from the Stork, Winchell acted as the club's resident publicist, keeping up its reputation as *the* place for elite folks to meet.

That night Winchell was there with a *Journal-American* reporter, Jack O'Brian, and his wife. They were about to go to a midnight sneak preview of Darryl Zanuck's film *Rommel*. Nearby sat Herman Klur-feld, one of Winchell's chief writers, responsible for Winchell's column, and much later his biographer. He was entertaining a journalist from Chicago. Also present were Shirley Eder, a print and radio gossip columnist, and her husband. Eder was young but had a certain amount of power because of her access to radio, so Billingsley treated her well. She was accustomed to receiving bottles of perfume and champagne.

When Josephine Baker came in, Winchell waved to her and she smiled back. He had written about her enthusiastically in his column. He thought she was gorgeous, loved her act, and admired her class. In prime Winchellese, he called her husband "Jo Bouillon, which is oo-la-la for soup."

Everyone must have noticed the Rico party because black faces were rarely seen at the Stork Club and never in the Cub Room. Billingsley let it be known that he did not welcome black patrons, even celebrities. Muriel Rahn, who had sung the lead in the 1944 production of *Carmen Jones*, once showed up for a guild-sponsored party at the Stork Club and was told that she had not been invited and so could not be admitted. When she produced her invitation, she was told that there was no more room.

The middleweight boxing champion Sugar Ray Robinson, who was a good friend of Walter Winchell's, had once volunteered to meet Winchell at the Stork Club. Winchell, who prided himself on his liberal credentials and particularly thought himself a friend of blacks and a fighter for civil rights, replied, "I wish you wouldn't, Champ.

Sherman Billingsley doesn't like Negroes, and he doesn't want them in his place, and if you came down there and he insulted you, I'd have to break with him although I've known him for twenty-three years."

Billingsley also did not like Jews much, but it would have been harder to keep them out of the Stork Club: Winchell himself was Jewish.

Shirley Eder says that just before the Rico group came in, Billingsley went over to Winchell looking pale and angry and whispered something in his ear. Then he disappeared.

The Ricos and their guests sat down and ordered drinks. Only Baker wanted to eat. She ordered a crabmeat cocktail, a steak, and a bottle of red wine. Drinks came. Then nothing. Far from receiving the usual lavish Billingsley treatment of celebrities, they were ignored. No perfume. No French champagne. No hello from Billingsley. He shunned their table. So did the waiters. The Ricos were not accustomed to being treated this way in the Cub Room, and Josephine Baker was not used to being ignored anywhere. They began to suspect that the waiters were pointedly ignoring them, and for Baker, the specialist in integrating nightclubs, it was not hard to figure out why.

When they finally forced a waiter to their table to explain why the food was so delayed, he said that there was no steak, no crabmeat, and they were still looking for the wine. When they said they would order something else, he went away again.

They waited between half an hour and an hour. Baker, the Ricos, and Bessie Buchanan said they waited close to an hour. Other observers said they waited little more than half an hour and that such delays were not unusual in the Stork Club, where service could be poor.

When the waiters continued to ignore them, Rico and Baker, certain now that they were being discriminated against, got up, walked past Winchell without saying a word, and went to the phone booth. There Baker made two calls, one to William Rowe, a black police commissioner, and another to her lawyer. She claimed that the Stork Club had refused to serve her because of her color and asked to have the incident investigated. If her charge of racial discrimination could be made to stick, the Stork Club would be in violation of both the State Civil Rights Act and the State Alcoholic Beverage Control Law.

When they returned to the table, a waiter rushed over with a menu and asked for their order. Finally, a steak appeared. By then, everyone at the table was too embarrassed to want to stay longer and Baker had lost her appetite. They left the club and went to see Walter White, the powerhouse of the NAACP, to tell him what had happened and discuss the possibility of legal action.

For some people, the mystery was why she made a fuss. What did she expect at the Stork Club? Other people, equally unable to credit such naïveté, imagined that she staged the whole thing. She must have gone to the Stork Club intending to dramatize the club's practice of discrimination. Why not complain to Billingsley if all she wanted was a steak? What she really wanted was exactly the publicity she got.

The Ricos and Baker denied that. Stork Club regulars, the Ricos had invited Baker there and were sufficiently concerned about the possibility of ugliness that they consulted several people beforehand, all of whom said there should be no problem taking Baker anywhere in New York. They were outraged at what happened, and Baker was genuinely humiliated.

Possibly she was oversensitive, perceiving an intentional slight where there was only bad service. She had been treated rudely before in America; she had known the humiliation of being turned away from hotels. Traumatized by those slights, she may have anticipated or imagined rudeness. Certainly she expected to be catered to and was quick to claim discrimination when she was not. On the other hand, people who knew Billingsley believed he was fully capable of telling his waiters not to serve Baker. "He was just that dumb," said one woman who went often to the Stork Club in those years. But investigating committees set up by the mayor's office and the State Liquor Commission failed to find evidence of systematic discrimination. Fact in this case may be in the hidden realm of intentions; however, given the pattern of hostility toward blacks at the Stork Club on the one hand and on the other Baker's pattern of sensitivity to slights and determination to resist them, the incident seems inevitable. What seems accidental—and became central—was the presence of Walter Winchell. Also accidental but rich with irony was the specific identity of Baker's host, Roger Rico.

Rico was the star of *South Pacific*, which had opened in April 1949 and proceeded to break Broadway records, running second only to Rodgers and Hammerstein's earlier hit, *Oklahoma!* Yet the backers of the show had been afraid its material was too sensitive and would offend many Americans. Based on James Michener's *Tales of the South Pacific*, it concerned a young American nurse stationed in the French Pacific in World War II who falls in love with an older French planter. These were the roles first and indelibly played by Mary Martin and Ezio Pinza. When Nellie, the nurse, discovers that Emile has previously been married to a Polynesian woman, she can't bring herself to marry him. Her racial disgust mobilized, she calls off the romance.

The story depends entirely on the planter's being French, for only a French colonist would believably have been so unconcerned about race as to marry a Polynesian woman. An English planter with a native wife is barely credible, and an American, out of the question completely. The play's whole point is the difference between American and French attitudes toward race.

In order for the play to end happily and for Nellie to find happiness with Emile, she has to overcome her race prejudice, a process helped and expressed by the song "You've Got to Be Taught."

> You've got to be taught to be afraid
> Of people whose eyes are oddly made
> And people whose skin is a different shade
> You've got to be carefully taught.

It is one of the most didactic songs ever to come out of Broadway, but it worked, becoming the achievement of which Oscar Hammerstein, the lyricist, was most proud.

Of all people to take Josephine Baker to the Stork Club, how suitable that it should have been the French star of *South Pacific*, forcing life to imitate art and to demonstrate the racial vulgarity of America in the face of the cosmopolitanism of France.

. . .

It was very late when the Ricos, Baker, and Buchanan arrived at White's apartment on East Sixty-eighth Street, and White and his wife were already in bed and asleep. In their nightclothes in the dining room the Whites heard their visitors describe what had happened. According to Mrs. White, Baker was quivering with humiliation and anger. "She told her story with enormous dignity but her hands trembled and there were tears in her eyes—like a little girl who had been hurt. 'If there had been a hole in the floor,' she said, 'I would have so gladly gone down into it. Everybody was looking at us and then looking away. Everybody could see how we were being humiliated.' " She was particularly angry with Walter Winchell because he had done nothing to protest what was being done to them.

The next day she sent Winchell a telegram complaining about his behavior. He was stunned. He hadn't seen anything unusual happen at the Stork Club that night. When she walked by him to call the police, she hadn't told him there was anything wrong. Everything, as far as he knew, was peaceful when he had left to go to his late-night sneak preview.

What had he done wrong? This powerful man was not used to people rebuking him, particularly not black people, whose gratitude was one of the pleasures of his life. Now he was in the position of losing two pleasures at once—his position as protector of the downtrodden and Billingsley's friendship. For the situation called on him to reproach his friend for bigotry. He had told Sugar Ray Robinson that he would do that if Billingsley ever insulted the boxer. But when push came to shove he couldn't bring himself to. Billingsley seemed to have insulted Baker, and Winchell stood by him, furious at having to do so—furious not at Billingsley but at Baker.

The writer of Winchell's broadcast, Ernest Cuneo, and Walter White met in an attempt to calm things down. They agreed that when Winchell did his usual Sunday-evening broadcast, he would rebuke the Stork Club for discrimination. In return, White gave Winchell a letter to read on the air, praising his civil rights record and exonerating him of complicity in the discourtesy to Baker. But when Winchell went on the air, this is what he said:

> After 20 years on the air and almost 30 in the newspapers, I thought my record was crystal-clear when minorities are getting kicked around. It irritates me now to have to recite that record and disgrace myself with my defense. . . . The facts are that whenever I have been called upon in the case of man's inhumanity to man I was always easily recruited. For anyone to demand of me where I stand when ANY person is discriminated against in a public place, means that that person is no friend of mine.
>
> I am appalled at the agony and embarrassment caused Josephine Baker and her friends at the Stork Club. But I am equally appalled at their efforts to involve me in an incident in which I had no part.

Winchell then read Walter White's letter, in which he said that he had examined the facts in the case and had determined that Winchell was unaware that Baker had been treated discourteously. "I know your record too well in your opposition to racial and every other kind of discrimination to believe that you would be a party to any insult to human dignity."

White, who had not been particularly angry at Winchell before, now was furious. Winchell had gone back on their deal by using his letter without the promised rebuke of Billingsley. In his anger, White agreed to do what Josephine Baker had wanted to do all along—throw up an NAACP-sponsored picket line in front of the Stork Club, protesting its policy of discrimination.

The picket line, unusual in nonlabor disputes, proved a highly successful means of drawing attention to the case. The first night, October 23, close to a week after the incident, a hundred people picketed in groups of six. In the first group were Walter White, Lindsay White, another important NAACP official, Bessie Buchanan, who marched as Baker's representative while Baker did her evening show, and Laura Hobson, the author of *Gentlemen's Agreement*, the novel about anti-Semitism. When picketing continued a second night, many of the picketers were supplied by the Manhattan Committee, a civic group headed by Duke Ellington's sister, Ruth James. There were also actors from some Broadway shows, including two from *South Pacific*, one of whom explained that they were there in part to support Roger Rico, but mainly because they believed in the message of the show's song "You've Got to Be Taught." The third night, politicians appeared on the picket line. New York elections were little more than a week away, and both Democrats and Republicans wanted to show themselves publicly opposing discrimination.

As days went by, the incident became increasingly a battle between Walter Winchell on the one hand and the NAACP and Josephine Baker on the other. Winchell's own writers and advisers—Herman Klurfeld, Ernest Cuneo, and Arnold Forster—were appalled. They tried to explain to Winchell in memo after memo that he had to take a stand against the Stork Club or get Billingsley to issue a statement denying a policy of discrimination. Klurfeld told him, "The public is beginning to think you would rather defend Billingsley than stand up for principles you have been fighting for." Forster said, "If the Stork Club was not guilty of discriminating against Josephine Baker—and it appears that a good case can be made for that position [that the slow service was the result of inefficiency or of simple discourtesy rather than a policy of discrimination]—the best public relations would have been (and may still be) for Sherman Billingsley to give you a simple one-paragraph letter in which he states the policy of no discrimination by the Stork Club, and adds to it an expression of regret for the discomfort caused Miss Baker from the combination of accidental circumstances. Had Billingsley given you such a letter to read along with the Walter White letter, it would successfully have choked off any further ado."

But Billingsley, far from issuing conciliatory statements, issued arrogant evasions which infuriated everyone. First he said that the Stork Club did not admit obnoxious people. When that produced howls of anger, he clarified: the Stork Club catered to the peoples of the world. Who exactly did he mean by "the peoples of the world"? "The peoples of the world. For the life of me, I can't see who's left out by that statement."

Winchell persisted in attacking the people who questioned his behavior and never disassociated himself from Billingsley. Thinking himself above reproach, he had also come to believe that nothing he said could please his attackers. "I have been accused, indicted, convicted and almost lynched by the very people who have asked and gotten me to fight such things." On his next broadcast, he called for Scotch tape: he wanted to lengthen his list of ingrates. His Drop-Dead List was also lengthened. Klurfeld, horrified by the paranoia that had suddenly been mobilized, saw that Winchell was determined to play the role of martyr.

The Stork Club incident pitted one child of poverty, ethnicity, and vaudeville against another. Walter Winchell had grown up in Harlem when Harlem was Jewish. His grandfather had been a rabbi, and Winchell himself spoke Yiddish fluently. Ultrasensitive to anti-Semitism all his life, he nonetheless felt entitled, when once attacked by *Time*, to call its writers and editors "smart-ass intellectual Jews."

Ten years older than Baker, like her he was no success at school, having been left back twice by the time he was twelve. At thirteen, on the verge of being left back again, he quit school as she did and went into show business. He had always loved performing. He had practiced tap dancing in the bathroom until the neighbors complained. He and his pal George Jessel started out as ushers at the Imperial Theater at Lenox and 118th Street. During intermission they led the audience in songs whose lyrics were flashed on the screen. They were then hired for a kid act called the "Newsboy Sextette," which included another friend, Eddie Cantor. Winchell played the role of a newsboy who went around hitting people with a rolled-up newspaper—emblem of things to come!

Around the time of World War I, he went out on his own with a woman he later married, Rita Greene. Their singing and dancing act got steady bookings, but never rose higher than the number two spot, just above the animal act that opened the show. But Winchell's passion for writing gossip now began to manifest itself. He wrote a newsletter about the doings of various vaudevillians which was posted backstage. Eventually he got some pieces published in *Billboard*, and by 1920 he left vaudeville—and Rita Greene—for show business journalism. Vaudeville helped create his sense of an audience, his conception of the journalist as entertainer, and the performance style of his radio show.

"Good evening, Mr. and Mrs. America and all the ships at sea. Let's go to press." After that signature opening, he rattled out 237 words per minute. "If I spoke slowly," he said, "people might realize I didn't have much to say." In the middle of the broadcast came a two-to-three-hundred-word segment he called the "eddy," the editorial, and at the end, a snappy line which he called the "lasty." Again in the vaudeville tradition ("Leave 'em wowed"), he considered this the most important part of the broadcast. Everyone connected with the broadcast worried about the lasty until sometimes just before airtime. A sample lasty: "Here's wishing you a Happy Father's Day with a toast to every mother's first child—her husband."

He broadcast on Sunday night at nine, and throughout the 1940s, before television, he had an influence and popularity unmatched in the history of journalism, the impact of a talk-show host and news anchorman rolled into one, of Dan Rather combined with Johnny Carson. But in many ways he was unprepared for the importance of his role and knew it, hence the paranoia that took so little to mobilize. At bottom he was a poorly educated, failed vaudevillian—in Arthur Miller's words, one of the "semiliterate sentimentalists [who] bestrode the world as powerful as Popes before the Reformation." And when the blanket respect and deference to which he had become accustomed failed, it provoked an almost existential panic.

With some reason, he saw Baker's attack on him as monumentally unfair. "Why didn't she tell me if she thought there was something wrong?" Usually, combat appealed to him. "It is the bullshit on which I thrive," he said. But this was different. Those who should have been grateful were attacking him, and his outrage was visceral. Years later he said, "The Baker story was my most frustrating experience. The unfairness of the whole thing was sickening. I had the same feeling when I was a kid in Harlem and was left back at school. I couldn't understand why the teacher had been so cruel."

This was a year and half after Senator Joseph McCarthy claimed to have a list of fifty-seven card-carrying Communists in the State Department. The witch-hunt was on, and the Robeson riots had shown how many people equated the demand for equal rights with anti-Americanism. So it occurred to Winchell that perhaps Baker's otherwise inexplicable behavior was part of a Communist conspiracy. He now began to see Communists everywhere. There were three people on the picket line outside the Stork Club, he said, whom reporters recognized from close-ups taken during the Robeson riots. Impelled by his sense of betrayal, Winchell, who really had been a voice for liberal causes, now became more than ever the friend of McCarthy, Roy Cohn, and J. Edgar Hoover, and hastened a drift to the right which had begun when Truman, whom he personally loathed, became President.

Shirley Eder, the gossip columnist who had been in the Stork Club on October 16, wanted to help Winchell out. She was furious at Baker, not for what she said about Billingsley, "which was obviously true," but for involving Winchell. "I don't discount the fact that he may have left knowing there could be trouble . . . But he honestly played no active part in whatever humiliation Miss Baker and her party may have been subjected to that night."

One day, Eder was having lunch with her friend Enid Haupt. Haupt was taking French lessons, and in her quest for material to read in French, she had found in a bookstore Josephine Baker's 1949 memoirs, a revision of the earlier Marcel Sauvage books, and had browsed through it, noting some passages that seemed hostile to Jews.

Eder perked up at this. She wrote down the name of the bookstore, and after lunch she found the book, bought it, and had the chapter in question translated. Then she tried to track down Winchell. It wasn't easy. She finally did it through Roy Cohn, who arranged a meeting at 1 A.M. in a private room at the Stork Club. Eder turned over the typed translation. She said she wanted to give him "at least some ammunition to defend himself against [Baker's] attack." Winchell threw his arms around her, saying he would never forget what she had done, and twenty-four hours later, the quotations appeared in his column.

The remarks were to the effect that discrimination against blacks by Jews was particularly sad because Jews had experienced the same kind of oppression as blacks had and the two groups should be allies. Winchell quoted so as to emphasize the accusation that Jews (specifically the merchants and landlords of Harlem) exploited blacks, but without any mitigating context—especially the reminder, which followed in the book, that Baker had been married to a Jew. Josephine Baker, he revealed, was anti-Semitic. In fact, she "out-Goebbels Hitler."

Other friends began providing other mud for him to sling in his column: Baker had supported Mussolini, she had not been anti-Nazi until the Nazis started losing, she had wanted no black patrons and had mixed with no blacks on her 1936 visit to New York, she was a provocateur who had made a career of this kind of incident—everything at the Stork Club had happened just as she planned it. No matter that it was hard to be both Fascist and Communist. Baker was both. She was everything bad.

Baker took his accusations seriously. Lots of people read Winchell—his column was syndicated in a thousand newspapers— and even if no one believed what he said, he did her harm by making her appear a troublemaker. Her manager complained that she seemed more interested in politics, what he called "flag-waving for the NAACP," than show business, and told her that her politics were beginning to cost her engagements. She didn't care. She put the question to Jo Bouillon, which should she devote herself to: her career or the cause she believed in? Jo Bouillon felt he didn't have a choice. If he told her to stick to her career, she would leave him. On the other hand, they had a vastly expensive enterprise at Les Milandes to support. The success of Josephine's American tour had seemed providential— the way out from under the enormous financial burden they had assumed in restoring the château and village at Les Milandes and beginning to make it a tourist attraction. Now she was letting that money slip away. She only cared about winning this fight, which was not so much with the Stork Club as with Winchell personally.

When Winchell accused her of provoking incidents, she replied, "People of color are not obliged to resort to provocation: incidents occur on their own." When he accused her of timeserving in World War II, she had Jacques Abtey fly to New York from North Africa to publicize her war record. And finally she sued Winchell and his employers, the Hearst Corporation and King Features, for $400,000 in United States District Court. She cited his concerted attack on her good name and reputation, his characterization of her as "a Fascist, a Communist, an anti-Semite, an anti-Negro, an enemy of the people of her own race, intellectually dishonest, a fraud, and a person of low or doubtful character." Her lawyer was Arthur Garfield Hays, the specialist in civil liberties cases. After several years, the case was dismissed in a pretrial hearing as various deadlines had passed with no further action by the plaintiff, but it was on record that she had sued him, and in the meantime, the war against Winchell had passed to other hands.

Ed Sullivan, then a columnist for the *New York Daily News*, the chief rival of Winchell's *Daily Mirror*, went on Barry Gray's midnight-to-three radio show and blasted Winchell. He was one of the few men in New York powerful and gutsy enough to do so. "I despise Walter Winchell for what he has done to Josephine Baker. Long before Senator McCarthy came into this character-assassination racket there was a guy by the name of Walter Winchell." Winchell, so fond of thinking of himself as a statesman, had never, Sullivan revealed, been to Europe. He was "dangerously ill-informed," a man of great power "unaccompanied by greatness or nobility of thinking," a "small-time Hitler."

Winchell refused to reply to Sullivan, taking the Olympian stance that he only cared what Presidents thought of him, not "small-timers" like his opposite number on the *News*. His revenge was not on the powerful Sullivan, but on Barry Gray, who, for providing the mike, went on Winchell's Drop-Dead List. It suddenly became hard for Gray to get performers to appear on his show.

Still, the very last stroke was Sullivan's, and it was indirect. For Sullivan, with his slow-paced delivery, his understatement, his dry irony, took well to the intimacies of television and became one of America's first television stars, hosting a weekly Sunday-night variety show. Whereas Winchell's frenetic style looked ludicrous in TV close-ups. He was dead in the media water.

The Stork Club incident was the beginning of the end for him. Never before had his enemies been able to attack him publicly. Now they began. The *New York Post* not only gave extensive coverage, highly sympathetic to Baker, to the flap at the Stork Club; it also planned and ran later that winter a major series of exposés of Winchell, detailing his vanities and weaknesses, illustrating his ignorance and petty tyranny. As he had with Baker, he tried to say the *Post* was Communist without actually saying it was Communist, for that was libelous. But the *Post* claimed he had gone beyond insinuation and threatened a suit. Backed by his network, ABC, Winchell settled the matter by publicly denying an intention to say the *Post* was Communist. The next day, he asked ABC to increase his libel insurance. They refused. He resigned, to signify how serious he was about his demand, assuming it was a move in a poker game. To his horror, his resignation was accepted.

Three weeks before the Stork Club incident, Winchell had signed a lifetime contract with ABC which guaranteed him $10,000 a week for as long as he was capable of broadcasting. Unable to broadcast, he still collected $1,000 a week. It was only four months since he had signed that contract. Now ABC, which did not like having to apologize to the *Post* and had seen that Winchell was no good on television, was letting him go. By the end of the decade, Winchell's syndication had dropped from a thousand newspapers to one hundred fifty. "Television has changed everything," he said. "Television is destroying New York nightlife, and the talk-shows are giving people the show-biz patter and prattle that belong in my column." The *Mirror* closed after a fourteen-day printers' strike in 1963, the year Josephine Baker did a benefit for the civil rights groups SNCC and CORE at Carnegie Hall. The Stork Club closed in 1965. Billingsley died broke.

Very close to the start of the Stork Club affair, Winchell had tried to deploy against Baker his own ultimate weapon, the Federal Bureau of Investigation. He had received some mail from people who agreed with him that Baker was a no-good ingrate. One person praised Winchell for seeing at last that Baker was a "#1 phoney." (Winchell took to calling her "Josa-phoney Baker.") Another, who signed himself "a colored student," thought that Baker should go back to France if she didn't like America. Another reported having seen Baker in Leningrad in 1936, drinking "to her heart's content" with important Reds and

French Commies. These important documents Winchell forwarded to the FBI's director with a covering note: "Hoover, can we check this please?" Later, when Winchell received a tip that Josephine Baker had been delayed entering the United States because she had with her a *Russian* maid, he hastened to send this information, too, to the government's fact-gatherers. "To Hoover," he scrawled. "True?"

The FBI never did an investigation of Josephine Baker. Its check in response to Winchell's request consisted of a summary of recent articles about Baker in *Time* and *Life* plus some newspaper items about her activity on behalf of Willie McGee, including one which praised her efforts to dissociate herself from Communists interested in the same cause. But Winchell's request did begin the FBI's file on Baker. The Bureau went on to collect many hundreds of pages of information about her over the course of years, much of it from laughably public sources. The *Life* article is cited over and over. To read the file is to marvel at the waste of time and taxpayers' money. But it did not escape the notice of the FBI that she was "not . . . procommunist but pro-Negro and primarily interested in [the] fight for racial equality."

In long retrospect, Josephine Baker seems to have come out well in the battle of the Stork Club, but at the time it seemed merely to have damaged her career. She was on the verge, finally, of making it big in America, which meant making a lot of money for the first time since the war began, money she badly needed, but all the political activity had a cost. She lost the rest of her American bookings and any chance she might have had for a Hollywood film career. She integrated Las Vegas nightclubs, but she never played a Las Vegas nightclub again after 1952.

She did herself even more damage and demonstrated the strange twistings of her political beliefs when she went to Argentina in 1952 and became devoted to the Peróns, making a series of violently anti-American and pro-Perón speeches. Her infatuation with Eva Perón seems inevitable. Both Josephine and Evita did things on a large scale with no thought of accounting; to both, it seemed mean-spirited to question where the money to fund their charities was coming from. Both were actresses, both had come from terrible poverty, both loved the poor with the sincerity of identification, and possibly, with their ditsy charities and mad display, spoke better to the fantasy life of those they aimed at helping than more efficient but imaginatively arid government programs. Evita, with her luxury hotels for working women, her luxury resorts, where poor people were housed for a while before being shunted back to poverty, thought in terms that Josephine, with her elaborate plans for Les Milandes, could understand. Given a wealthy South American country to bankrupt, Josephine might have managed it. As it was, all she had was a village in the Dordogne.

Her speeches in Argentina alienated even more people than had her civil rights activism. When it looked as though the Immigration Service might punish her for them by forbidding her to reenter America, she countered angrily that to be excluded from America would be an honor. The United States, the most lucrative market for her talents, was largely cut off for her. She had cut it off for herself.

She had asked Jo Bouillon a question which, he correctly saw, there was no way for him to answer. Money or beliefs. If he told her to make money, she would hate him. If he told her to ignore money and devote herself to her beliefs, they would be ruined. But what was no-win for him was no-lose for her. If they were ruined, she got to play a role she had flirted with but never played in real life, a role which was as seductive to her as it was, for similar reasons, to Walter Winchell—the role of martyr.

After seven years of marriage to Jo Bouillon, in her late forties, at an age when other people are starting to wind down, Josephine Baker began a family. Whereas for most of us families are biological events that generate meanings and intensity as they endure, for Baker the family was a willed event whose meaning preceded it. Her family was to prove that all races and nationalities could live together in harmony. With deadpan concreteness, she would bring to life and make her own the idea of the family of man. To this end, she and Jo Bouillon originally planned to adopt four children—one black, one white, one yellow, one red—who would be raised at Les Milandes and serve as the centerpiece of her *domaine*. She even had a name for her family: the Rainbow Tribe.

Her sister Margaret Wallace believed the seed for the Rainbow
Tribe had been planted in their childhood, when their mother made
a point of allowing no distinction between the child of Eddie Carson
and her siblings, whose father was Arthur Martin. Carrie Martin's
children were raised not to say half sister or half brother, because, as
their mother explained, "half" wasn't good enough. God had given
them all to her, and each child had her whole love. Margaret Wallace
thought this had inspired Josephine to prove to the world that universal
brotherhood is possible and that all of us are children of God.

But Baker's matriarchy was in several ways a rebuke to her mother's. If Carrie had sent her children out, her daughter would take
children in. If the little Martins had been poor and deprived, forced
to work, these children would be pampered. Where the Martins had
been strictly disciplined, these children would never be punished. If
there had been differences in skin color that distinguished Josephine
from her sisters and brother no matter what Carrie said, her own
children would be so different in color that difference would be the
norm.

She adopted the first child in Japan, when she was touring there
in the spring of 1954. He was close to two years old when she chose
him in a Japanese orphanage. He had been found abandoned by his
Korean mother (his father was probably an American soldier) and
given the name Akio, for "autumn," the season in which he was found.
Before she was out of the orphanage door, she saw another child she
could not resist and scooped him up, too—another half-American
occupation baby whose name, Tenuya, was soon changed to the more
pronounceable Janot.

Josephine was constantly traveling and performing, and beginning
in 1954 she brought back children from her travels as one might bring
back souvenirs. For her white child, she went to Scandinavia, adopting
Jari from an orphanage in Helsinki when he was close to two. From
Colombia in South America, she sent back Luis, a black child. His
mother already had seven children and offered Baker her eighth upon
hearing of her search. The child traveled to France from Canada with
the French consul's secretary and was met at Le Havre by Margaret
Wallace.

She now had four children—two Orientals, a Caucasian, and a black. Jari was Protestant, Akio Buddhist, Luis Catholic, and Janot Shinto. According to plan, she needed an American Indian. But she returned from Paris one day to the country with Jean-Claude, a French child. Jo Bouillon was bewildered and slightly appalled. He pointed out that Jean-Claude was white like Jari and Catholic like Luis. Strictly speaking, they didn't "need" him. "I thought you'd be bringing us an American Indian," he said. "They're very hard to find," she replied. "We'll simply have to be patient."

It occurred to her that, given the difficulty of finding Indians, a Jew might do. After all, they didn't yet have examples of all the major religions. And who had suffered more from racism than Jews? She and Bouillon agreed, after some discussion, that they must have an Israeli, and she went to Israel with the firm intent of adopting another child. For once, she was thwarted. They had agreed to adopt only boys, to avoid sexual problems in the future, and the Israeli government, needing its male children, would not allow her to take one out of the country. After more discussion back at Les Milandes, Mr. and Mrs. Bouillon decided they would make do with a Jewish child from France and adopted their sixth son, Moïse (Moses). Moïse at ten months was the youngest. The oldest was four. To have that many children so close in age had they been biologically hers, she would have had to bear three sets of twins in three years.

The pace of acquisition slowed down somewhat between 1956 and 1960. But now, every time Josephine adopted a child, she provoked a fight with Jo Bouillon, who was more than content with six. He tried to convince her that children cost money to raise, but this was a point she would not accept. "Her left hand was busy squandering all that her right hand amassed," he said. Not that adopting children was squandering in the same way buying shoes or dresses was. Bouillon admired his wife's big heart. And he loved the children, even when he was dead set against adopting them. But he saw something she thought it petty to consider, that all this love had a cost.

Initially excited by her high spirits and daring, as their marriage went on he grew increasingly exasperated by the underside of those same traits, recklessness and improvidence. Every new adoption seemed more proof that Josephine was irresponsible and that he would be unable to keep them from financial ruin. She, in turn, had married him for his practicality and his malleability, but as the marriage went on she began to despise him for thwarting her without being as strong as she was. Once, when they had a fight about her expenditures at Les Milandes, Bouillon said he did not know what to do with her. He thought slapping her might help, but the men of his family would never hit women—they were too middle-class. "I know," said Josephine. "That's one of the reasons I married you." She could manage him—but only up to a point. He was a man who, pushed beyond his limits, simply retreated. At times he locked himself in his room. Eventually he would threaten to leave her, and finally he would.

The theater remained the only way she really knew of making money. She had to fall back on it. Having announced to her French audience that she was leaving the stage in 1950, a departure marked by a farewell performance, she returned triumphantly in 1956. She would "leave" again in 1959, then "return" again in 1964. In fact, there would be twenty-five years between her first farewell performance and her last and so many farewells that one wit said a goodbye performance by Josephine was just an elegant way of announcing she was back again. When she said goodbye, it was to devote herself to her children. When she returned, it was to make money for her children. Cynics said she used the children as a show business ploy, but on the whole the French press accepted her chameleon explanations as offered in good faith, as did her closest friends, who believed her incapable of insincerity.

In the early fifties, Josephine had brought her mother and her surviving brother and sister, Richard Martin and Margaret, with her husband, Elmo Wallace, to live at Les Milandes, creating an even more extended family. She put her family members to work, tolerating very little individual initiative on their parts. Richard started as her chauffeur, later was promoted to running the filling station. Margaret helped run the house, eventually opening a patisserie. Josephine gave her money for the patisserie, but resentfully: she was sure that Margaret would not be able to make a go of it. Her brother, who fought with her over how to run the gas station and finally left Les Milandes, said that Josephine used to talk a lot about liberty, equality, and fraternity, but always told everyone else what to do. In the fairy tale, Cinderella marries the prince and forgives her stepsisters, marrying them off to gentlemen. What if instead she installed them in a château in France, buried them in magic pumpkins and pastry, and showed them how it should have been done?

Some people react to aging and the threat of death, over which no one has control, by exaggerating just how much control they have in other areas of life. They pride themselves on their competence and are the only people they know who get things right. With the world resting on their shoulders, they are simultaneously proud of their burden and tired of it. If they lose control, if circumstances stymie them, they often fall to pieces with surprising speed. If they cannot be the center of the world in triumph, they are the center in despair, martyred, everyone against them.

Fifty years old in 1956, Baker would continue to perform for close to twenty years. Onstage, where all the elements were under her control, she could maintain the illusion of defying time and never aging and maintain along with it her good nature and plucky spirit, but in her private life the effort to be in total control was increasingly draining—not just on her but on the people around her.

From a 1956 tour in North Africa, she returned with two children, a boy and a girl, although she and Bouillon had agreed they would have only boys. Marianne clearly had French blood and was to be raised Catholic. Brahim was Moslem. The two babies were found together, hidden under a bush, the sole survivors of a massacre during the Algerian war. Josephine, who had a hunger for symbolic meaning that made it impossible for her to resist two such children saved from a warring country for a common happy fate, brought them both home.

In 1957, from another tour in Africa, she brought back Koffi, an ebony-skinned child from the Ivory Coast whose mother had died in a hospital Josephine was visiting and whose father was unknown. She finally got her Indian child in Venezuela in 1959—a boy named Mara, who was undernourished and required some nursing back to health.

In the same year, just before Christmas in Paris, a ragpicker going through a bunch of trash slightly in advance of the garbage truck, discovered an infant boy. By this time, journalists knew whom to bring the news to, and her friends were just as anxious to keep it from her. But Josephine, performing the first of her comeback runs at the Olympia to support her children, heard about the child from a stranger at a party, dashed over to the hospital where he was being cared for, and took him home, changing André, the name the nurses had given him, to Noël to underline the symbolism of her Christmas act. Her twelfth and final child was another girl, born in France of a Moroccan mother, named Stellina after a child once seen in an Italian orphanage whose mother just managed to reclaim her before Josephine got her. But this final adoption did not take place until 1962, by which time Jo Bouillon and Josephine Baker had separated.

In addition to children for herself, Josephine had come home one day with a baby for her sister. Her name was Rama, a girl of Hindu background, found in a Belgian orphanage and carried home to Margaret with Josephine's characteristic generosity. And besides the children she formally adopted and raised from babies, who bore the name Bouillon, there was one she took on informally, Jean-Claude Rouzaud, who is now known as Jean-Claude Baker and runs a restaurant called Chez Josephine in New York. He was grown, a teen-aged bellboy at a Paris hotel when Josephine met him and volunteered to be his mother—somewhat superfluously, as he already had a mother—eventually paying for him to attend hotel school in England. He was quite a bit older than the Rainbow Tribe and sometimes helped Baker manage the kids, at least some of whom grew up to resent his irregular position in the family and his using the name of their mother, although it is also possible to feel that he had more than earned both.

Pavlova had adopted a whole village of orphans, and Isadora Duncan, who tragically lost her own children, ran a school for young Russian dancers whom she treated like her own. Seen in that tradition, Josephine Baker's twelve adoptions do not seem excessive. But the Bouillon children remembered no other family; Bouillon and Baker were literally their father and mother. Bouillon regarded them with equal literalness as his, and twelve was more than he could handle.

He accused his wife of loving their children in the same way she loved all other children—children she saw in the street and thought beautiful. While he understood the impulsive adoptions as signs of Josephine's good-heartedness, he also regarded them as signs of her shallowness. "I think I would have admired Josephine Baker even more if she had been content to adopt two, three, or four children. She would have been able to bring them up more easily, more discreetly, and even maybe have been able to love them better."

Margaret Wallace, who shared with Bouillon the burden of raising the children, also shared his disenchantment with Josephine as mother. She was delighted to be given a child of her own to raise, because she found her nieces and nephews unbearable. She thought—and her mother, Carrie Martin, agreed—that they were given too many presents, were taken to stay too often in luxury hotels, and in general were exposed to a life that was unsuitable for children. Moreover, there had been too many nurses to care for them and tutors to teach them their native languages and traditions. There was no central source of discipline.

Adopting children away from their ethnic and cultural backgrounds is not looked upon with favor these days, even when, as in Baker's case, the goal is to create an interracial family. The resistance the Israeli government put up to her adoption efforts prefigured that. There had been trouble, too, in Colombia, where she originally fastened upon a different child from the one she eventually adopted. The villagers seemed upset when she took the child from its mother, and later there were angry demonstrations. Her lawyer told her that according to local superstition, white people stole black babies to drink their blood. Baker replied in astonishment that she was black herself. But the lawyer explained that to the natives she was not. Her wealth made her white. They were slightly ahead of her in their understanding of the connection between race and colonial appropriation. She managed to bring Luis away in the end only because his mother herself had offered him and accepted in return a small house and garden.

Close to predatory in her search for children, vulnerable to the charge of buying them, imperialist in her efforts to bring into being her grand design, she had no idea that what she was doing was in any way morally ambiguous or ethnocentric. Ethnocentric, because her "point" seemed ultimately directed at whites. To take black children and raise them as white—or use them for white purposes—was not uncommon, as the Colombian villagers' fear revealed. To take a white child and give it a black mother was more provocative. Josephine got the kind of effect she wanted in Scandinavia, when an old man said that Jari would always be a Finn no matter what and Jari, left in the care of a roomful of Finnish relatives while Josephine went to perform, cried inconsolably until he was reunited with his black mother.

Still, it was not a bad life for the children. They had plenty of playmates. Their home was an amusement park. They had animals and space, a house that was perfect for hide-and-seek. They had a flamboyant mother who spread energy through the household, who always came home from trips with presents for everyone, who was forever organizing special events. They knew she was famous, and that reinforced their sense of her uniqueness: the world agreed their mother was special. Their father, who played what was usually the feminine role, stayed at home and was a source of some stability. In France, he was famous, too; he came from a well-established family of musicians.

If, from Jo Bouillon's anxious point of view, there was not enough money or even perhaps enough love to go around for so many children, for Josephine in her later years, the more she could gather around her—the more feathers and furs, the more bangles and beads, the more children—the happier she was. But whatever the differences in Bouillon's and Baker's styles of loving them, the children did not doubt that they were loved. Nor did they feel that their parents expected them to be especially grateful because they had been adopted. Whatever problems they had growing up were no different in kind from the problems of other people in families. In that sense Baker and Bouillon succeeded. They took a bunch of kids with nothing in common and turned them into a family.

CHAPTER 8
THE OVERDRESSED
YEARS

What she had taken to calling the capital of world brotherhood demanded more and more money. In the late fifties, in the heyday of the establishment, 300,000 visitors were making their way to Les Milandes a year. With such attendance, it might have been a financial success, but Josephine Baker had never been cost-effective. Her good heart was expensive. Although the operation at Les Milandes was strictly seasonal, she insisted on keeping the staff on throughout the winter. In general she ran the place on whim, instinct, and theatrical gesture. When the sow gave birth to a litter of piglets, she covered them with one of her fur coats. When

Michel Gyarmathy came to visit, she had him string up the name of each cow in lights and thought this made hers a model farm.

More disastrously, she and Jo Bouillon often canceled each other's direction: he hired one orchestra for the summer and she hired another; he hired one man to run the farm and she fired him. Their constant battles about the running of Les Milandes—he concerned about its financial viability, she wanting to put every idea into practice no matter the cost—was what finally led them to separate. He left in 1960, first moving to Paris and then to Buenos Aires, where he opened a French restaurant. Eventually some of the children joined him there, and four of them still live in Argentina.

After his departure, Les Milande's debts grew even more astronomical than they had been in the 1950s. The local people, sympathetic to the project at the start, grew distinctly hostile. Conservative country people, they did not take kindly to the Rainbow Tribe, and it was their hostility as much as Baker's love that welded the children together, forcing them to put up a solid front against their neighbors. The local people also did not like Baker's way of doing business, which largely consisted of asking for credit and postponing payment as long as she could. Perhaps as a result, and perhaps knowing that with such poor financial supervision there could be nothing to combat the practice, they raised their prices on anything they knew was going to Les Milandes. Eventually Baker shopped in Paris for food which was produced locally, because it cost her less in the city.

In 1962, even she began to get discouraged. "They steal from me. They ruin me. I've lost everything. Look at this farm. You remember how beautiful it was? It had the best equipment in the country. Ultramodern machinery. People have taken advantage of my good nature. I've been weak." When a local child took one of her cars and smashed it up, she forgave him. "I don't want people saying, 'Josephine threw an employee in the street. Josephine makes a human being suffer.'" Another young person came to work for her. She paid him; he ate with the staff; he had a room to himself. At the end of a month, she realized he was doing no work at all and spending all his time by the swimming pool. She was too worn out to deal with these problems. She felt she couldn't do it by herself anymore and needed a man to help her. "Sometimes I feel so abandoned, so misunderstood that I want to give up on Les Milandes. I imagine leaving for a more welcoming place. Toward Africa, where I came from."

She talked readily to the public about her private life. She had a whole other audience in France which followed her personal drama in the papers, fascinated by her roles of crusader and wholesale mother. Whenever possible, she liked to reinforce the real-life maternal role with stage roles. In 1962, she got the idea of staging Bizet's *L'Arlésienne* at Les Milandes, playing the title role of a mother who loves her child more than herself but cannot save him. Onstage, she bent over the body of her son and gave a cry which sent the fifteen hundred spectators into tears. She felt it was one of her greatest, most emotional performances as an actress, but just in case her acting could not carry the show, she saw that it was accompanied by an elaborate and expensive deployment of local color: a nineteenth-century Arlesian costume, an expensive lace dress, twelve tambourine players, and twenty-one farandole dancers all imported from Provence. As it turned out, the support was needed. When the production moved to Paris, without the torches and outdoor setting, it failed. This was her last attempt at a dramatic role.

In 1963 Jack Jordan, a black producer, got the idea of bringing Baker from France for the August 28 demonstration that became known as the March on Washington. It turned out to be a high point of her life. Its stated aim was to press for "jobs and freedom" for black Americans. Its underlying aim was to put pressure on Congress to pass the Civil Rights Bill by showing Washington lawmakers how much power the black civil rights groups—the NAACP, the Urban League, the Southern Christian Leadership Conference, SNCC, and CORE—could mobilize. Four hundred and fifty chartered buses left Harlem for Washington at four-thirty in the morning. From Penn Station between four and eight in the morning, fourteen special trains left. People came by plane from Los Angeles and Seattle, and one man roller-skated from Chicago. By eleven, there were 90,000 people in front of the Lincoln Memorial. By the early afternoon, over 200,000, from all over the country.

Baker wore her World War II uniform, the uniform of the Women's Auxiliary of the French Air Force. Early in the afternoon, before the main speeches, there was entertainment to warm up the crowd. Odetta, Josh White, Bobby Darin, Bob Dylan, Joan Baez, and Peter, Paul and Mary sang. Baker was asked to say a few words. She was deeply moved by the sight of all those thousands of people, black and white, "united in a common dream." She was moved to be standing in front of the memorial to Lincoln. What she saw before her did not seem a demonstration of power in an ongoing effort, but the culmination of thirty years of struggle, a celebration of brotherhood achieved, ripe fruit. To the crowd she said, "You are on the eve of a complete victory. You can't go wrong. The world is behind you." She looked at them contentedly. "Salt and pepper. Just what it should be."

Commentators noted that of all the speakers that day, Baker and Martin Luther King were the most hopeful. When he spoke, she was on the platform, along with the officials, the politicians, the heads of the organizations, and a few figures from the arts. She heard him say, "I have a dream that one day on the red hills of Georgia the sons of former slaves and the sons of former slave owners will be able to sit down together at the table of brotherhood." Her point exactly.

"Until the March on Washington," she said, "I always had this little feeling in my stomach. I was always afraid. I couldn't meet white American people. I didn't want to be around them. But now that little gnawing feeling is gone. For the first time in my life I feel free. I know that everything is right now."

For Baker, the civil rights struggle in America virtually ended with the March on Washington. In the years that followed, living in France and out of touch with America, she never really understood the way the civil rights movement developed. She never got used to the term "black power." She was of the generation that preferred the word "colored" to "black," and "power" seemed a dirty word to her no matter what came before it. "Black power" seemed to suggest mistreatment of whites by blacks, for which she had no more sympathy than mistreatment of blacks by whites. She told a reporter who came to quiz her on black power that sometimes violence was "the only way of saving your dignity," but she did not have a militant temperament, preferring intermarriage as the solution to racial problems. "I think

In rehearsal for the 1949 Folies-
Bergère show, with dancers dressed as
stained-glass figures and a cathedral
backdrop.
Keystone, Paris.

Baker at the end of World War II in
the uniform of the Women's Auxiliary
of the Free French Air Force. She won
her lieutenancy by secret intelligence
work and later propaganda efforts for
de Gaulle and the resistance.
Courtesy of Mme. Maryse Bouillon.

With Jo Bouillon, the French orchestra leader,
her fourth husband.
Courtesy of Mme. Maryse Bouillon.

With her mother, Carrie McDonald, who came
to live in France in 1948.
Keystone, Paris; courtesy of Mme. Maryse Bouillon.

At Les Milandes, Josephine Baker's home
in the Dordogne, her sister Margaret
Wallace and mother listen to the radio.
Courtesy of Mme. Maryse Bouillon.

In rehearsal for *Paris Mes Amours*
at the Olympia in Paris. She is
fifty-three years old.
Keystone, Paris.

In 1961, Baker received the Légion
d'Honneur wearing her World War II
uniform and medals.
Keysone, Paris.

The exotic-cosmopolitan look for her
American tour, 1951.
*Billy Rose Theater Collection, Performing Arts
Research Center, New York Public Library at
Lincoln Center; Astor, Lenox, and Tilden
Foundations.*

INSET: Les Milandes, Baker's château in the Dordogne, which she opened as a tourist attraction and model community after the war.
Courtesy of Mme. Maryse Bouillon.

RIGHT: A birthday party for one of Baker's twelve adopted children.
Courtesy of Mme. Maryse Bouillon.

On stage at the Olympia, 1968.
Keystone, Paris.

Evicted.
Robert Cohen/ AGIP.

With Robert Brady at his home in Cuernavaca, 1973. The painting of a woman above them is a self-portrait by Frida Kahlo.
Courtesy of Mr. John Brady, Jr.

With all her children, 1969.
Keystone, Paris.

Baker with her children, Koffi, Noël, and Stellina Bouillon.
Keystone, Paris.

Baker's funeral at the church of the Madeleine in Paris,
April 15, 1975.
Ginies/ SIPA.

Party at the Bristol in Paris on April 8, 1975, opening night of what
would be her final run. Jean-Claude Brialy is behind Baker, Alain
Delon offering congratulations, Mireille Darc behind him, and Princess
Grace, seated, looking on.
Keystone, Paris.

they must mix blood, otherwise the human race is bound to degenerate. Mixing blood is marvelous. It makes strong and intelligent men. It takes away tired spirits."

Jack Jordan and his partner, Howard Saunders, a publicist and advertising man, were responsible for Baker's playing New York's Carnegie Hall in 1963. A benefit for civil rights groups, it was also a way of reintroducing her to American audiences, and it succeeded in getting her bookings that season in New York at the Strand and at the Brooks Atkinson Theater.

Baker was fifty-seven when she appeared in America in 1963. She made no attempt to hide her age; in fact, she exaggerated it. "Not bad for sixty, huh?" she said to open her show. In the early 1960s fashion was hard-edged: Jacqueline Kennedy was wearing her rectangular suits and pillbox hats. But Josephine Baker wore exaggeratedly feminine dresses with big hips and bust and narrow waists, strapless dresses with wired curves and feathers. Her glamour was a holdover from another age, courting in every way possible a softening of vision, a flattering illusion. She wore light-reflecting spangles not only under her eyes, to hide the bags she had had even when young and which grew worse with age, but also on her lips.

Usually, her own past was her theme—her revues were often tableaux of scenes from her own life—and that theme shaded into the larger one of the passage of time. In between her dances and songs, she monologued about her projects, her children, her charities, her outrage at racial injustice, and her bittersweet feelings about the brevity of existence. In fact, some things got better for her as she aged: her voice was lower, richer, more mellow, more sure, more interesting. But the humanity she projected—her genuine love of her audience— never changed. Time passes, she said to her audience in various ways, and we are getting older every day, but I still love you, love is still the most beautiful thing in life. On recordings of these performances, you can hear the audience roar back its affection.

Her sentimentality was trendy, echoing the refrain of the Beatles and other Aquarians which told us that all we needed was love. The message was more usually purveyed in a setting of tie-dyed T-shirts and thrift-shop regalia than of feathers and fur, but Baker had a way of wearing her preposterous headdresses and finery so as to mock them. One of her routines was to come onstage in a white fur cape, drop it onto the floor, and walk on it as though it didn't exist. An audience that took material goods more seriously might find the gesture offensive. But the woman who had once left Paul Poiret dresses in heaps on her floor shared the hippie love of finery and disrespect for possession and somehow communicated this. It was part of the historical accident that continued to give Baker some viability when other nightclub performers were seeing their audiences disappear.

By her later years, she had become a legend, especially meaningful to blacks. One man who followed her triumphs from a distance was the dancer Geoffrey Holder, who had grown up in Trinidad, "behind God's back," as he says. There were people of color all over the world like Geoffrey Holder and his brother Boscoe taking a special interest and a special pleasure in Josephine Baker's career. Langston Hughes, like Boscoe Holder, collected every scrap of information he could find about her. So did many less famous men and women whose clipping collections have ended up in research archives. When she made her rare appearances in the States in the 1950s, 1960s, and 1970s, there were some members of her audience who came to honor her as much as to enjoy her performance.

So when Geoffrey Holder worked with Baker on her 1963 American tour, he was getting to know an idol, someone he thought existed in another sphere. He was surprised to find her easy to work with, remarkably lacking in the airs and vanities of most American stars, a performer of enormous discipline. At the finale, she would not move from her position onstage until the orchestra had finished playing her theme song, even after the curtain came down. If she went off key, she apologized to the conductor. All this Holder found extraordinary.

He was keenly aware of the deference due her as a great star, but she seemed never to want to claim it. When she asked him and his wife, Carmen de Lavallade, to go back to Paris with her and perform at the Olympia, Holder said he would not come unless he was presented as her discovery. "You discovered us," he said. But she replied, with equal courtesy, "No, Holder, you have discovered yourself."

During the show, they took turns dancing. Holder and Carmen

de Lavallade danced as Josephine changed her costumes. Carmen would dance and top Josephine. Josephine would come on and top Carmen. It wasn't competition, says Holder. Neither of them was competitive. They were spurring each other on, like soloists in a jazz band. On opening night in Paris, Josephine said to Carmen, "Paris is going to love you tonight, like they loved me forty years ago. I can't go on like this. I need someone to take my place."

The French press called the Holders "a royal gift" that Baker had given the French public. They appreciated the gift while finding it astonishing that a woman her age would willingly bring onstage with herself someone as young and lovely as Carmen de Lavallade. A lesser person than Baker would certainly have seen as a rival the woman she chose to see as her successor.

In France, it was harder to get bookings as she aged. The years between her Paris appearances became longer: 1956, 1959, 1964, 1968. She played the more provincial cities of Europe: in Scandinavia, for example, which goes on welcoming stars long after the rest of Europe is through with them. And she could always find an audience in Latin America. She was as popular in Cuba under Castro as she had been in Cuba under Batista. But locating her audience meant constant travel, more money for more elaborate costumes, and she never made enough to bail out Les Milandes.

By February of 1964, Les Milandes was about to be seized to pay debts amounting to two million old francs. At the request of Josephine and some of her friends, Brigitte Bardot, then at the height of her fame, appeared on French television to appeal for funds to save Les Milandes. She spoke for two and a half minutes. Her plea brought in 1.2 million francs, and the sale of Les Milandes was temporarily postponed, but Baker said, "I would need twenty times more to save my *domaine* and my children."

She had no difficulty seeing Les Milandes as worthy of the nation's support. It embodied the principle of interracial harmony, and money given to her was given to that good cause. Others did not see it that way and resented Brigitte Bardot's appeal to the nation in the name of *devoir* to support Josephine Baker and her children. Some wrote angry letters to newspapers saying that they had children, too, but didn't think it was the nation's duty to help support them—especially not to live in a château. "If everyone who adopted children held out his hand for help to raise them (in luxury) what merit would it have? The hand Josephine holds out lacks neither rings nor bracelets." At moments, Baker herself came to question her style, if not her ideal. "Even generosity can be a form of egotism," she said.

In July 1964, during the fight to save Les Milandes, she had her first heart attack. She was hospitalized in Paris and returned very weak to Les Milandes in August. That fall, according to her sister Margaret, she was still wrought up, not only about Les Milandes but also about the racial situation in America and the upcoming election. In October, she suffered another minor attack.

The children, too, created difficulties for her as they aged. It is one sort of problem to have six babies, all more or less the same age. It is quite another problem to have adolescence doubled and redoubled and redoubled again in the same household. With her kids in their teenage years and herself approaching sixty, Josephine found herself in the position of trying to contain an unruly force of nature. As they got older, their amity was increasingly paraded and photographed and held up to strangers as an example. Under these circumstances, it would have been hard for many people to refrain from fighting. But the Bouillon children were intensely loyal to each other. As they moved into adolescence, some of them took out their irritation on Josephine, with her eccentricity and her self-importance—obnoxious traits to adolescents who want to be normal and their own masters.

According to Margaret Wallace, their harshest critic, the children were liars, thieves, and spongers, one of whom had stolen the money she had saved for medical treatment for her own daughter. They certainly were wild—what group of twelve kids close in age who had never been disciplined would not be?—and Josephine in the late 1960s was perpetually worried about them. Was one of the girls sleeping with someone? Had one of the boys been stealing? Would they ever grow up to earn their own livings? She took to sending some of them to England for the summer, to the care of Harry Hurford Janes and his wife. He was an Englishman she had met in North Africa during the war, when he was working for ENSA. He wanted to be her professional representative in England, but about all Baker ever let him do was take care of her children. Childless themselves and no longer young, the Janeses were hardly the ideal caretakers for teenagers, and they were shocked by the irreverence and bad manners of their summer charges. Still, a few of the children were sent back there summer after summer.

Sometimes Baker thought her experiment had failed. In a conversation she reported to Harry Janes, she, Jean-Claude Bouillon, and Moïse were discussing "complexes," the catchword of the moment for neurotic problems. Moïse said Jean-Claude, a Catholic in France, could not have complexes, whereas he and Josephine, in some sense outsiders in France, had them. Jean-Claude boasted in reply that even were he to go to live in Africa, he would have no complexes, knowing full well that as a white he was superior to all the blacks, who were lazy, dirty, and stupid. Josephine was horrified. Was Jean-Claude any better than Hitler? A racist among her children? What had gone wrong? After some thought she decided it had to be "outside influences" rather than her "educational system" that was at fault. Still, she asked herself if it had been right to bring these children together as a symbol of universal brotherhood.

Throughout the latter part of the 1960s, Les Milandes hovered on the verge of confiscation by creditors and was rescued at the last minute by Josephine's exertions or those of friends. People close to the situation claimed that she could have saved Les Milandes by selling off some of the land, but she refused to let any of it go. In 1968, by now over sixty, she was again performing at the Olympia to save Les Milandes, with the active help of the Olympia's director, Bruno Coquatrix, but without his enthusiasm. Personally, he thought she should give up Les Milandes: it was a bottomless pit.

Although Coquatrix applied himself to Baker's affairs, he was no more successful than Jo Bouillon had been at getting her to act prudently. In that year of political turmoil, when her run at the Olympia was suspended because of the student strikes in May, she risked alienating some of her audience by participating in a march down the Champs-Élysées in support of de Gaulle. A few days after that, Robert Kennedy was assassinated, and Josephine, who revered him, felt it behooved her to fly to America for his funeral, along with five of her sons. Coquatrix was in despair, watching her squander whatever profit she would make from the show at the Olympia, to say nothing of her energy. In July after that turbulent spring, she suffered a mild stroke, just managing to get through the end of her run before she collapsed.

Les Milandes was actually sold in early 1968, but Coquatrix arranged to have the sale annulled and Baker was given until May to clear a debt of close to half a million dollars. A second sale took place in May, bringing in much less than the property was worth, and Coquatrix tried to get that sale annulled, too, but unsuccessfully. The local people were fed up with Baker, and the sale was conducted in an atmosphere of hatred which appalled Coquatrix and Baker's eldest son, sixteen-year-old Akio Bouillon, who witnessed the sale and saw the creditors go after his mother's property like "ferocious animals."

By the end of September, she was due to be evicted. She still had all twelve children with her. She managed to get a local court to postpone the eviction until December 1, which meant she didn't really have to move until the spring, French law forbidding evictions between October 15 and March 15. But she had irrevocably lost Les Milandes. It only remained to play the finale. Some people might have left gracefully, but that would have been to pass up a chance to enact a role that had until now eluded her—the role of welfare mother. As she had done all her life, she acted out her fantasies and left others to write them down.

At Christmas, *Figaro* announced: Josephine still barricaded at Les Milandes. The heat and water had been turned off by the new owners. Josephine, her sister, and the twelve kids were living in one room huddled around a fireplace for warmth. The children had to go out to gather fallen branches to make a fire. They all washed their face and hands in the same small pail of water. The new owner pointed out indignantly that he had not taken possession and had no way of turning off the heat and water. If they were lacking, it was because Josephine had removed and sold all the fixtures—sinks, faucets, radiators—making the place unlivable entirely on her own. He accused her of keeping her children there for show, when they could very well have gone to live in their aunt Margaret's house in the village.

At last, quietly, she moved the children to a two-bedroom apartment in Paris, leaving Les Milandes empty, and began preparing for an appearance at a nightclub owned by Jean-Claude Brialy. But when word reached her that the new owner of Les Milandes intended to take possession, she returned alone to play her final scene. She camped out in the kitchen and was seized when she opened the door to go out to get some water. Burly men hired by the new owner pushed their way in and carried her bodily out of the house. She was in her nightdress without the wig she always wore now to cover her hair, damaged by years of straightening. They picked her up by her arms, legs, and head and carried her out into the rain, hurting her shoulder and banging her head against the stove in the process.

On the back steps, she put on a shawl and something resembling a shower cap and sat herself down near a pile of garbage. This was the end of the story of Les Milandes, and Baker had had the foresight to arrange for reporters and photographers to be there to record it. She had been turned inside out by her own idealism and reduced to the poverty from which she began: the Folies star as bag lady, Josephine Baker as her own mother. When her sit-in ended, she was devastated physically as well as emotionally. An ambulance was called to take her away and she was hospitalized again.

The hospital stay was brief: her powers of resilience were remarkable. She soon resumed her run at Brialy's nightclub in Paris and from there went to Monte Carlo to do the prestigious annual fund-raiser for the Monacan Red Cross. At this point her plight—she was virtually homeless, with twelve children—attracted the attention of Princess Grace of Monaco. An admirer of Baker's crusade for civil rights and interracial brotherhood, the former American movie star got the Monacan Red Cross to subsidize a villa in Roquebrune, near Monte Carlo, for Baker and her children. Arys Nissotti, the producer of Baker's early films, then living in Monte Carlo, guaranteed the mortgage. At four bedrooms, it was hardly palatial, but it was virtually free, it had a good view of the bay, and it became Baker's permanent home. She was endlessly grateful to Princess Grace and her husband, Prince Rainier, whom she considered to have rescued her Rainbow Tribe. "If he asked me to go jump in the water, I'd do it in a second," she said.

For the rest of her life, Baker continued to try to interest people in a "college of universal brotherhood." She had lawyers draw up papers for a Geneva-based "Josephine Baker Foundation" to support such an enterprise. She asked anyone she thought had money for donations. She got Marshal Tito and his wife to offer an island off the coast of Yugoslavia as the headquarters for such a center. She thought, too, about locating it on another island, one near Ischia. She conned architects into drawing up plans for the college without fee. But she never came as close again to bringing her vision into existence as she had at Les Milandes.

It is hard to see Les Milandes, even now—its facilities run-down, the playground deserted, grass growing through the cement floor of the outdoor nightclub—and not be impressed by the scope of Baker's ambition, the insistence on an idea which she might have put into operation if she had not kept expanding it beyond any possibility of realization. This Renaissance château with its black-tiled Art Deco bathroom, its terraced grounds and outlying tourist facilities, the whole enclosed by a wrought-iron fence with the initials JB at regular intervals, is evidence—as the Pyramids seemed to Dr. Johnson—of the hunger of the imagination, people's need to create monuments to their aspirations or beliefs.

There are many Josephine Baker fans for whom the *real* Josephine Baker began to exist only after 1950. The stage persona they like is the one she began to project as she settled into middle age: the totally fabricated woman, singing into a rhinestone-studded microphone, wearing knock-'em-dead designer dresses, feather headdresses, and sequins all over her face.

Jack Jordan, though wary of Baker as a client, took her on again in 1973 and booked her for a four-day run at Carnegie Hall in New York. He and his partner, Howard Saunders, cleverly realized that although from one point of view Baker was an overaged has-been, from another she was just what the increasingly politicized zeitgeist ordered—someone who would appeal both to black audiences and to the camp sensibility which seemed to be a growing power in the theater world. Susan Sontag defined that sensibility in her "Notes on Camp" as the playful, ironic, subversive spirit of the "theatricalization of experience," out to dethrone pomposity and elevate style, and Josephine Baker in her later years was the theatricalization of experience incarnate, her lush, preposterous artificiality an important part of her appeal to her new and, in America at least, significantly homosexual audience. Jordan and Saunders, in their promotional efforts for the 1973 Carnegie Hall performances, targeted the gay community and produced a highly enthusiastic audience.

In her interaction with the audience, she had come to resemble somewhat the black preachers of her youth, asking to be confirmed in her beliefs, giving the audience the chance to participate, to endorse, to bear her up. But sometimes in these late performances she talked about love and how it filled the theater and "really, you know," said a man who saw her, "it wasn't there." Age was getting to her, and her memory slipped. She compensated as best she could. "Now Mummy's getting older," her daughter Stellina explained to Harry Janes, "she la-la's when she can't remember the words."

Dotson Rader followed her through a rehearsal in New York in 1973 when she forgot lyrics, forgot patter, and forgot the names of people from her past. Was it Billie Brice? The stagehands, musicians, and theater personnel treated her coolly. "She is an old woman now," Rader thought, "and worn through by the years, and she is among people who pay her no regard, do not understand what she remembers of life, who think she is over the hill. Time for your travelin' shoes, sweet Josephine." Nonetheless, she pulled herself together for the performance, sang some dozen songs, did the costume changes, the monologues, the Charleston, and received a standing ovation. Afterward, she was so exhausted, she couldn't speak to Rader again. "Child, leave me be. Josephine has talked and talked. She has given you a . . . book. Enough, child."

When she went onstage, a transformation took place in which she lost twenty years. The bags under her eyes and the jowls of age disappeared thanks to the makeup and lights, but equally important was some magic of inner alignment by which her posture grew erect and buoyant. People who sat with her in her dressing room before she performed were stunned to see her metamorphose in front of their eyes from a bent and frumpy old lady into a glamorous star.

Barbara Chase Riboud, the American writer and sculptor, then living in Paris, described it vividly. "I thought, 'Anybody's aunt from St. Louis. What is all the fuss about?' The bright but melancholy eyes, the extravagant eyelashes behind bifocals, the aging jowls, the slight dowager's hump, the small, rather dumpy figure looked ridiculous in the chorus-girl costume cut high into the hip. Yet in the midst of a rather grandmotherly conversation La Josephine, then 64, received her cue to go onstage. And before my unbelieving eyes, the superstar emerged from the frump and folds of age.

"She appeared to shed pounds. The line of her back straightened, her upper thighs tensed and lengthened, her stomach flattened, her jowls disappeared. Her eyeglasses were hurriedly exchanged for a rhinestone microphone, her chin lifted, her head went back, and the Josephine of Parisian dreams suddenly appeared as if by magic onstage. A huge and collective sexual sigh seemed to rise from the audience upon her entrance, the smooth siren voice slid out over the audience. I turned to Geoffrey [Holder] in amazement. He just shrugged his shoulders and said, 'I told you she was something else.' "

Defying nature, relying on art, she poured herself, at the age of sixty-two, sixty-four, sixty-eight into flesh-colored body stockings with spangles and looked good in them. On the eve of her final comeback, when someone asked if she wasn't scared to show herself onstage at the age of sixty-nine, she replied, "With makeup, lights, and a little intelligence, I'll be okay."

A female impersonator named Lynne Carter had received from Baker in about 1970 the gift of three taxicabfuls of her 1950s Paris gowns—her famous Diors and Balenciagas. Carter, who had served in the Navy, wore two pairs of stockings onstage because he refused to shave his legs and took an hour and a quarter to put on makeup; he was thoughtful about the gender differences that allowed him to make his living. "I have found that women always wear a mask. It's made of cosmetics and fashion. Women consider it a masculine trait simply to be yourself. But they end up being caricatures of themselves, which makes them easy to mimic."

In the overdressed years which succeeded her underdressed years, Baker was a sister of Lynne Carter, speaking to fantasies of the defeat by artfulness of biological imperatives like age and gender, finding a new audience among men who made similar icons of the artifice of femininity out of Marlene Dietrich and Mae West. She was a female impersonator who happened to be a woman.

Like many women who have lived hard sexually, she had reached the end of her interest in sex. Sometimes she said it did not befit a woman who symbolized maternity as she did. Sometimes she said she was too busy working for world brotherhood and bringing up her kids to give it much time. When sex arrived, as it were, on her doorstep, she had nothing against it—it was nature, after all—and she enjoyed a week-end reunion with Simenon, a good forty years after their original affair, both of them as passionate as they had been before. But she was not in good health and not very eager to display a body that had been operated on so many times. On the whole, she had given up on the active search for sexual excitement which can take up so much energy earlier in life.

Even for someone with a strong heart, the strains of performance plus the strains of mothering twelve children would have taken a toll. In June 1973, she was so worried about her daughter Marianne, who had run away, that her heartbeat became radically irregular. At the American Hospital in Paris, her heart was stopped and started up again. But she insisted on meeting an obligation to perform in Denmark, where, later that month, she had a massive heart attack. Her face was partially paralyzed, and when three of her sons came to see her, she did not recognize them. Her doctors recommended at least four months' rest, but she was up and working again within a week. Two months later she would go to Israel to participate in the nation's twenty-fifth anniversary celebration.

She did not want anyone to realize she was sick. If word got

around that she had a bad heart, it would be even harder for her to
find work; no producer wants to book a performer who is going to
be stricken in the middle of a run. She, especially, depended on continuing to stun her audiences with her vitality and health. But in fact,
from a medical point of view, she was a mess: not only did she have
a bad heart, not only had she had a stroke, but there was also her
stomach, a problem since the war. She was devoted to spaghetti, the
one food that never upset it.

While she was still in the Copenhagen hospital in June 1973 re-
cuperating from her heart attack, she got a call from a friend, Robert
Brady, who wanted to cheer her up. She had met Brady, a wealthy
American artist based in Cuernavaca, in 1967, when she was performing in Mexico City. The friendship between them developed at a
distance over the years. Charming and good-looking—dark, lean,
mustached—he moved in an international jet set and was a close friend
of several extraordinary women: Peggy Guggenheim, the heiress and
art collector; Eugenie Prendergast, the widow of the painter's brother;
Dolores del Rio, the beautiful Mexican actress; and Helen Hayes.
Known for the tapestries he designed and had executed in wool by
local Mexican craftsmen, he had good business sense and an impeccable
eye. He was used to escorting women to social functions and helping
them with their business affairs.

Baker was sixty-seven, working desperately to support her family,
and the sudden illness had been devastating. She had no one to lean
on. Although she and Jo Bouillon were not officially divorced, they
had been separated for over a decade and he was in Argentina. Out
of nowhere, help came in the appealing form of a well-off and attractive
man in his forties offering devotion. On the telephone, Brady suddenly
told Baker that he loved her, and he followed the call with a gallant
letter proposing that—in spirit—they be married to each other.

She was wild with delight and only worried that she had not
understood correctly what he suggested. "Did I rightly understand . . .
that you do want us to be married? If so I am so happy, because you
are the only man I can trust with my ideas and life etc. but we will
do it with the understanding that nothing changes your life, that it
will be a pure marriage without sex etc. etc. because sex spoils

everything—that we stay free—that we be married by God and not by man."

She was in love in the way a lonely person can be in love when someone abruptly turns up offering devotion: suddenly, totally, and gratefully. Perhaps she was all the more in love because there was no question of sexual involvement. "It makes me so happy, Bob, and stupidly young like a girl in love for the first time. I can't stop thinking about you and see you in my dreams continuously."

It did not matter that he was not physically with her. It did not matter how little they would be able to see each other. As they worked out the details of their platonic marriage in letters, the fact that they would *not* see each other often was all to the good. They were both nomads, free desert spirits who needed to be loose to wander. If they did not impinge on each other, the marriage would last. She made a point of saying that she did not want him to stop seeing Eugenie Prendergast. "You see I am so natural and africain inside that I think it is natural that a man has several wives—and he can love all of them in different ways."

In September 1973, when she was feeling better, she went to Mexico to stay with him. One Sunday, in a church in Acapulco, they made their marriage vows without benefit of clergy. Brady was Catholic; Baker, since her marriage to Jo Bouillon, considered herself Catholic, too. Each in his or her eccentric way was devout. They took their private oath seriously. They were both too nervous to take communion and would both regret it afterward. She was scared about what they were doing but certain they were doing the right thing. They planned to tell no one about it because publicity would debase it. *Pour vivre heureux*, she quoted to him, *vivre caché*. But they were married nonetheless. "You are my husband, Bob dear. I am your wife before God."

There is a lot to be said for an imaginary marriage. It has the same stabilizing effect as a real marriage, the comfort of thinking oneself part of a pair rather than alone, and none of the friction of actual contact. It is particularly appropriate for people who travel a lot and like to have someone they can write to. It helps establish the fixed point from which they are wandering. Josephine was on the move incessantly: Jerusalem one week, California the next, Barcelona, Hamburg, Copenhagen, Paris, New York. Relationships in those circumstances tend to *be* imaginary or symbolic, and it is easy enough to imagine why Josephine Baker would have welcomed this tie to Robert Brady.

As for Brady, on one level the alliance between the rich and the famous is so natural as to require little comment. A man who was known to some extent for the people he knew, Brady became much more noticeable with Josephine Baker on his arm. There were other advantages for him in this alliance, particularly in conservative Cuernavaca, where even in 1973 an unmarried man was a "bachelor" who did well to maintain his heterosexual credentials. And the somewhat repetitive nature of society in Cuernavaca—the same foreigners saw each other at one house or another all winter long—may have stirred the imaginative Robert Brady to some "enfant-terriblism." What better way to shock his neighbors than by bringing his black guest to swim in their pools?

He was not a man who loved easily; his disdain for most people was ill concealed. Once, he said to the woman seated next to him at dinner, "Nothing you could possibly say would have the slightest interest to me." But he seems to have genuinely loved Josephine—in a circumscribed way, but genuinely. Her triumphant sweetness must have soothed his waspishness, and the distance between them—geographical and otherwise—perhaps allowed him to feel more warmly than usual. However, as they both had feared, being together did not prove to be good for their relationship.

The Casa del Torre, Brady's Cuernavaca residence, housed a museum-quality collection of African and Pacific sculpture, Spanish colonial sculpture, furniture, textiles, and paintings. In the cool, thick-walled rooms whose walls and shelves were filled with beautiful objects, Baker could live for her brief stays a life of easeful luxury, with plenty of servants to care for her. At a time when poverty was making her life so little gracious, the Casa del Torre was a fairy-tale castle, and she had no desire to leave it, wanting only to stay home with Brady. But for him to shock the local gentry, Baker had to be willing to be seen. She had to swim in other people's pools, not theirs. She had to participate in the nightly gathering at someone else's house. On a visit she made to Cuernavaca in January 1974, they disagreed violently about whether to stay home or go out.

He put it that her demands for love weighed too heavily, and she, deciding to leave the next day, stayed up all night to write a letter explaining how she felt in distracted Franglais. *"Je suis un pure sang. Pour moi*, to be or not to be. I who love freedom it is torture to me to be here where all eyes are on me judging my every moment or move. Why why can't I have a moment of freedom with you. I don't want anything else." She had always said she would not impinge on him, and now that he had accused her of impinging, she must leave. She returned his ring and chain. She left him with advice: "Don't drink too much. Sleep a lot. Work even over time. As I said, dear, work is our best friend." Later, when she was less upset, she would write a fairy tale about their romance. She already had the idea. "Now I have the title—*the straw prince*—remember I told you that I was clinging to you—you are my straw prince."

Despite this rupture, the two kept in touch for the rest of Baker's life—which would only be two more years. She continued to ask Robert Brady and his savvy brother John for advice. She continued, in four-and five-page single-spaced letters, to keep him apprised of her thoughts on world brotherhood or the racial situation in America. Shortly before Robert Brady died of cancer in 1986, he told his brother that he still considered himself to have been married to Josephine Baker.

In 1974, the Société des Bains de Mer of Monte Carlo asked her to star in their annual gala to benefit the Monacan Red Cross. She had done this in 1969—it was how she attracted the attention of Princess Grace and came to live on the Riviera—and again in 1970. But four years had gone by since her last appearance in Monaco, and at her age, as someone did not hesitate to tell her, every year counts double. Moreover, Monte Carlo audiences were difficult, filled with celebrities, sophisticates, and connoisseurs of the good life. The appeal to them could not be camp. She really had to be youthful, dynamic, beautiful, and sensational onstage.

The designer, André Levasseur, imagined an extravagant show

which would once more—definitively—tell the story of Baker's life in a series of scenes: childhood in Louisiana (sic), opening in the Revue Nègre, service in the war, and so on. Josephine was enthusiastic. Everyone hoped that if the show was successful, it might go to Paris. She had not been asked to play Paris since 1968, at least in part (she thought) because of her conspicuous support of de Gaulle in that year. America's left-wing threat was in France a right-wing dinosaur whose Gaullist allegiance made her seem even older, more "retro" than she was.

Joséphine was a success in Monte Carlo and did move on to Paris. However, the Casino de Paris, which would have seemed the most appropriate place, did not want the show, and it was booked into the small Bobino Theater on the rue de la Gaieté in Montparnasse. Baker, whose tastes were Right Bank, told Jean-Claude Brialy, who was acting as her master of ceremonies, that she felt she was returning to Paris through the back door. Still, she was returning to Paris.

Her opening on April 8, 1975, was yet another celebration of her career. She had been in show business for fifty years. Brialy read a congratulatory letter from the President of the Republic, Giscard d'Estaing. In the audience were de Gaulle's son-in-law General de Boissieu, along with Sophia Loren, Mick Jagger, Mireille Darc, Alain Delon, Jeanne Moreau, Tino Rossi, Madame Sukarno, and Pierre Balmain. At nine, Princess Grace, the guest of honor, came in and was given an orchid bouquet by the management and a warm greeting by the audience. After the show two hundred and fifty people were invited to dinner at the Bristol.

The show was completely sold out for weeks in advance, and the reviews were almost all ecstatic. Naturally, the one that was not is the most amusing. In the eyes of the reviewer for *Libération*, the lively, widely read left-wing daily, the most reactionary characters in Paris had gathered to pay tribute to Josephine Baker, "vestige of the past and notorious Gaullist." When she walks onto the stage, there is delirium in the audience. "The fossils congratulate each other. 'She' is still there, as in 1925 at the Casino de Paris." She herself never has enough of getting worked up, tears in her eyes, about her own past, a past of no interest to anyone but "privileged nostalgics for whom between the wars was that charming period when such a good time was to be had in Monte Carlo."

The next night, Wednesday, she gave her performance with her usual energy and humor—twelve changes of costume and all. "I'm carrying thirty-four years on one shoulder and thirty-five on the other. You add them up!" That was her parting shot to the audience. Afterward she went to eat spaghetti at La Barate, across the street from the theater, with the show's director, Jean-Claude Dauzonne, and her three co-stars, Jean-Marie Proslier, Laurence Badie, and Annie Siraglia. She wanted to go somewhere afterward to dance, but her tired co-stars wanted to go home to sleep. Baker, two months short of her sixty-ninth birthday, said, "I'm the youngest of all of you."

On Thursday she got up, made phone calls, had a light lunch, lay down for her afternoon nap. She was scheduled to meet a journalist at five o'clock, but she appeared to be sleeping so soundly at five that Pepito Abatino's niece Lélia, who was staying with her, was reluctant to wake her up. Finally Lélia decided it would be rude to make the journalist wait any longer. But when she tried to wake Baker up, she couldn't. She was in a coma. She had had a stroke an hour before, about the time she wanted to get up for her interview and evening performance. Dauzonne came with a doctor, but there was nothing to do except transport her to the hospital—it was La Salpêtrière—where she died.

As deaths go, this was a good one—quick, clean, at a moment of triumph. She had done it again, bowled Paris over against all the odds. They found her in bed surrounded by newspapers. No doubt before she fell asleep she had been looking for some more ecstatic tributes to the sixty-nine-year-old woman who never seemed to relinquish the beauty and vitality of youth. Officially, she died of cerebral hemorrhage, but some thought she died of joy.

Her nationally televised state funeral was almost unprecedented for an entertainer. The coffin was carried slowly through the city in a hearse, past the Bobino Theater, whose marquee was turned on in the dreary day to blaze her name, across the Seine to the church of the Madeleine, where Napoleon had been crowned emperor. Twenty thousand people crowded the streets outside the church, spilling back almost to the Place de la Concorde. Many of the celebrities and dignitaries who had been present on her opening night three days before were there again for the funeral—including Princess Grace and Sophia Loren. In addition, on the steps of the majestic church, paying tribute to Baker, stood the mayor of Paris, the Minister of Culture, the chancellor of the Legion of Honor, a representative from the President of the Republic, and, again, de Gaulle's son-in-law, who was also commander-in-chief of the French Army. Her flag-draped coffin was carried through an honor guard of two dozen flags, as is done for French Army veterans.

It is hard not to wonder what was being honored here beyond the talented and irreplaceable individual. Mistinguett had been a beloved music-hall figure, but she had not received such a funeral. "I would never have thought a woman of color would be buried in Paris like a queen," said Margaret Wallace. But it may have been her color, in addition to the love the French people felt for her, that produced this spectacular funeral.

So much had changed since she was briefly queen of the Colonial Exposition in 1931. In France as in England, the empire was striking back. Black people from former colonies were changing the demographics of metropolitan France. The kind of racism that France had prided itself on lacking was being mobilized by the pressure of numbers. Most of it was directed at North Africans, at Arabs, rather than at sub-Saharan blacks, because there were more of them in France, competing with the French for jobs. Throughout the 1970s and into the 1980s, spasms of racism shook and shocked France. In the spring of 1975, racial tension was already enough of a problem in France so that it made political sense to call attention to and honor a black woman who had loved France signally and to whom France had been notably good.

Even in her death, Josephine Baker, in addition to being a unique and beloved individual, functioned as a symbol, a magnet for other people's meanings. During the funeral mass, her coffin rested beneath a massive flower cross, a floral Star of David, a wreath from the President of the Republic, and another in the shape of a heart. But inside the coffin, Baker lay without makeup. Her sister had laid her out and insisted on that, as well as on a closed coffin. There would be no photographs of Josephine Baker dead. She would have wanted people to remember her alive.

FINALE
STAGING LOVE

∫he was Venus in a black body
with an irresistible smile. She was Cleopatra, another embodiment of
that contrary character about whom Shakespeare wrote, "Age cannot
wither her, nor custom stale her infinite variety." She riveted attention
by being unpredictable, by surprising always—like jazz. She was one
aspect of the eternal feminine, the best loved, the one that embodies
unthreatening good-natured life-enhancing sexuality. Later, her sexuality channeled differently, she became the embodiment of maternal
love, with which love she seemed as promiscuous as the other.

Like many performers, she believed the essential business of stage performance was communicating love. First you had to feel it, then you had to let your audience see that you felt it, then they loved you back, and their love gave you the energy to go on. The more disappointment she felt with the families life gave her, the more she sought solace in the family she imagined. Offstage, she might get things wrong, be scared, come on too strong, but onstage, she was at home. When she did not have a live audience in front of her, she suffered from stage fright. For that reason she did not like recording or radio work. She was stiff and strained on film, unless she was playing a performer.

Langston Hughes said of Baker in performance that she sort of reached out and took everybody's heart in her hands. Providing the illusion of intimacy without requiring the experience of intimacy was her great gift as a performer. Somehow she managed to convince large numbers of individuals that she was directing her attention to them alone. Whereas in drama the boundaries between stage and audience are exaggerated by differences in lighting and the inactivity of the spectators, in Baker's vaudeville and music-hall tradition, performers worked to break down those differences. Baker knew better than most how to bridge the distance between herself and her audience, sometimes by a gimmick like passing out vegetables or flowers, sometimes by the size and style of her gestures.

In daily life, too, she went about making intimates of strangers. When she took taxis, she always rode in the front seat. She said it was to have more room for her legs, but one person who knew her was sure it was to give herself a chance to talk to the drivers, asking them immediately about their families. Cabdrivers in New York were so fond of her that thirty of them waited to greet her when she finished lunch at La Grenouille in 1973, tipped off by the man who dropped her there. Her daughter Marianne describes how, driving a narrow road on the Riviera, they came nose to nose against a truck which refused to back up. Josephine sent Marianne to find a policeman, but by the time she got back, her mother was in the cab of the truck drinking wine with the driver and exchanging photos of their children.

She had a mimic's facility for picking up the rudiments of languages, and on the road she made a point of addressing her audiences no matter where—Japan, Hungary, or Yugoslavia—in their native tongue. In addition to French and English, she knew enough Spanish, Italian, German, and Portuguese to sing in them and get the accent right. Knowing a bit of all these languages led her to a Platonic vision of each song as having an essence that was merely clothed in different nationalities. "Only when you've sung a song in many languages is it ready for everyone. What was too local in it, too special in the lyrics, too banal, all that disappears."

By performing for most of her career to a multilingual, international audience, she had learned how to get beyond words in communication. Often audiences found her very errors of language charming—so charming they copied them. In Cuba for a long while it was fashionable in certain circles to say "Se cambia, se cambia," when you were going to change your clothes, even though this means nothing in Spanish. It was what Josephine Baker had said to announce her costume changes in Havana, aiming at Spanish and hitting something closer to Italian, and Cubans loved it.

At the celebration of Israel's twenty-fifth anniversary in 1973, she made herself the most popular of the visiting celebrities by befriending the Arab porter who cleaned her room at the Jerusalem Intercontinental, accepting an invitation to visit his home in a West Bank village, spending two hours over coffee with him, and, upon returning to the city, sending him and his family a refrigerator she could not afford. At a torchlit gala in the Citadel of Jerusalem, when the wind blew dust, scattered sheet music, and reduced most of the entertainers to nonentities, Baker with her grand-scale gestures descended the stone steps of David's Tower in a black dress and a white feather cape and made a regal impact, not at all dwarfed by the setting.

Carrying across the windswept Citadel and reaching out across the social, cultural, and economic barriers to an Arab porter were equivalent gestures. She was best with people separated from herself by some sort of barrier—the barrier of class or money, or the physical barrier of the stage. Animals, on the other side of an ultimate barrier, the one that divides human from nonhuman, evoked particular warmth. But intimacy seemed to stimulate a different reaction: she came down too hard on the people closest to her. Perhaps because she did not fundamentally trust them to be good to her, she tended to overdirect their every move.

Her seemingly reckless spontaneity onstage when she was young had always in fact been carefully contained and strategically released. Offstage, her need to control, as strong as the countervailing urge to abandon, grew ever stronger as she aged. Even when she made love, she took charge, deciding what to do, unwilling or unable to be passive. To be the object of someone else's desire made her feel frighteningly powerless. Throughout her life she had found ways of restoring the balance, above all onstage.

All performance is a ritualization of the exchange of love, and in Baker's case staging love solved a particularly large number of problems. In front of an audience, she could control the desire she faced, turning it on with seductiveness and off with laughter. Nor did she get into struggles over who was running the show, as she did with individuals. In performance her own centrality was clear: the audience was there for *her*.

In another attempt to exercise a control over her own past that she had not felt when she lived it, she caused the story of her life to be told over and over. Like any celebrity, she was besieged by reporters wanting to know about her life, and because she was exotic in France, people were more than usually curious. Still, she told the story of her own life so many times and in so many different ways that one wonders what she was trying to get straight.

The first of her memoirs, *Les Mémoires de Joséphine Baker*, came out in 1927, written by the poet Marcel Sauvage. In 1931 he updated the story in *Les Voyages et aventures de Joséphine Baker*, adding some anecdotes about her tours in Central and Eastern Europe. In 1935 another journalist, André Rivollet, came out with her "recollections," in a book called *Joséphine Baker: Une Vie de toutes les couleurs* (a many-colored life). Marcel Sauvage combined his previous two books and added new material for *Les Mémoires de Joséphine Baker* of 1949, the book that figured in Winchell's attack. About the same time, her partner in the war, Jacques Abtey, produced the memoir called *La Guerre secrète de Joséphine Baker*. Throughout the 1960s and 1970s she was gathering material for another autobiography and looking for someone to co-author it. After her death, Jo Bouillon took on the project and the last version of her memoirs appeared in 1976 as *Joséphine*.

Books alone do not represent the extent of her instincts for self-mythologizing. At Les Milandes, she established a museum of autobiographical tableaux which she called the Jorama, and in her later years, the stage shows in which she appeared offered singing and dancing versions of scenes from her own life. *Joséphine*, the revue at the Bobino Theater in which she was starring when she died, was a sequence of these *tableaux vivants*, beginning with Josephine dancing in her basement as a child (a twelve-year-old played the little Josephine) and including Josephine in uniform, making her entrance on the hood of a wartime jeep.

A couple of times, she edged up on comparing herself to Christ, most notably in the illustrations for *My Blood in Your Veins*, and, understandably, the people of Les Milandes were upset when she commissioned a sculpture of herself ministering to the little children in "biblical" dress and in the posture of St. Francis of Assisi. But sympathetically understood, her behavior was the reverse of presumption. People who are born to power and privilege do not have to work so hard to conceptualize themselves. They tend to know better where they belong, who they are. Baker was not so sure who she was or where she fitted into the scheme of things.

Her fans' attempts to use her life for their own ends and their tendency to turn her into a screen on which they projected their fantasies were unsettling to her. Through her autobiographies, she reclaimed her life for her own ends, asserting herself as subject rather than object. *She* was the one in control of the facts of her own life, distorting them or rearranging them however she wanted. In some ways, the more contradictions the better. Surface lies protected the truth. Proliferating versions of her past were the narrative equivalent of her eye-crossing, attempts to thwart the public gaze by interposing her own gaze, doubled back on itself. She protected her deep self—

which was more fearful than she would have wanted anyone to know—by a surface exhibitionism; her mythomania was a way of deflecting attention while appearing to satisfy it.

She was continually on the lookout for other people to collaborate with her in projecting who she was. She went from one person to another, whoever she thought might serve her turn, saying, "You will write the story of my life." The books she got them to write were more or less charming and sympathetic, depending on the collaborator, but they were never exactly what she wanted, or what she wanted changed, and eventually she had to try again.

A powerful part of her wanted her life to be figurative—that is, not her own life at all, not an individual life, but the life of a people. So in later versions she underscored her identification with black Americans. In 1964 she tried to interest Langston Hughes in writing at least part of her life story. She wanted him to write about her childhood and James Baldwin to write about what she called her "revolutionary side," including her wartime service, her civil rights efforts, and her adoption of the children. Someone from France could write about her professional life. If not, she could do it herself. "Three Negros writing about a Negro woman's life," as she put it. "There will be three books because my life is so full."

As the ideology of the civil rights and black consciousness movements spread, she recast the story again. Henry Louis Gates, Jr., just out of college, went to the Riviera in 1973 to interview her for a *Time* piece on black expatriates. He asked her why she had left the States, and seeing that he was a young black intellectual, she replied: "One day I realized I was living in a country where I was afraid to be black. It was only a country for white people. Not black. So I left. I had been suffocating in the United States. . . . A lot of us left, not because we wanted to leave, but because we couldn't stand it anymore. . . . I felt liberated in Paris. People didn't stare at me. But when I heard an American accent in the streets of Paris, I became afraid. I would tremble in my stomach. I was afraid they'd humiliate me."

As rewritings go, that was not extreme. It was true that she had been unhappy in the United States, true that she felt liberated in Paris, and true that white Americans in Paris scared her. All she had dropped from her account was the relatively superficial circumstance of Caroline Dudley's coming to her at the Plantation Club and offering her a job. In a more extreme autobiographical revision, she let Gates go on thinking that she had not been allowed back into the United States between 1925 and 1963, until President Kennedy personally arranged for her visa so she could attend the March on Washington. Thus the beginning and the end of her period of exile were marked by historic events—the Revue Nègre and the March on Washington—and there was no messy middle period.

Gates quickly located the hole in the story of "All for Race." Why did she not go back after 1963? Particularly in the years of civil rights struggle, didn't she feel guilty letting others do the work? She had no good answer to this question, although she said it had troubled her. Indeed, it threw her back onto a whole different narrative: "It's a sad thing to leave your country," she said. "How often I've felt like the Wandering Jew with my twelve children on my arms."

If Josephine Baker invented herself as she went along, multiplying stories to suit her purposes, the basic story, the one that underlay all the others, was the story of a black woman's success in Europe, un-fettered by race. That her success was entwined with the perception of race in ways she preferred not to explore is part of the story I have told in this book, which is as much about the European exoticism that embraced her as about the American-style racism she sought to escape.

Unique and unreproducible in its details, in outline Baker's story is that of many people who make themselves over, who manage to scramble out of a restrictive childhood, see a wider world, and claim it for themselves. In America, where the restrictiveness of childhood is so often connected with ethnic identity, many people grow up want-ing to shape larger identities while at the same time wanting to prove the value of the ties that made them. One immigrant group after another produces children who want simultaneously to vindicate and to transcend the groups that produced them. The rhetoric of cultural pluralism—this is the land of the melting pot—obscures the difficulties each individual suffers in negotiating the borderline between family pride and wariness of family. How does anyone with an ethnic identity—black, Jew, Hispanic, Irish, or Armenian—participate in a national culture without seeming to reject his or her origins?

By living in Europe, by adopting French citizenship, by speaking French, by dressing in Parisian clothes, Baker transformed her surface identity. Yet beneath these exchanges of one style of living for another, something remained which triggered her inventiveness, set her pace, choreographed her melding of moment to moment, allowed her to go on inventing herself over and over until the moment of her death. Her whole life was a jazz improvisation, turning itself inside out every few years. One way or another, she forced herself to live on the edge, never settling into predictable patterns. Whether we call it her black identity or her American identity or, metaphorically, as in the title of this book, jazz, something beneath the French superstructure formed the core of a self that endured.

From the American work ethic and from Christianity's encouragement to love, Baker derived a few truths that she clung to passionately and acted on with consistency and vigor. She had little subtlety and less angst, but that does not mean she had no depth. About her there was the poignancy of a Memorial Day parade in a small town, the poignancy of great ideas reduced to the lowest common denominator.

She never understood the vocabulary of black pride that started being used in the 1960s. For her, whose ideology was of the 1920s, it sounded like the old vocabulary of racism, and she did not follow the brilliant twist by which it was used precisely to transform "black" from a racial put-down used by whites to a quasi-nationalist rallying cry used by blacks, beginning at last to create African-Americans as an ethnic group rather than a racial one. Nonetheless, she demonstrated black pride if she did not understand its rhetoric. As the first international black star, Josephine Baker transcended her ethnic identity without in the slightest repudiating it, managing in her art and in her rapport with her audience to triumph over her old antagonists—rejection, time, and the many forms of the limiting fiction of race.

ПОТЕ $

New York Public Library at Lincoln Center = Library for Performing Arts of the New York Public Library (Astor, Lenox, and Tilden Foundations), New York.

Schomburg = The Schomburg Center for Research in Black Culture of the New York Public Library, New York.

Arsenal = The Bibliothèque de l'Arsenal of the Bibliothèque Nationale, Paris.

Beinecke = The Beinecke Rare Book and Manuscript Library, Yale University, New Haven, Conn.

CHAPTER I: SAVAGE DANCE

PAGE 5, *the managers were not happy with the Revue Nègre*: see Jacques Charles, *De Gaby Deslys à Mistinguett* (Paris: Gallimard, n.d.).

PAGE 6, "In spite of her magnificent body": Josephine Baker and Jo Bouillon, *Josephine*, transl. by Mariana Fitzpatrick (New York: Harper & Row, 1977), p. 49. See also Paul Colin *La Croûte: Souvenirs* (Paris: Table Ronde, 1957), and Jack Rennert, *100 Posters of Paul Colin* (New York: Images Graphiques, 1977).

PAGE 8, *dressed in white robes*: Janet Flanner, "Letter from Paris," *The New Yorker*, October 25, 1925.

PAGE 8, "We don't understand their language": Paul Achard, "Tout en Noir ou la 'Revue Nègre,' *Paris-Midi*, September 27, 1925, Arsenal Pressbook (RO 15.702), Vols. I and II.

PAGE 9, *she could be a princess*: Aristocratic cultures like to hear this story—the Pygmalion story with a couture emphasis—perhaps because it belittles power, making it seem accessible to anyone who can scrape together the price of a nice outfit. Democratic cultures may understand that power is harder to get.

PAGE 10, *formed by poverty and rejection*: For accounts of Baker's childhood, see Marcel Sauvage, *Les Mémoires de Joséphine Baker* (Paris: Éditions Kra, 1927); André Rivollet, *Joséphine Baker: Une Vie de toutes les couleurs* (Grenoble: B. Arthaud, 1935); and *Josephine*. Lynn Haney's research into Baker's early years is especially valuable. See her *Naked at the Feast: A Biography of Josephine Baker* (New York: Dodd, Mead, 1981), pp. 1–34.

PAGE 10, *he earned lessons at the local dance academy*: Haney, *Naked at the Feast*, pp. 6, 9.

PAGE 11, *Richard had taken someone's bicycle*: Notes of an interview by Harry or Peggy Janes with Margaret Wallace, August 18, 1975. Janes Papers, Beinecke.

PAGE 12, *The dog and a chicken were her only friends*: Rivollet, *Une Vie de toutes les couleurs*, p. 42. See also *Josephine*, p. 4.

PAGE 14, "There is no Santa Claus": Haney, *Naked at the Feast*, p. 19.

PAGE 16, "identifying with the aggressor": Anna Freud, *The Ego and the Mechanisms of Defense* (New York: International Universities Press, 1966), pp. 109–21.

PAGE 19, "Is it a man? Is it a woman?": Pierre de Régnier, "La Revue Nègre," in *Candide*, November 12, 1925, Arsenal Pressbook (RO 15.702), p. 123. Some details also taken from Gérard Bauer, *Annales*, November 18, 1925, Arsenal Pressbook (RO 15.702), p. 93.

PAGE 21, *moves related to the Belly Dance*: See Marshall and Jean Stearns, *Jazz Dance: The Story of American Vernacular Dance* (New York: Macmillan, 1968), pp. 104–7, 234–35.

PAGE 21, "the triumph of lubricity": Régnier, "La Revue Nègre."

PAGE 22, "manifestation of the modern spirit": *De Gauguin à la Revue Nègre*, pp. 224–26.

PAGE 23, *bare-breasted Algerian women*: See Malek Alloula, *Le Harem Colonial* (Geneva and Paris: Éditions Slatkine, 1981).

PAGE 23, "Their lips must have the taste of pickled watermelon": Blanche, *De Gauguin à la Revue Nègre*, p. 221.

PAGE 23, "Our romanticism is desperate for renewal": *Annales*, October 18, 1925, Arsenal Pressbook (RO 15.702), p. 93.

PAGE 24, "walking like a little hummingbird": Mura Dehn, interview with the author, December 1984.

PAGE 24, "The rear end exists": Sauvage, *Les Mémoires de Joséphine Baker*, p. 89.

PAGE 24, *opening and closing the legs*: It was a development of one detail in the sequence of moves called Patting Juba. See Stearns, *Jazz Dance*, p. 29.

PAGE 24, *made her legs seem endless*: Mura Dehn interview.

PAGE 25, *a little heavy*: ("Tiens, du cellulite!" said a Frenchwoman I know, with relief.)

PAGE 25, *African dance*: For much of what I say about African dance and its influence on American vernacular dance I am indebted to Robert Farris Thompson, *African Art in Motion* (Berkeley, Los Angeles, and London: University of California Press, 1974), and to Marshall and Jean Stearns, *Jazz Dance*. I am grateful, also, to the late Mura Dehn, whose films of black dancing in America, made lovingly over many years, are preserved in the Dance Collection of the Library for Performing Arts, Lincoln Center, New York.

PAGE 25, *stylized instability*: Thompson, *African Art in Motion*, p. 24.

PAGE 26, *as if he or she had no bones*: Ibid., p. 9.

PAGE 26, *the carryover from African religion*: Music and dance were part of all African religious ritual. Their rhythmic patterns helped produce the experience central to African religious life—possession by the god. Supported by the community of worshippers dancing and singing around him, the worshipper went into a kind of frenzy, an unconscious state, in which his movements—jerky and expressive—were controlled by the spirit that had taken possession of him. When blacks were taken from Africa and shipped to America as slaves, they adapted their religious life to the new forms of worship that were imposed on them. African possession became Christian testimony, and when little Josephine went to church for the fun of seeing the newly converted make public confession of their sins, she was watching a practice that had survived, transformed but with the spirit intact, a transplantation over thousands of miles and hundreds of years. See Melville J. Herskovits, *The Myth of the Negro Past* (Boston: Beacon Press, 1958), pp. 210–13, and Zora Neale Hurston, *The Sanctified Church* (Berkeley: Turtle Island, 1983), p. 104.

PAGE 27, *dizzy with excitement*: *Josephine*, p. 7, and Rivollet, *Une Vie de toutes les couleurs*, pp. 23–25, for differing accounts.

PAGE 28, "The dance of the Negresses": J.-F. Roger, *Fables sénégalaises*, quoted by Léon-François Hoffman, *Le Nègre romantique: Personnage littéraire et ob-*

session collective (Paris: Payot, 1973), pp. 214–15, to which I'm indebted for much of the information in this paragraph. The idea that black women were more erotic than white women was such a cliché that Flaubert listed it in his Dictionary of Received Ideas, under "Negress."

PAGE 29, "from the valley of the Niger to the lights of Broadway": "The Negro Dance," *Theatre Arts Monthly*, Vol. II (April 1927), p. 292. This is a translation of part of his book *La Danse d'aujourd'hui* (Paris: Éditions Duchartre et Van Buggenhoudt, 1929).

PAGE 29, *form squeezes out spirit*: Spontaneity is always located in an earlier time. A recent article compares the dying Romantic breed of pianists, Horowitz and Rubinstein, with the arid modern perfectionists being turned out by music schools and music competitions today (*The Atlantic*, August 1986). This perception—that arid intellectual performance is replacing spirited performance—is so recurrent as to seem to me archetypal and not historical. Perhaps it reflects the fact that each individual experiences in his own life the passing of spontaneity and passion and its reluctant consignment to the past, as he or she proceeds to perform on sheer will.

PAGE 30, "The Negro stepper": Levinson, "The Negro Dance," p. 287.

PAGE 31, "There seemed to emanate from her violently shuddering body": Ibid., pp. 291–92.

PAGE 31, "She made her entry entirely nude": *Paris Was Yesterday: 1925–1939* (New York: Viking, 1972), pp. xx-xxi. Despite the minor inaccuracies (the Danse Sauvage was the finale, not her first appearance, and she wore a whole skirt of feathers, not one), this is, I think, a truer account of Josephine Baker's opening night than virtually all written at the time. It was actually written many years after the event described. In her first effort to write about Baker's debut, the one printed in 1925, Flanner wrote, by her own account, "like a dullard." "Precisely at the moment when black is being worn again, Josephine Baker's Colored review has arrived at the Champs-Élysées Theater and the result has been unanimous. Paris has never drawn a color line. It likes blondes, brunettes, or Bakers, more now than ever." In the early 1970s, when she collected her Paris letters, Flanner was appalled at what she had written in 1925 and gave herself the chance to do right by Baker, whose excitement and sensuality had never faded in her mind. However, even this account bears the marks of ideology. In 1925 Flanner noted that black was fashionable, in 1972 that black was beautiful. Would she have remembered Baker's dance as establishing in 1925 that black was beautiful if that had not been what one was encouraged to see in 1972?

PAGE 33, "All masterworks of the human spirit": For this man, the success of the Revue Nègre was connected with the admission of the Douanier Rousseau into the Louvre—a painter praised, as he put it, for knowing neither how to draw nor how to paint. Clément Vantel, *Journal*, November 17, 1925.

PAGE 34, "The cross between a white man and an Indian": *The Passing of the Great Race, or The Racial Basis of European History* (New York: Scribner's, 1918; orig. publ. 1916), p. 18.

PAGE 34, *the three European races*: Actually, the three races had been discovered by William Z. Ripley, author of *The Races of Europe*, a large, scholarly volume of 1899. Ripley called the three races Alpine, Mediterranean, and Teutonic.

PAGE 35, "the right of merit to rule": Lothrop Stoddard, *The Rising Tide of Color Against White World-Supremacy* (New York: Scribner's, 1920; reprinted Westport, Conn.: Negro Universities Press, 1971), p. xxx.

PAGE 37, "We do not descend from the ape": "Nous ne descendons pas du singe, mais nous y allons." Quoted in Thomas F. Gossett, *Race: The History of an Idea in America* (Dallas: Southern Methodist University Press, 1963), p. 344. See pp. 342–48 for an account of Gobineau's thought. See also Léon Poliakov, *The Aryan Myth: A History of Racist and Nationalist Ideas in Europe*, transl. by Edmund Howard (New York: Basic Books, 1974).

PAGE 37, "Why is it art?": *Women in Love*, Chapter 7, "Totem."

PAGE 38, "The white races" and "Was he fated?": Ibid., Chapter 19, "Moony."

PAGE 40, *Josephine Baker's body . . . one of many African "objects"*: See James Clifford, "Histories of the Tribal and the Modern," *Art in America*, April 1985, pp. 169–70, and also Thomas McEvilley, "Doctor Lawyer Indian Chief," *Artforum*, November 1984, pp. 54–60, and ensuing correspondence, *Artforum*, February 1985, pp. 42–51, and May 1985, pp. 63–71.

PAGE 40, *Paris had been the city*: Jean-Louis Paudrat, "The Arrival of Tribal Objects in the West from Africa," in *"Primitivism" in 20th Century Art: Affinity of the Tribal and the Modern*, ed. William Rubin (2 vols.; Boston: Little, Brown, and New York: The Museum of Modern Art, 1984), Vol. I, pp. 125–32.

PAGE 41, *his work on that seminal painting*: See Rubin, "Picasso," in *"Primitivism,"* Vol. I, pp. 241–345, and also his "Modern Primitivism: An Introduction" in the same volume.

PAGES 41–42, "It was disgusting": André Malraux in *La Tête d'obsidienne*, quoted by Paudrat in *"Primitivism,"* Vol. I, p. 141.

PAGE 43, *female sexuality and blackness*: Sander Gilman, "Black Bodies, White

Bodies: Toward an Iconography of Female Sexuality in Late-Nineteenth-Century Art, Medicine, and Literature," in *Critical Inquiry*, Autumn 1985, pp. 232–34. Included (Fig. 16) is a reproduction of Picasso's black *Olympia*.

PAGE 43, "The fact that rather abruptly": Clifford, *Art in America*, April 1985, p. 170. Following quote, ibid.

PAGE 44, "She was incited to make an impression": Quotations from *Quicksand* (Westport, Conn.: Negro Universities Press, 1969; orig. publ. New York: Knopf, 1928), pp. 114, 155, 160, 162–63.

PAGE 45, *to ally themselves with the children against the fathers*: Rubin, "Picasso."

PAGE 45, "She just wiggled her fanny": Maria Jolas, telephone interview with the author, May 1985.

CHAPTER 2: BLACK BROADWAY, BLACK PARIS

PAGE 47, *she learned a lot from mimicking rag dolls*: Sauvage, *Les Mémoires de Joséphine Baker*, pp. 55–56.

PAGE 47, *Through-the-Trenches*: Identified, along with other steps, by the knowledgeable Mr. Ernie Smith.

PAGE 49, *a spectacle of glamour for their audiences*: See Linda Dahl, *Stormy Weather: The Music and Lives of a Century of Jazzwomen* (New York: Pantheon, 1984), p. 119.

PAGE 50, *balancing her weight on high-heeled shoes*: *Josephine*, p. 21.

PAGE 51, *distract the usher*: James Weldon Johnson describes the humiliating process of getting into a white theater before 1921. See *Along This Way: The Autobiography of James Weldon Johnson* (New York: Viking, 1933).

PAGE 51, *Tough on Black Asses*: See Lynn Emery, *Black Dance in the United States from 1619 to 1970* (Palo Alto, Calif.: National Press Books, 1972).

PAGE 51, *no better off than wandering minstrels*: Al Rose, *Eubie Blake* (New York: Schirmer Books, 1979), p. 60.

PAGE 52, *the gospel of ballroom dancing*: See Irene Castle, *Castles in the Air* (Garden City, N.Y.: Doubleday, 1958).

PAGE 52, *the one who stood at the end of the line*: According to Harry Sampson, a midwestern vaudeville producer introduced this innovation at the time of World War I. See "Billy King" in Harry T. Sampson, *Blacks in Blackface:*

A Source Book on Early Black Musical Shows (Metuchen, N.J., and London: The Scarecrow Press, 1980).

PAGE 54, *demanded an encore*: Robert Kimball and William Bolcom, *Reminiscing with Sissle and Blake* (New York: Viking, 1973), p. 93. For "I'm Just Wild About Harry," see p. 106.

PAGE 55, "Every sinew in their bodies danced": Ibid., p. 99.

PAGE 55, *upper floors did not sell out*: Ibid., p. 98.

PAGE 59, "Her emotions": "How Jo Baker Got Started," *Negro Digest*, August 1951, pp. 15–19.

PAGE 59, "NAACP-type production": Billie Holiday with William Dufty, *Lady Sings the Blues* (Garden City, N.Y.: Doubleday, 1956), p. 74.

PAGE 60, "She began to realize": "How Jo Baker Got Started," *Negro Digest*, November 17, 1951.

PAGE 61, "pretentious": Kimball and Bolcom, *Reminiscing with Sissle and Blake*, p. 178.

PAGE 61, "People who went to a colored show": Ibid., p. 181.

PAGE 61, "movement was a blues": Ibid., p. 181.

PAGE 61, *black writers and composers had gathered at the Marshall Hotel*: See James Weldon Johnson, *Black Manhattan* (New York: Arno Press and The New York Times, 1968; orig. publ. 1930).

PAGE 62, "I am the world's greatest violinist": Edward Kennedy (Duke) Ellington, *Music Is My Mistress* (Garden City, N.Y.: Doubleday, 1973), p. 97, and Sidney Bechet, *Treat It Gentle* (New York: Hill and Wang, 1960), p. 125.

PAGE 62, "ashamed of it": Sampson, *Blacks in Blackface*, p. 132.

PAGE 62, "Only at the very end": Ibid.

PAGE 66, "To be able to live well on very little money": *Memoirs of Montparnasse*, with an introduction by Leon Edel (Toronto and New York: Oxford University Press, 1970), p. 14.

PAGE 66, "But the younger and footloose intellectuals": *Exile's Return: A Literary Odyssey of the 1920s* (New York: Viking, 1951), p. 79.

PAGE 67, *the Harlem Hellfighters*: See Jervis Anderson, *This Was Harlem: A Cultural Portrait, 1900–1950* (New York: Farrar, Straus & Giroux, 1982) pp.

107–8. On General Pershing, see Nathan Huggins, *Harlem Renaissance* (New York: Oxford University Press, 1971), pp. 54–55. Also, on blacks in World War I, especially black musicians, National Public Radio's "Fanfare for the Warriors," written by Thulani Davis.

PAGE 67, *one day of glory*: The best description of this event is in Huggins, *Harlem Renaissance*, pp. 55–56.

PAGE 68, "blues on the clarinet": Bechet, *Treat It Gentle*, p. 127. See also, for Bechet's deportation from England, p. 133.

PAGE 68, "crazy to be doing": Ibid., p. 149.

PAGE 69, *Gene Bullard*: Bricktop, with James Haskins, *Bricktop* (New York: Atheneum, 1983), p. 84. Bessie Coleman, the first black woman to get a pilot's license in America, also had gone to France to get her training.

PAGE 69, "risk of humiliating experiences": Schomburg Clipping File, *Logan*. Especially "Confessions of an Unwilling Nordic," in *The World Tomorrow*, July 1927, pp. 297–300. Logan was an officer in the American Expeditionary Force from 1918 to 1919.

PAGE 70, *Langston Hughes*: See Faith Berry, *Langston Hughes: Before and Beyond Harlem* (Westport, Conn.: Lawrence Hill, 1983), and Arnold Rampersad, *The Life of Langston Hughes* (2 vols.), Vol, I: *1902–1941, I, Too, Sing America* (New York and Oxford: Oxford University Press, 1986), pp. 82–91. Also Langston Hughes, *The Big Sea: An Autobiography* (New York: Knopf, 1940).

PAGE 71, "Less you can play": Berry, *Langston Hughes*, p. 45. Also, for Hughes at the Grand Duc, p. 47.

PAGE 72, "Do you mean to say": *Bricktop*, p. 85.

PAGE 73, "Paris does not reproach the person bent on going to the devil": *Town and Country*, December 1, 1922.

PAGE 73, *Harold Stearns himself proved to be one of the "morally malnourished"*: See Hugh Ford, "Introduction" to Stearns's *Confessions of a Harvard Man: Paris & New York in the 1920s & 30s* (Sutton West, Ontario, and Santa Barbara, Calif.: The Paget Press, 1984), and *Four Lives in Paris* (San Francisco: North Point Press, 1987), pp. 83–135.

PAGE 73, *continuity against which violent artistic gestures can be played*: See *Paris France* (New York: Liveright, 1940), esp. pp. 8, 11–12. For her attitude toward the avant-garde, compare Flaubert's advice to be bourgeois in your life so that you can be violent and original in your art. About her attitude toward Basket, note that she replaced him with a similar and similarly named dog against the advice of Picasso, who wondered rhetorically whether, if he himself died, she would look for another friend named Pablo.

PAGE 74, "Liquor was an important factor": James Charters, *This Must Be the Place*, as told to Morrill Cody, with an introduction by Ernest Hemingway (New York: Lee Furman, 1937), p. 306 for "wild-oats field" and p. 150 for Duchamp.

PAGE 74, "I was suddenly free": *Along This Way*, p. 209.

PAGE 74, "a normal human atmosphere": "American Negroes in France," *The Crisis*, June–July 1951, p. 381.

PAGE 75, "No more bars to beat against": "The American Negro in Europe," *The American Mercury*, XX:77 (May 1930), pp. 1–10.

PAGE 75, *Bricktop*: Most of my information about Bricktop comes from the memoir she co-authored with James Haskins. See above.

PAGE 76, *Gwendolyn Bennett*: Her journal is in the Schomburg Center for Research in Black Culture of the New York Public Library and is quoted by permission of the library and of the executor of her estate, Mrs. Martha O. Tanner.

PAGE 77, *Harry T. Burleigh*: He had studied with Dvořák and had interested Dvořák in black spirituals. A man with an extraordinary voice, Burleigh was soloist for two fashionable white congregations in New York, St. George's Episcopal Church and Temple Emanu-El. Along with the two Johnsons and Bob Cole, he was, in the black community, a supreme authority on musical theory. The group that gathered at the Marshall Hotel also tended to frequent Burleigh's Park Avenue apartment. See Johnson, *Along This Way*, pp. 172–74.

PAGE 80, "The prostituting of Negro talent": "Deplores 'High Yellow' Revues," *Chicago Tribune* (Paris edition), November 18, 1925, clipping file, James Weldon Johnson Collection, Beinecke.

PAGE 80, *the real renaissance in Harlem*: See Huggins, *Harlem Renaissance*, pp. 9–11.

CHAPTER 3: TOP BANANA

PAGE 81, "The white imagination sure is something": Marcel Sauvage, *Voyages et aventures de Joséphine Baker* (Paris: Éditions Marcel Sheur, 1931), p. 16.

PAGE 82, *the Revue Nègre moved*: It reopened at the Théâtre de l'Étoile on November 21. Baker was out for a few days around November 13 with an "indisposition."

PAGE 82, "Josephine, you will hurt your soul": Interview with Michel Fabre. Caroline Dudley later married Joseph Deltheil, a surrealist writer, and lived into her eighties in the South of France. Professor Fabre is France's expert on black American writers in Paris. See his fascinating *La Rive Noire: De Harlem à la Seine* (Paris: Éditions Lieu Commun, 1985).

PAGE 82, "She wouldn't go around the corner": Bricktop, with James Haskins, *Bricktop* (New York: Atheneum, 1983), p. 108.

PAGE 83, *Berlin at that time*: See Hans Heinsheimer, *Best Regards to Aida: The Defeats and Victories of a Music Man on Two Continents* (New York: Knopf, 1968), pp. 22 ff. This is a marvelously written account of Berlin between the wars and a fine memoir of one man's transition from Europe to America. For more on Berlin between the wars, see Charles Higham, *Marlene: The Life of Marlene Dietrich* (New York: Norton, 1977), and Marion K. Sanders, *Dorothy Thompson: A Legend in Her Time* (New York: Avon), pp. 100–1.

PAGE 84, *a cross between Madison Square Garden and St. Patrick's*: Heinsheimer, *Best Regards to Aida*, p. 26.

PAGE 84, *absorbed by the dazzling city*: Ibid., p. 22, describing Brecht in Berlin.

PAGE 84, "Fame is a ladder with many rungs": *Josephine*, p. 58.

PAGES 84–85, *Reinhardt and black vaudeville*: See Alain Locke, "Max Reinhardt Reads the Negro's Dramatic Horoscope," *Opportunity*, Vol. II (May 1924), pp. 145–46, reprinted in *The Critical Temper of Alain Locke: A Selection of His Essays on Art and Culture*, ed. Jeffrey C. Stewart (New York and London: Garland, 1983). Locke interviewed Reinhardt at the time of his visit to New York. What Reinhardt said to Locke about black comedians generally I represent him as addressing to Baker specifically. Locke adopted Reinhardt's view that black vaudeville, rather contemptible in its Broadway incarnation, could be the source of great art in the future. See "The Negro and the American Stage," *Theatre Arts Monthly*, Vol. X (February 1926), pp. 112–20, also reprinted in Stewart, *The Critical Temper of Alain Locke*.

PAGE 85, "*Feathered mannequin?*": *Josephine*, p. 59.

PAGE 85, *the "Red Count"*: Otto Friedrich, introduction to *In the Twenties: The Diaries of Harry Kessler*, transl. by Charles Kessler (New York: Holt, Rinehart and Winston, 1976). Publ. in Germany as *Harry Graf Kessler, Tagebücher 1918–1937* (Frankfurt am Main, Insel Verlag, 1961). Engl. transl. orig.

publ. as *The Diaries of a Cosmopolitan: Count Harry Kessler, 1918–1937* (London: Weidenfeld & Nicolson, 1971).

PAGE 86, *like a limp bowstring*: Kessler, *In the Twenties*, p. 282.

PAGE 86, "Watching her": Ibid., p. 282.

PAGE 86, "perhaps by Richard Strauss": Ibid., p. 280.

PAGE 87, *Genius was addressing genius*: This account of Baker's dance to the sculpture is based closely on Harry Kessler's diary entry for February 24, 1926, Ibid., pp. 283–84.

PAGE 89, "Herr Reinhardt hadn't mentioned Irving Berlin": *Josephine*, p. 60.

PAGE 90, *an instance of racial revenge*: Ibid., p. 58.

PAGE 91, "She was Parisian in tone": Jacques Damase, "Le Music-Hall," in *Histoire des Spectacles*, a volume of *Encyclopédie de la Pléiade* (Paris: Éditions Gallimard, 1965), pp. 1543–75.

PAGE 91, *twenty-one-foot train*: Charles Castle, *The Folies Bergère* (London: Methuen Paperback, 1984), p. 223.

PAGE 92, *"The Flea"*: Paul Derval, *Folies-Bergère*, transl. by Lucienne Hill (New York: Dutton, 1955), p. 51.

PAGE 92, *the Folies were fairly vulgar*: A popular act of the time was the "Pétomane," who appeared in tails and white tie and made sounds like music without opening his mouth or indeed making use of his vocal cords. *Péter* means "to fart," and you could say that the Pétomane was a "fart artist."

PAGE 93, *Barthes*: "Au Music-Hall," in *Mythologies* (Paris: Éditions du Seuil, 1957), pp. 199–201.

PAGE 93, *Colette*: When the Théâtre des Champs-Élysées opened as a music hall in 1925, Colette at the inaugural gala read two of her dialogues for animals and reminisced about her days as a performer on the music-hall stage.

PAGE 94, "plotless drama": "Vive la Folie! An Analysis of the *Revue* in General and the Parisian Revue in Particular," *Vanity Fair*, September 1926, p. 55.

PAGE 94, "The whole world is at our disposition": Louis Léon-Martin, *Le Music-Hall et ses figures* (Paris: Les Éditions de France, 1928), pp. 29–30. See also Jacques Damase, *Les Folies du Music-Hall: Histoire du Music-Hall à Paris de 1914 à nos jours*, preface by Bruno Coquatrix (Paris: Éditions Spectacles, 1960). Compare the way in which Bloomingdale's still features the goods of a chosen country, turning "Japan," "Italy," or "Ireland" into a promotional theme and serving in a strange way an educational purpose. The geo-thematic orientation of high school proms seems to me another avatar of the same practice, which I might call "spurious access."

PAGE 94, "The voice has to be in the legs": Louis Roubaud, *Music-Hall* (Paris: Louis Querelle Éditeur, 1929), p. 57. "C'est dans les jambes qu'il faut avoir de la voix."

PAGE 95, "A gradual buildup and perfect timing": Derval, *Folies-Bergère*, p. 23.

PAGE 96, *Her business was to win them over*: Ibid., p. 22.

PAGE 96, "the land of dream-fulfillment": Ibid., p. 31.

PAGE 97, "O magic, O joy": Pierre Loiselet, *Soir*, January 30, 1927.

PAGE 99, "a wand of golden flesh": E. E. Cummings, "Vive la Folie!" *Vanity Fair*, September 1926, p. 116.

PAGE 99, *genuinely Cubist*: Louis Léon-Martin, "La Revue des Folies-Bergère," *Paris-Midi* (May 1, 1926). The "Flower Ball" number was encased in a brief but tasteless comic narrative. The Folies comedy star, Dorville, played a professor who fell in love with Josephine Baker as she danced the Charleston. He pursues her but she eludes him by substituting a black male dancer, Benga, for herself. The professor is so myopic he does not notice the difference.

PAGE 99, "There's no need to regret": "La Folie du Jour," *Comoedia*, April 30, 1926.

PAGE 99, *A furious attack: Bulletin d'Informations Anti-Pornographiques*, July 1926, Arsenal Pressbook (Ro 18.757), p. 39.

PAGE 100, *many French people resented it*: For an imaginative rendering of how Parisians felt about Americans in 1926, see Harold Stearns, "Letter from Paris," *Town and Country*, September 1, 1925. He told Americans to imagine how they would feel if, at the very end of a devastating war, Germany had come in on our side and tipped the balance in our favor. Technically our benefactors in war, they appall us. Their money is worth more and more against ours, so they have all the best apartments in New York, crowd the bars and restaurants, squander money while we hardly have enough to buy food, and fill the streets with the sound of German.

PAGE 100, *Alexander Calder*: H. H. Arnason, *Calder* (Princeton: Van Nostrand, 1966), p. 17.

PAGE 100, "might very easily be called rotten": Nancy Cunard, "Letter from

Paris," reprinted in Carolyn Hall, *The Twenties in Vogue* (New York: Harmony Books, 1983), p. 49.

PAGE 100, "tall, vital, incomparably fluid nightmare": Cummings, "Vive la Folie!," pp. 55, 116.

PAGE 101, "marry the prince": "The Dark Tower," *Opportunity*, February 1927, p. 53. The article is unsigned, but its author may well have been Countee Cullen. The observations about "small, brown, and rather plump" are from G. de la Fouchardière, writing in *L'Oeuvre*, translated and quoted in the *Opportunity* piece.

CHAPTER 4: FRESH BLOOD

PAGE 106, "Oh, Bricky": Bricktop, with James Haskins, *Bricktop* (New York: Atheneum, 1983), p. 107.

PAGE 106, *Le Tumulte noir*: These were done in a stencil technique called *pochoir*, which produces particularly intense color.

PAGE 107, "You don't know what it's like to write": "Vous ne savez pas ce que c'est: écrire, oh là là! moi, je danse, j'aime ça la danse, je n'aime que çela, je danserai toute ma vie." *Les Mémoires de Joséphine Baker* (1927), p. 14.

PAGE 108, *turned sex into a gymnastic exercise*: "She was in charge, in the driver's seat. She decided what to do and how to do it." Frédéric Rey, quoted by Haney, *Naked at the Feast*, p. 205.

PAGE 109, *he did not want to be Mr. Baker*: Georges Simenon, *Mémoires intimes* (Paris: Presses de la Cité, 1981), p. 24, and Leslie Garis, "Simenon's Last Case," *The New York Times Magazine*, April 22, 1984, and interview.

PAGE 110, "*I* was the instrument that I must care for": *Josephine*, p. 58.

PAGE 110, "A frequent visitor to Paris": Ibid., p. 67.

PAGE 110, "His real name was Giuseppe Abatino": *Bricktop*, p. 109.

PAGE 112, *5,000 francs out of 285,000*: I would estimate the 1989 equivalent of her total bill as $280,000, of which $5,000 was unpaid.

PAGE 112, "someone to help me fight my battles": *Josephine*, p. 69, also p. 74.

PAGE 114, "But how much resistance": Letter (April 18, 1927) in Arsenal Pressbook (Ro 18.757).

PAGES 114–15, "Fifteen years ago in California": Pierre Lazareff, *Soir*, January 16, 1927, Arsenal Pressbook (Ro 18.757).

PAGE 115, *her parents fell in love in school: Les Mémoires de Joséphine Baker*, p. 44, 47.

PAGE 115, "I got all the family jewels": *New York Herald* (Paris edition), July 1927, Beinecke Library, Yale University, Van Vechten collection.

PAGE 116, "My husband in the film": *Paris-Soir*, June 26, 1927, Arsenal Pressbook (Ro 15.816).

PAGE 116, "Count's Father Glad": *The Defender*, February 7, 1927, Schomburg clipping file.

PAGE 117, "If that boy sticks with me": *New York World*, July 10, 1927, Schomburg clipping file.

PAGE 117, *book-signing party: Chantecler*, July 13, 1927.

PAGE 118, "I had no stockings": *Les Mémoires de Joséphine Baker*, p. 57.

PAGE 118, "I've heard a lot of talk about the war": Ibid., p. 82.

PAGE 119, "it would be pretty picturesque": See Pierre Humbourg, "Va-t-il y avoir un nouveau procès Joséphine Baker?" *Presse*, October 22, 1927, and Pierre Lazareff "Pourquoi Joséphine Baker veut intenter un procès à Marcel Sauvage," *Paris-Midi*, November 2, 1927.

PAGE 120, *She was humiliated*: She discusses her early film career in Sauvage, *Voyages et aventures de Joséphine Baker*, pp. 130 ff. For Pierre Batcheff and Buñuel, see Denise Tual, *Le Temps dévoré* (Paris: Fayard, 1980), p. 60. Also, author's interview with Denise Tual, May 1985.

PAGE 120, "The finished film brought tears to my eyes": *Josephine*, p. 73.

PAGE 123, *as long as she is never the same*: Ibid., p. 90.

PAGE 123, "It is a sin": *Mein Kampf* (New York: Reynal and Hitchcock, 1939), p. 640.

PAGE 123, *Colonial Office complained*: Keith L. Nelson, "The 'Black Horror on the Rhine': Race as a Factor in Post-World War I Diplomacy," *Journal of Modern History* Vol. XLII (1970), p. 608.

PAGE 123, "barbarians": Ibid., p. 615.

PAGE 124, "the playground of black African hordes": *Mein Kampf*, p. 917.

PAGE 124, *The French Army was being used*: Ibid., pp. 448–49.

PAGE 125, *the impact of jazz was more substantial*: See Susan Cook, *Opera for a New Republic: The* Zeitopern *of Křenek, Weill, and Hindemith* (Ann Arbor, Mich.: UMI Research Press, 1987), pp. 46 and 51. I am indebted to Professor Cook of the Music Department of Middlebury College for her imaginative research on jazz in Germany between the wars.

PAGE 125, *not a bad introduction to jazz for the Germans*: Ibid., p. 49; for *The Chocolate Kiddies Revue*, see also pp. 47–50 and Duke Ellington, *Music Is My Mistress* (Garden City, N.Y.: Doubleday, 1973), p. 65.

PAGE 126, "transfusion of fresh Negro blood": Quoted by Cook, *Opera for a New Republic*, p. 57.

PAGE 126, *an enthusiasm for America*: See John Willet, *The Weimar Years: A Culture Cut Short* (New York: Abbeville Press, 1984).

PAGE 126, "a child of nature": Ernst Křenek, *Horizons Circled: Reflections on My Music.* (Berkeley, Los Angeles, and London: The University of California Press, 1974), p. 38. Křenek said he knew so little English when he wrote the opera that he accepted the spelling "Jonny," which had been used in a popular German song. Later, when American friends asked him where the "h" was, he said his character's name was Jonathan.

PAGE 127, "You put on a shirt with your eyes open": Hans Heinsheimer, *Best Regards to Aida: The Defeats and Victories of a Music Man on Two Continents* (New York: Knopf, 1968), p. 153.

PAGE 127, *a black saxophonist in a top hat on whose lapel is a Jewish star*: Reproduced in George Mosse, *Toward the Final Solution: A History of European Racism* (New York: Howard Fertig, 1978), pp. 34–35.

PAGE 127, *which shows how well it had rooted there*: Cook, *Opera for a New Republic*, p. 65.

PAGE 127, "an anti-negro feeling that Vienna never knew existed": March 4, 1928.

PAGE 129, "like a Congo savage": Unattributed news item, February 25, 1928, in the *New York Post* clipping file.

PAGE 129, "Who fights nudity blasphemes God": *Voyages et aventures de Joséphine Baker*, p. 68.

PAGE 129, "in atonement for outrages on morality": *The New York Times*, March 12, 1928.

PAGE 129, *a sermon against Josephine Baker and the Charleston*: Voyages et aventures de Joséphine Baker, p. 66.

PAGE 129, *she had always wanted to be a stranger*: Ibid., p. 36.

PAGE 131, *barrier to the existence of a gymnosophic utopia*: *Nudism in Modern Life: The New Gymnosophy*, with an introduction by Havelock Ellis, orig. publ. 1927 (New York: Knopf, 1931), p. 237.

PAGE 131, *Leni Riefenstahl*: See Susan Sontag's brilliant essay on Nazi primitivism and fascist aesthetics, "Fascinating Fascism," in *Under the Sign of Saturn* (New York: Farrar, Straus & Giroux, 1980).

Parmalee concedes in a footnote that racist German nationalists had turned nudity to their own ends, using the pursuit of physical culture to promote racial superiority. "The gymnosophic movement, like nearly every movement in post-war Germany, has been a battlefield between the liberal and radical forces and the conservative and reactionary forces." *Nudism in Modern Life*, p. 264, n. 1.

PAGE 132, "Now it will grow": Richard Sterba, *Reminiscences of a Viennese Psychoanalyst* (Detroit: Wayne State University Press, 1982), p. 72.

PAGE 132, *Baker continued to provoke controversy*: Information about Baker's European tour in this paragraph comes largely from unattributed clippings in the *New York Post* clipping file.

PAGE 133, "It would have been evidently disagreeable": "Joséphine Baker indésirable à Munich," February 16, 1929, Arsenal Pressbook (Ro 15.816), II.

PAGE 133, "Since the occupation of the Rhineland": Hélène Saurel, "La petite 'idole noire' nous raconte quelques pages de sa vie d'artiste," *Marseille-Matin*, November 21, 1931, Arsenal Pressbook (Ro 15.816), II.

PAGE 133, "It certainly must be irritating": May 10, 1928, Arsenal Pressbook (Ro 15.816), I, 86.

PAGE 133, *The sax was certain to win*: Lucien Farnoux-Reynaud, "Les Heures Typiques," *Gaulois*, February 18, 1928, ibid.

PAGE 134, "by a black one transgresses": Dagran, "Joséphine Baker abandonnera-t-elle la danse?" *Volonté*, August 25, 1929, Arsenal Pressbook (Ro 15.816), II, 25.

PAGE 134, "The old Catholic parties hounded me": *Voyages et aventures de Joséphine Baker*, p. 35.

PAGE 136, "the somatic determinant of whatever one wished to explain": D. Van Arkel, "Racism in Europe," in *Racism and Colonialism*, ed. Robert Ross (The Hague: Martinus Nijhoff, 1982), p. 12.

PAGE 136, "it no longer has the same blood in its veins": Quoted in Thomas F. Gossett, *Race: The History of an Idea in America* (Dallas: Southern Methodist University Press, 1963), p. 344. On mixing blood, see J. A. Gobineau *Essai sur l'inégalité des races humaines* (4 vols.; Paris: Firmin Didot, 1853–55), I, 39.

PAGE 137, *blood transfusions were new on the scene*: Maurice Sachs, *Au Temps du Boeuf sur le toit* (Paris: Éditions de la Nouvelle Revue Critique, 1939), p. 267.

PAGE 137, *Blood transfusion caught the popular imagination*: For a contemporary analogue to transfusion stories, see transplant stories. In a recent case, a teenaged boy, prophesying with no evidence his own early death, instructed that his heart be donated to his girlfriend. The girl, who did in fact come to need a transplant, lived for a while by the gift of his heart. As a human-interest story, transfusion has totally disappeared and current news about the blood supply focuses on fears of transmitting AIDS.

PAGE 138, "on her shoulders—and hips": Robert Mountsier, "A Girl from Harlem Abroad" (October 1928), Schomberg clipping file.

PAGE 138, "Every new country is a new dance": *Voyages et aventures de Joséphine Baker*, p. 29.

PAGE 139, "It's crazy how clean everything is": Ibid., p. 23.

PAGE 139, "They're just samples": Ibid., pp. 31–33.

PAGE 140, "So much for Rumania": Ibid., p. 44.

PAGE 140, "I don't want to live without Paris": Georges Schmitt, "Joséphine Baker passant à Paris nous dit . . . ," *Volonté*, April 9, 1929, Arsenal Pressbook (Ro 15.816), II.

PAGE 140, "But I *am* French": Pierre Lazareff, "Joséphine Baker sage est revenue à Paris," *Paris-Midi*, April 20, 1929, ibid. "Mais je suis française. Je suis une Française noire."

PAGE 140, "Yours is the only country": Pierre Lazareff, "Joséphine en bourgeoise," *Canard*, May 30, 1929, ibid., p. 17. "Votre pays est le seul où l'on puisse vivre tranquillement."

PAGE 140, "I have no pretension to being pretty": Hélène Saurel, "La petite 'idole noire' nous raconte quelques pages de sa vie d'artiste," *Marseille-Matin*, November 21, 1931, Arsenal Pressbook (Ro 15.816), II.

PAGE 141, "The *danse sauvage* is finished": Pierre Rocher, interview with

Josephine Baker, *L'Éclaireur* (Nice, 1932), Arsenal Pressbook (Ro 15.816), IV, 68.

PAGE 141, "You shouldn't make fun of the tools of a person's trade": André Rivollet, *Gringoire*, February 13, 1931, Arsenal Pressbook (Ro 15.816), II, 109.

CHAPTER 5: QUEEN OF THE COLONIES

PAGE 143, *The applause was her due: Josephine*, p. 86.

PAGE 144, *Mistinguett was not happy*: Jean Prasteau, *La Merveilleuse aventure du Casino de Paris* (Paris: Noël, 1975), pp. 208–17.

PAGE 146, *a favorite place for Parisians to go*: Jean de Brunhoff, for one, took his little sons Laurent and Mathieu. He had just illustrated *The Story of Babar*, about an orphaned elephant who ran from the jungle to a nearby city resembling Paris. For that one season, the summer of 1931, as in the Babar books, there was a little bit of Africa right outside of Paris. The third book in the series, *Babar the King*, would tell a story much like the one told by the Colonial Exposition, about the blessings of civilization brought to creatures who start in a state of nature. But because these were stories for children, whose primary business *is* to acquire the skills of civilization, the colonial myth was transformed in these books into something universal.

PAGE 148, "The territory is not just raw material": Robert Delavignette, *Freedom and Authority in French West Africa* (London, New York, and Toronto: Oxford University Press, 1950), a translation of *Service Africain* (Paris: Gallimard, 1946).

PAGE 149, "Queen, Where Is Yo' Kink": *New York World-Telegram*, March 4, 1931, Schomburg vertical file. "Harlem's No French Colony" is the subhead.

PAGE 149, "Belleville—that is the native island of Maurice Chevalier": Clipping, Arsenal Pressbook (Ro 15.816), II, 119.

PAGE 149, *The equipment seemed predatory: Les Mémoires de Joséphine Baker* (1949), p. 219.

PAGE 149, *Sometimes she would giggle*: René Silon, "Quand Joséphine enregistre," *Gringoire*, January 6, 1933, Arsenal Pressbook (Ro 15.816), V.

PAGE 149, "*Bye Bye Blackbird*" et al.: These recordings are part of the James Weldon Johnson Collection of the Beinecke Library, Yale University, in the care of Yale's Historical Sound Recordings Collection.

PAGE 150, "We said goodbye to a perky and amusing but primitive little black girl": Pierre Varenne, *Paris-Soir*, October 10, 1930, Arsenal Pressbook (Ro 15.816).

PAGE 151, "as pure as a child's voice": Undated, unattributed clipping, Arsenal Pressbook (Ro 15.816), II.

PAGE 151, "Mademoiselle Josephine Baker descended the traditional staircase": Antoine, *Information*, October 14, 1930, Arsenal Pressbook (Ro 15.816).

PAGE 151, "Her caramel-colored body": Janet Flanner, *Paris Was Yesterday: 1925–1939* (New York: Viking, 1972), pp. 72–73.

PAGE 152, "Didn't being a *black* star in a *white* show prove something too": *Josephine*, pp. 88–89.

PAGE 152, *Le Corbusier*: Haney, *Naked at the Feast*, pp. 156–58, and *Josephine*, pp. 80–81.

PAGE 153, "Just a few lines and not even straight": F. de Rudbeck, "Une demi-heure intime avec Joséphine Baker," *Marseille-Matin*, September 20, 1933, Arsenal Pressbook (Ro 15.816), V, 28.

PAGE 154, "She is the most likable": "Femmes d'Aujourd'hui," unattributed clipping (1930), Arsenal Pressbook (Ro 15.816), IV.

PAGE 154, "How can I convey the spontaneity": Jean Guyon-Gesbron, "Une soirée avec Joséphine Baker," *Européen*, July 30, 1931, Arsenal Pressbook (Ro 15.816) III, 2.

PAGE 154, "Do you prefer white men or black": Dany Gérard, "Joséphine noircie par ses soeurs," *Paris Music-Hall*, April 1, 1933, Arsenal Pressbook (Ro 15.816).

PAGE 155, "Art is an elastic sort of love": F. de Rudbeck, "Une demi-heure intime avec Joséphine Baker," *Marseille-Matin*, September 20, 1933, Arsenal Pressbook (Ro 15.816), V, 29.

PAGE 155, "I had no talent when I started": Interview with Earl Wilson, *New York Post*, January 12, 1948, *Post* clipping files.

PAGE 156, *she was the spike*: André Rivollet, *Joséphine Baker: Une Vie de toutes les couleurs* (Grenoble: B. Arthaud, 1935), p. 116.

PAGE 157, "At the age of eight": This English version was run by the black Chicago newspaper *The Defender*, October 10, 1931, under the headline "Atta Girl, Jo." The French version is slightly more polished and the effect-cause structure more systematically sustained:

on dit que j'étais laide . . . nature
j'ai dansé comme un singe . . . zoologie humaine
enfin j'étais moins laide . . . cosmétique

. . . .

j'aide les pauvres . . . j'ai souffert beaucoup
j'aime les animaux . . . ils sont les plus sincères

PAGE 158, *Josephine of the Casino de Paris and Josephine of Le Vésinet*: *Josephine*, p. 87.

PAGE 160, *improvised films with joyous mediocrity*: Raymond Borde, " 'The Golden Age': French Cinema of the 30s," in *Rediscovering French Film*, ed. Mary Lea Bandy (Boston: Little, Brown and the Museum of Modern Art, 1983), p. 70. For valuable discussions about French films in the 1930s and Baker's films in particular, I am grateful to Jeanine Basinger, professor of film studies at Wesleyan University.

PAGE 161, "We may wonder": Ibid., p. 71.

PAGE 161, *the best things in the movie*: Her own favorite scenes had to do with animals. One scene doesn't exist in the version of the film I saw, but publicity stills confirm her description. Gabin stands next to her as she frees a bird from a cage. She said she wanted to rehearse this scene over and over, setting another bird free with every take, but the first bird wouldn't budge. There were similar problems with a puppy she found on the street and insisted on using in the film over the producer's objections that a trained animal would be better. After twenty takes the puppy still refused to eat a chop the script called for him to eat.

PAGE 162, "Zou-Zou is a star": *Josephine*, p. 94.

PAGE 163, "The film enchants me": G. L. George, "Joséphine Baker revient à l'écran," September 27, 1934, Arsenal Pressbook (Rk 10154).

PAGE 165, "Ça ne jazze pas": *Joséphine*, p. 135.

PAGE 165, "high, airy voice": *Paris Was Yesterday*, p. 131.

PAGE 165, "strictly French actors": *Les Mémoires de Joséphine Baker*, p. 213.

PAGE 165, "Who doesn't have his vanity?": Ibid.

PAGE 166, "This goes": Billie Burke, *With a Feather on My Nose* (New York: Appleton-Century-Crofts, 1948), pp. 245–46.

PAGE 167, *the new and elegant French liner* Normandie: The *Normandie* didn't last long. Launched in June 1935, it burned in 1939.

PAGE 167, *Bob Hope, to Eve Arden*: William Robert Faith, *Bob Hope: A Life in Comedy* (New York: Putnam, 1982), pp. 99–102.

PAGE 168, "You are from Paris": *Afro-American*, February 15, 1936, Schomburg clipping file.

PAGE 168, *turned into something ugly and aggressive*: "Look what they've done to her," Geoffrey Holder said in horror when I showed him pictures of Baker in this costume. "They've made her look ugly."

PAGE 168, *barely audible*: clipping, *The Ziegfeld Follies of 1936* scrapbook. Billy Rose Theater Collection of the New York Public Library at Lincoln Center.

PAGE 169, "Josephine Baker is a St. Louis washerwoman's daughter": "The Theatre," *Time*, February 10, 1936.

PAGE 169, "rolling those eloquent eyes": *The New York Times*, January 31, 1936.

PAGE 170, "Any artist must develop a technique of his own": Lucius Beebe, *New York Herald Tribune* (1936), clipping file, Billy Rose Theater Collection, New York Public Library at Lincoln Center.

PAGE 171, *As Thousands Cheer*: The revue was based on the idea of a newspaper. "Heat Wave," for example, was the weather report.

PAGE 171, "Honey, you is full of shit": Haney, *Naked at the Feast: A Biography of Josephine Baker*, p. 201.

PAGE 172, "Time was when I lived in a cabin": *Afro-American*, February 8, 1936, Schomburg clipping file.

PAGE 172, "She had no business trying to be white": "Hectic Harlem" (March 28, 1936), James Weldon Johnson Collection clipping file, Beinecke Library.

PAGE 173, *Fredi Washington*: See Donald Bogle, *Brown Sugar: Eighty Years of America's Black Female Superstars* (New York: Harmony Books, 1980), p. 79.

PAGE 173, *Alice Delano Weekes*: Haney, *Naked at the Feast*, p. 203.

PAGE 173, "That is enough for me": *Afro-American*, February 1, 1936, Schomburg clipping file. In her final autobiography, her only complaint against the hotel was that she and Pepito, because of American puritanism, had to take separate suites.

PAGE 174, *when it opened again in the fall*: It was perhaps Brice's last appearance in the Follies. After that, she took Baby Snooks onto radio and to the end of her life never performed onstage again.

PAGE 175, *it was not her color that disqualified her*: Author's interview with Maurice Bataille, May 1985.

PAGE 177, *never had a chance to get to know each other*: Haney, *Naked at the feast*, p. 216.

CHAPTER 6: VENUS IN JEEPS

PAGE 181, *a very small percentage took part in the resistance*: See Robert O. Paxton, *Vichy France* (New York: Knopf, 1972), p. 292.

PAGE 182, *a novelized account*: "Rémy" [pseud.], *J.A.: Épisodes de la vie d'un agent du S.R. et du contre-espionnage français* (Paris: Éditions Galic, 1961).

PAGE 183, "France made me what I am": Jacques Abtey, *La Guerre secrète de Joséphine Baker* (Paris and Havana: Éditions Siboney, 1948), p. 21. My account of Baker's wartime activity is based on this book, corroborated, wherever possible, by other sources.

PAGE 186, "the flame of the French resistance must not go out": Henri Noguères, *Histoire de la Résistance en France: juin 1940–juin 1941*, (4 vols. to date), Vol. I (Paris: Laffont, 1967), p. 21.

PAGE 186, *Paillole*: See ibid., p. 69.

PAGE 187, *written in invisible ink on Josephine's sheet music*: *Joséphine*, pp. 168–69.

PAGE 188, *to go from a nightmare to an amusement park*: Abtey, *La Guerre secrète*, p, 58.

PAGE 188, *"Il faut!" she said*: *Joséphine*, p. 170.

PAGE 190, *Rodolphe Solmsen*: The information about Solmsen comes from a MS memoir in French entitled "The One Who Got Away," for generous access to which I am indebted to his daughter, Liliane Tuck of New York.

PAGE 193, *Paillole's information written again on her sheet music*: Abtey, *La Guerre secrète*, p. 96.

PAGE 195, *her former husband, Jean Lion*: *Les Mémoires de Joséphine Baker* (1949), p. 270.

PAGE 195, "not the time to get hitched up": "Josy Baker Blames It on Bananas," *Variety*, May 8, 1941, clipping file, James Weldon Johnson Collection (Langston Hughes Bequest), Beinecke Library.

PAGE 196, *According to her own account*: *Josephine*, pp. 126–28.

PAGE 196, *Baker was pregnant*: Haney, *Naked at the Feast*, pp. 225–26.

PAGE 197, *a zipper in her stomach*: *Les Mémoires de Joséphine Baker* (1949), p. 221.

PAGE 197, "Don't leave me, Maurice": Abtey, *La Guerre secrète*, p. 142.

PAGE 198, *Americans liked his sense of humor*: See Kenneth Crawford, *Report on North Africa* (New York and Toronto: Farrar and Rinehart, 1943), pp. 41–42.

PAGE 198, *in Baker's hospital room*: Ibid., p. 42.

PAGE 198, "Let me go": *La Guerre secrète*, p. 151.

PAGE 199, "It was strictly out of Arabian Nights": Kenneth Crawford, "Josephine Baker in North Africa," *PM*, April 1, 1943, clipping file, James Weldon Johnson Collection (Langston Hughes Bequest), Beinecke Library.

PAGE 200, "I couldn't leave French territory": Crawford, *Report on North Africa*, p. 43, and "Josephine Baker in North Africa."

PAGE 200, *Lawrence Pool*: Letter to the author, March 25, 1985.

PAGE 203, "Isn't it wonderful?": Abtey, *La Guerre secrète*, p. 176.

PAGE 203, *ENSA show*: "Operational," typescript by H. Hurford Janes, Beinecke Library.

PAGE 203, *350,000 old francs*: About $900, worth at least ten times as much in contemporary dollars.

PAGE 205, *she berated the commander*: Madame Olivier Ziegel, in conversation with the author, June 1988.

PAGE 205, *General de Gaulle sent a letter*: Printed in Abtey's book as a foreword.

CHAPTER 7: THE FAMILY OF MAN

PAGE 207, *Paul Robeson's civil rights work*: When Robeson played Othello, the first black to do so on an American stage with a white Desdemona, the event made theater history. So incendiary was the concept of a black actor appearing to strangle a white actress that no established stars could be recruited to play either Desdemona or Iago for the 1943 production. Uta Hagen and Jose Ferrer thus got to make their reputations by playing these roles early in their careers. Robeson furthermore had an unusual provision written into his contract for out-of-town performances of *Othello*, whereby a certain number of orchestra seats were to be at his disposal, to be made available to black theatergoers.

Throughout the 1940s, Robeson worked with Walter White of the NAACP to promote integration in the theater. Among other efforts, he helped White in shaping Lena Horne's film career, aware that she was an important precedent for blacks in the film industry the way Jackie Robinson was in baseball. See Gail Lumet Buckley, *The Hornes: An American Family* (New York: Knopf, 1986), pp. 154–58.

But when Robeson became known as sympathetic to Communism, his usefulness to the NAACP was at an end. In 1949 he gave a concert in Peekskill, New York, in support of civil rights, and the ensuing melee with anti-Communist groups became known as the Robeson riots.

PAGE 207, *backdrops of stained-glass windows*: So perfect was this moment that the Folies management held on to the sets and was still using them thirty-five years later when I saw the show.

PAGES 207–8, *continued to sing "Ave Maria"*: Earl Wilson, the *Post* columnist, asked if religious people didn't mind her "Ave Maria" act. "Mind?" she replied. "They love it. I'm the spirit coming back to life. This act is the talk of the whole world."

PAGE 208, "We cannot keep the world permanently at war": See Antony Penrose, *The Lives of Lee Miller* (New York: Holt, Rinehart, and Winston, 1985).

PAGE 209, "They're the only things around here that remind me of my music-hall days": *Josephine*, p. 201. For a novel about an aging show girl who raises peacocks for the same reason, see Larry McMurtry's *The Desert Rose*.

PAGE 210, "This is the most important moment of my life": *Josephine*, p. 175. For her and Jo Bouillon's accounts of the Copa City negotiations and appearances, see pp. 174–76.

PAGE 211, "The showmanship that is Josephine Baker's": *Variety*, March 7, 1951.

PAGE 211, "I have no talent": Arthur Pollack in *The Daily Compass*, March 13, 1951.

PAGE 212, *class performer*: *Variety*, January 17, 1951, clipping file, New York Public Library at Lincoln Center.

PAGE 213, *occupying the table herself*: The NAACP "Outlook" said, "Miss

Baker's purpose is to let people get used to seeing Negroes in places. 'When people see that Negroes know how to act, and hotel officials find that their customers are not going to walk out, there will be no need for such discrimination,' Miss Baker stated. She proved herself right on both points, playing to a capacity audience for every show, every night of her Las Vegas appearance."

PAGE 213, "the first manifestation of protest by a minority group": May 14, 1952, clipping file, Theater Collection, New York Public Library at Lincoln Center.

PAGE 213, *she refused to go to Atlanta*: Under Georgia law, a white hotel granting accommodations to blacks could have its innkeeper's license revoked. The black delegates to the NAACP convention had to stay in segregated hotels, in private homes, or in black colleges nearby. The situation wasn't any better in 1962 when Ralph Bunche was due to address an NAACP convention in Atlanta and couldn't book a midtown hotel room. Change came only with the Civil Rights Act of 1964.

PAGE 213, *she visited the head of the Illinois Central Railroad*: Joseph V. Baker, *Philadelphia Inquirer*, May 16, 1951, clipping file, James Weldon Johnson Collection, Beinecke Library.

PAGE 214, *her father had been a policeman: The Daily Compass*, July 22, 1951, clipping file, Theater Collection, New York Public Library at Lincoln Center.

PAGE 215, "Her appearances have been marked": Joseph V. Baker, *Philadelphia Inquirer*, May 16, 1951.

PAGE 216, *Bessie Buchanan*: She retired from the stage to marry Charles Buchanan, an important businessman in Harlem, manager of the Savoy Ballroom and head of an insurance company.

PAGE 217, "Sometimes I think life's a terminal illness": Herman Klurfeld, *Winchell: His Life and Times* (New York: Praeger, 1976), p. 94.

PAGE 217, "I wish you wouldn't, Champ": Ted Poston, *New York Post*, October 24, 1951, Schomburg clipping file. "Sugar Ray Tells Billingsley: 'End Bias or Quit Cancer Fund.' "

PAGE 218, *The Ricos and their guests sat down and ordered drinks*: This account of the incident from the point of view of the Baker-Rico party is based on statements by Mrs. Rico and Mrs. Buchanan in a report by Ted Poston, *New York Post*, October 18, 1951.

PAGE 221, "She told her story with enormous dignity": Poppy Cannon [Mrs.

Walter White], "What is she really like . . . Josephine Baker?" typescript, James Weldon Johnson Collection, Beinecke Library.

PAGE 222, "After 20 years on the air": *Daily Mirror*, October 22, 1951.

PAGE 223, "The public is beginning to think": Klurfeld, *Winchell*, p. 154. Through Arnold Forster, Winchell had been allied to the Anti-Defamation League and prided himself on using his influence to oppose bigotry. Forster said, "He was read, heard, and admired by millions. His readers and listeners believed him. If he said bigotry was wrong, then it was wrong. He was Mister America." (Klurfeld, *Winchell*, p. 98.)

PAGE 223, "If the Stork Club was not guilty": Ibid., p. 158.

PAGE 224, "I have been accused, indicted": Ibid.

PAGE 224, "smart-ass intellectual Jews": Ibid., p. 130.

PAGE 225, "If I spoke slowly": Ibid., p. 103.

PAGE 225, "semiliterate sentimentalists": Ibid., p. 203.

PAGE 225, "Why didn't she tell me": Ibid., p. 152.

PAGE 225, "It is the bullshit on which I thrive": Ibid., p. 132.

PAGE 225, "The Baker story was my most frustrating experience": Ibid., p. 164.

PAGE 226, "I don't discount the fact that he may have left knowing there could be trouble": *Not This Time, Cary Grant! and Other Stories About Hollywood* (Garden City, N.Y.: Doubleday, 1973), p. 258.

PAGE 226, "at least some ammunition": Ibid., p. 259.

PAGE 227, "out-Goebbels Hitler": *Daily Mirror*, November 20, 1951.

PAGE 227, "People of color are not obliged to resort to provocation": *Josephine*, p. 181.

PAGE 228, "small-time Hitler": Article 20 in the *New York Post* series on Winchell (March 11, 1952).

PAGE 229, *a lifetime contract with ABC*: Klurfeld, *Winchell*, p. 150.

PAGE 229, "Television has changed everything": Ibid., pp. 183, 186.

PAGE 230, "Hoover, can we check this": November 5, 1951, Josephine Baker file, FBI.

PAGE 230, "not . . . procommunist but pro-Negro": Memo 62-95834, February 10, 1960, Josephine Baker file, FBI.

PAGE 232, *Margaret Wallace*: From a statement dated February 8, 1977, in the Janes Papers, Beinecke Library.

PAGE 233, "We'll simply have to be patient": *Josephine*, p. 199.

PAGE 233, "Her left hand was busy squandering": Ibid., p. 217.

PAGE 234, "That's one of the reasons I married you": Ibid., p. 212.

PAGE 235, *talked about liberty, equality, fraternity*: Quoted by Haney, *Naked at the Feast*, p. 280.

PAGE 237, "I think I would have admired Josephine Baker even more": Michel Castel, *France-Dimanche*, August 16, 1962.

PAGE 237, *she found her nieces and nephews unbearable*: *Josephine*, p. 218. See also statements in the Janes Papers.

PAGE 238, *the children did not doubt that they were loved*: Interview with Akio Bouillon, July 1988.

CHAPTER 8: THE OVERDRESSED YEARS

PAGE 240, *even she began to get discouraged*: Quotations in this paragraph from *France-Dimanche*, August 16, 1962, Arsenal Pressbooks.

PAGE 241, *March on Washington*: See Doris Saunders, ed., *The Day They Marched* (Chicago: Johnson Publishing Co., 1963). Also "March on Washington," Schomburg clipping file.

PAGE 242, "united in a common dream": Autograph letter, Josephine Baker to Jack Jordan, Monte Carlo, 1974, Bricktop papers, Schomburg Center for Research in Black Culture.

PAGE 242, *a few figures from the arts*: Lena Horne, Langston Hughes, Marian Anderson, and Mahalia Jackson.

PAGE 242, "Until the March on Washington": "Josephine Baker: A Lion Abroad, But More Like a Lamb at Home," *The National Observer*, April 6, 1964, p. 16.

PAGES 242–43, "I think they must mix blood": John Vinocur, "Josephine Baker and Black Power," *Washington Post*, October 4, 1970.

PAGE 244, *Geoffrey Holder*: Information in this and the next three paragraphs from interview with the author, November 24, 1985.

PAGE 245, *A lesser person would have seen as a rival the woman she chose to see as her successor*: When they took their curtain calls, Carmen de Lavallade appeared in a simple black velvet dress with big sleeves and a train, designed to show off her magnificent neck and head. Baker had never seen the dress, and it was so striking that she did a double take. When de Lavallade stepped back from her bow, Baker pushed her forward again, so she could take another look at the dress and her beauty. "That to me is class," said Holder. "She was the queen's mother, which is even more elegant than being the queen."

PAGE 246, "If everyone who adopted children held out his hand": *Riverol*, September 5, 1968, Arsenal Pressbooks.

PAGE 246, "Even generosity can be a form of egotism": *France-Soir*, April 4, 1968, Arsenal Pressbooks.

PAGE 246, *intensely loyal to each other*: See Haney, *Naked at the Feast*, p. 298.

PAGE 246, *liars, thieves, and spongers*: Harry or Peggy Janes, interview with Margaret Wallace, August 18, 1975, Janes Papers, Beinecke Library.

PAGE 247, *she, Jean-Claude Bouillon, and Moïse were discussing "complexes"*: Josephine Baker to Harry Hurford Janes, September 28, 1971, Beinecke Library.

PAGE 248, "ferocious animals": Jacqueline Cartier, *France-Soir*, May 17, 1968, Arsenal Pressbooks.

PAGE 251, *targeted the gay community*: Haney, *Naked at the Feast*, p. 303.

PAGE 251, "she la-la's": Janes Papers, Beinecke Library.

PAGE 251, "She is an old woman now": Dotson Rader, "Down, But Not Out at the Palace," *Esquire*, June 1973.

PAGE 252, "I thought, 'Anybody's aunt from St. Louis' ": Barbara Chase Riboud, "The Life and Death of Josephine Baker," *Essence*, February 1976.

PAGE 252, "With makeup, lights, and a little intelligence, I'll be okay": Gilberte Cournand, *Le Parisien Libéré*, March 24, 1975, Arsenal Pressbooks.

PAGE 252, *Lynne Carter*: Carter's professional triumphs included doing Pearl Bailey successfully at the Apollo (as star of the Jewel Box review in 1965) and having a Carnegie Hall one-man show in 1971. He scorned impersonators who depended on makeup rather than gesture and mannerism to capture a likeness. He did Pearl Bailey without blackface in a blond wig.

PAGE 252, "I have found that women always wear a mask": Marian Christy, *Boston Globe*, March 12, 1971. See also Judy Klemesrud, "Lynne Carter, Female Impersonator Who Will Perform at Carnegie Hall," *New York Times*, January 16, 1971.

PAGE 253, *she had reached the end of her interest in sex*: "Es geht auch ohne" ("You can get along without it"), Marlene Dietrich is reported to have said in her later years.

PAGE 254, "Did I rightly understand": Josephine Baker to Robert Brady, undated letter [June 1973].

PAGE 255, "It makes me so happy, Bob": Josephine Baker to Robert Brady, June 23, 1973.

PAGE 255, "You are my husband, Bob dear": Josephine Baker to Robert Brady, October 15, 1973.

PAGE 257, "Je suis un pure sang": Josephine Baker to Robert Brady, January 15, 1974.

PAGE 258, "The fossils congratulate each other": André Visok, "Pipi de Chat et Vieille Rosette," *Libération*, April 5, 1975, Arsenal Pressbook.

PAGE 259, "I'm the youngest of all of you": *L'Aurore*, April 12, 1975, Arsenal Pressbook.

PAGE 259, *but some thought she died of joy*: See Haney, *Naked at the Feast*, p. 324.

PAGE 260, "I would never have thought a woman of color would be buried like a queen": Quoted by Barbara Chase Riboud, "The Life and Death of Josephine Baker," *Essence*, February 1976.

FINALE: STAGING LOVE

PAGE 263, *reached out and took everybody's heart in her hands*: Paraphrase of Langston Hughes to Josephine Baker, TLS, October 16, 1963, Beinecke Library.

PAGE 263, *Her daughter Marianne describes*: *Josephine*, p. 271.

PAGE 264, "Only when you've sung a song in many languages": Ibid., p. 216.

PAGE 264, *In Cuba it was fashionable to say "Se cambia"*: Néstor Almendros, in conversation with the author.

PAGE 267, "revolutionary side": ALS Josephine Baker to Langston Hughes, December 23, 1964, Beinecke Library.

PAGE 267, "three Negros writing about a Negro woman's life": Ibid.

PAGE 267, "There will be three books because my life is so full": Josephine Baker to Langston Hughes, August 15, 1964, Beinecke Library.

PAGE 267, "One day I realized I was living in a country where I was afraid to be black": Henry Louis Gates, Jr., "An Interview with Josephine Baker and James Baldwin." I am grateful to Mr. Gates for making the original transcript of this interview available to me. A slightly edited version, with an account of the interview's circumstances, appeared in *The Southern Review*, Summer 1985, pp. 594–602.

PAGE 268, "How often I've felt like the Wandering Jew": Ibid.

PAGE 268, *to vindicate and to transcend the groups that produced them*: See, for example, Peter Collier and David Horowitz, *The Kennedys: An American Drama* (New York: Summit Books, 1984).

PAGE 269, *an ethnic group rather than a racial one*: See Michael Banton, *The Idea of Race* (Boulder, Colo.: Westview Press, 1978), p. 11.

BIBLIOGRAPHY

On Josephine Baker (by date):

MARCEL SAUVAGE. *Les Mémoires de Joséphine Baker.* Paris: Éditions Kra, 1927. Illustrated with drawings by Paul Colin.

MARCEL SAUVAGE. *Voyages et aventures de Joséphine Baker.* Paris: Editions Marcel Sheur, 1931. Preface by Fernand Divoire. Illustrated with photographs and drawings.

ANDRÉ RIVOLLET. *Joséphine Baker: Une Vie de toutes les couleurs.* Grenoble: B. Arthaud, 1935.

JACQUES ABTEY. *La Guerre secrète de Joséphine Baker.* Paris and Havana: Editions Siboney, 1948.

MARCEL SAUVAGE. *Les Mémoires de Joséphine Baker.* Paris: Corréa, 1949.

"RÉMY" [pseud.]. *J.A.: Épisodes de la vie d'un agent du S.R. et du contre-espionnage français.* Paris: Éditions Galic, 1961.

STEPHEN PAPICH. *Remembering Josephine: A Biography of Josephine Baker.* New York and Indianapolis: Bobbs-Merrill, 1976.

DIETER KUHN. *Josephine: Aus der öffentlichen Biographie der Josephine Baker.* Frankfurt: Surkamp Verlag, 1976.

JOSEPHINE BAKER and JO BOUILLON. *Joséphine.* Paris: Laffont, 1976.

JOSEPHINE BAKER and JO BOUILLON. *Joséphine.* Transl. by Mariana Fitzpatrick. New York: Harper & Row, 1977.

LYNN HANEY. *Naked at the Feast: A Biography of Josephine Baker.* New York: Dodd, Mead, 1981.

BRYAN HAMMOND, compiler. *Josephine Baker.* With biography by Patrick O'Connor. London: Jonathan Cape, 1988.

On the Revue Nègre:

JACQUES CHARLES. *De Gaby Deslys à Mistinguett.* Paris: Gallimard, n.d.

PAUL COLIN. *La Croûte: Souvenirs.* Paris: Table Ronde, 1957.

JANET FLANNER. *Paris Was Yesterday: 1925–1939.* New York: Viking, 1972.

JACK RENNERT. *100 Posters of Paul Colin.* New York: Images Graphiques, 1977.

On dance:

LYNN EMERY. *Black Dance in the United States from 1619 to 1970.* Palo Alto, Calif.: National Press Books, 1972.

MARSHALL and JEAN STEARNS. *Jazz Dance: The Story of American Vernacular Dance.* New York: Macmillan, 1968.

ROBERT FARRIS THOMPSON. *African Art in Motion.* Berkeley, Los Angeles, and London: University of California Press, 1974.

On Afro-American culture:

DONALD BOGLE. *Brown Sugar: Eighty Years of America's Black Female Superstars.* New York: Harmony Books, 1980.

JOSEPH BOSKIN. *Sambo: The Rise and Demise of an American Jester.* New York and Oxford: Oxford University Press, 1986.

LINDA DAHL. *Stormy Weather: The Music and Lives of a Century of Jazzwomen.* New York: Pantheon, 1984.

HENRY LOUIS GATES. *Figures in Black: Words, Signs, and the "Racial" Self.* New York: Oxford University Press, 1984.

MELVILLE J. HERSKOVITS. *The Myth of the Negro Past.* Boston: Beacon Press, 1958.

ZORA NEALE HURSTON. *The Sanctified Church.* Berkeley: Turtle Island, 1983.

LAWRENCE LEVINE. *Black Culture and Black Consciousness: Afro-American Thought from Slavery to Freedom.* New York: Oxford University Press, 1977.

PAUL OLIVER. *Songsters and Saints: Vocal Traditions on Race Records.* Cambridge: Cambridge University Press, 1984.

HENRY PLEASANTS. *The Great American Popular Singers.* New York: Simon & Schuster, 1974.

ARNOLD RAMPERSAD. "Biography, Autobiography, and Afro-American Culture," *The Yale Review,* Autumn 1983, pp. 1–16.

EILEEN SOUTHERN. *The Music of Black Americans: A History.* New York and London: Norton, 1983.

On twenties Harlem and black Broadway:

JERVIS ANDERSON. *This Was Harlem: A Cultural Portrait, 1900–1950.* New York: Farrar, Straus & Giroux, 1982.

ARNA BONTEMPS, ed. *The Harlem Renaissance Remembered.* New York: Dodd, Mead, 1972.

IRENE CASTLE. *Castles in the Air.* Garden City, N.Y.: Doubleday, 1958.

JEAN COCTEAU. *My Journey Round the World.* Transl. by W. J. Strachan. London: Peter Owen, 1958. (Orig. publ. as *Mon Premier Voyage.* Paris: Gallimard, 1936.)

NANCY CUNARD, ed. *Negro: An Anthology.* Edited and abridged, with an introduction, by Hugh Ford. New York: Frederick Ungar, 1970. (Orig. publ. 1934.)

EDWARD KENNEDY (DUKE) ELLINGTON. *Music Is My Mistress.* Garden City, N.Y.: Doubleday, 1973.

NATHAN HUGGINS. *Harlem Renaissance.* New York: Oxford University Press, 1971.

JAMES WELDON JOHNSON. *Along This Way: The Autobiography of James Weldon Johnson.* New York: Viking, 1933.

JAMES WELDON JOHNSON. *Black Manhattan.* New York: Arno Press and The New York Times, 1968. (Orig. publ. 1930.)

ROBERT KIMBALL and WILLIAM BOLCOM. *Reminiscing with Sissle and Blake.* New York: Viking, 1973.

DAVID LEVERING LEWIS. *When Harlem Was in Vogue.* New York, Knopf, 1981.

CLAUDE McKAY. *A Long Way Home.* New York, Harcourt, Brace, 1970. (Orig. publ. 1937.)

CLAUDE McKAY. *Harlem: Negro Metropolis.* New York: Dutton, 1940.

AL ROSE. *Eubie Blake.* New York: Schirmer Books, 1979.

HARRY T. SAMPSON. *Blacks in Blackface: A Source Book on Early Black Musical Shows.* Metuchen, N.J. and London: The Scarecrow Press, 1980.

CHARLES W. STEIN, ed. *American Vaudeville As Seen by Its Contemporaries.* New York: Knopf, 1984.

On Americans in twenties Paris:

SIDNEY BECHET. *Treat It Gentle.* New York: Hill and Wang, 1960.

FAITH BERRY. *Langston Hughes: Before and Beyond Harlem.* Westport, Conn.: Lawrence Hill, 1983.

BRICKTOP, with JAMES HASKINS. *Bricktop.* New York: Atheneum, 1983.

JAMES CHARTERS, as told to Morrill Cody. *This Must Be the Place.* With an introduction by Ernest Hemingway. New York: Lee Furman, 1937.

MALCOLM COWLEY. *Exile's Return: A Literary Odyssey of the 1920s.* New York: Viking, 1951.

MICHEL FABRE. *La Rive Noire: De Harlem à la Seine.* Paris: Éditions Lieu Commun, 1985.

HUGH FORD. *Four Lives in Paris.* San Francisco: North Point Press, 1987.

HUGH FORD, ed. *The Left Bank Revisited: Selections from the Paris Tribune 1917–1934.* University Park, Pa., and London: Pennsylvania State University Press, 1972.

JOHN GLASSCO. *Memoirs of Montparnasse.* With an introduction by Leon Edel. Toronto and New York: Oxford University Press, 1970.

LANGSTON HUGHES. *The Big Sea: An Autobiography.* New York: Knopf, 1940.

ROBERT MCALMON. *Being Geniuses Together: 1920–1930.* Revised with supplementary chapters by Kay Boyle. Garden City, N.Y.: Doubleday, 1968.

ARNOLD RAMPERSAD. *The Life of Langston Hughes* (2 vols.). Vol. I: *1902–1941, I, Too, Sing America.* New York and Oxford: Oxford University Press, 1986.

MAURICE SACHS. *Au Temps du Boeuf sur le toit.* Paris: Éditions de la Nouvelle Revue Critique, 1939.

GEORGES SIMENON. *Mémoires intimes.* Paris: Presses de la Cité, 1981.

HAROLD STEARNS. *The Confessions of a Harvard Man.* Sutton West, Ontario, and Santa Barbara, Calif.: The Paget Press, 1984.

GERTRUDE STEIN. *Paris France.* New York: Liveright, 1940.

GEORGE WICKES. *Americans in Paris.* Garden City, N.Y.: Doubleday, 1969.

WILLIAM CARLOS WILLIAMS. *The Autobiography of William Carlos Williams.* New York: New Directions, 1967.

WILLIAM WISER. *The Crazy Years: Paris in the Twenties.* New York: Atheneum, 1983.

On Berlin in the twenties:

PETER GAY. *Weimar Culture: The Outsider as Insider.* New York: Harper & Row, 1968.

HANS HEINSHEIMER. *Best Regards to Aida: The Defeats and Victories of a Music Man on Two Continents.* New York: Knopf, 1968.

HARRY KESSLER. *In the Twenties: The Diaries of Harry Kessler.* Transl. by Charles Kessler. New York: Holt, Rinehart and Winston, 1976.

On French music-hall:

CHARLES CASTLE. *The Folies Bergère.* London: Methuen Paperback, 1984.

Colette. "Backstage at the Music Hall," in *The Collected Stories of Colette.* Ed. by Robert Phelps. Transl. by Matthew Ward. New York: Farrar, Straus & Giroux, 1983.

JACQUES DAMASE. *Les Folies du Music-Hall: Histoire du Music-Hall à Paris de 1914 à nos jours.* Preface by Bruno Coquatrix. Paris: Éditions Spectacles, 1960.

PAUL DERVAL. *Folies-Bergère.* Transl. by Lucienne Hill. New York: Dutton, 1955.

JACQUES FESCHOTTE. *Histoire du Music-Hall.* (Que Sais-Je? 1169.) Paris: Presses Universitaires de France, 1965.

ARTHUR KING PETERS et al. *Jean Cocteau and the French Scene.* New York: Abbeville Press, 1984.

JEAN PRASTEAU. *La Merveilleuse aventure du Casino de Paris.* Paris: Noël, 1975.

On primitivism and race:

JEAN-CLAUDE BLACHÈRE. *Le Modèle nègre: Aspects littéraires du mythe primitiviste au XXᵉ siècle chez Apollinaire, Cendrars, Tzara.* Dakar: Nouvelles Éditions Africaines, 1981.

GEOFFREY G. FIELD. *Evangelist of Race: The Germanic Vision of Houston Stewart Chamberlain.* New York: Columbia University Press, 1981.

THOMAS F. GOSSETT. *Race: The History of an Idea in America.* Dallas: Southern Methodist University Press, 1963.

JOHN HIGHAM. *Strangers in a Strange Land: Patterns of American Nativism 1860–1925.* New York: Atheneum, 1971.

LÉON-FRANÇOIS HOFFMAN. *Le Nègre romantique: Personnage littéraire et obsession collective.* Paris: Payot, 1973.

JEAN LAUDE. *La Peinture française (1905–1914) et "l'art nègre."* Paris: Éditions Lincksieck, 1968.

GEORGE L. MOSSE. *Toward the Final Solution: A History of European Racism.* New York: Howard Fertig, 1978.

WILLIAM RUBIN, ed. *"Primitivism" in 20th Century Art: Affinity of the Tribal and the Modern.* 2 vols.; Boston: Little, Brown, and New York: The Museum of Modern Art, 1984.

On France in World War II:

HENRI NOGUÈRES. *Histoire de la Résistance en France: juin 1940–juin 1941,* Vol. I. Paris: Laffont, 1967.

ROBERT O. PAXTON. *Vichy France.* New York: Knopf, 1972.

Miscellaneous:

HERMAN KLURFELD. *Winchell: His Life and Times.* New York: Praeger, 1976.

ACKNOWLEDGMENTS

It is a pleasure to record my gratitude to the many people who took time to speak with me or who otherwise, with generosity, helped my research: Angelica and Euan Baird, Jean-Claude Baker, Mary Lea Bandy, Sally Banes, Serge Barret, Jeanine Basinger, Maurice Bataille, Helen Gary Bishop, Robert Bishop, Walter Bonsall, Akio Bouillon, Maryse Bouillon, John Brady, Jr., Colette and Charles Cachin, Hazel Carby, Susan Cook, Thomas Quinn Curtiss, Douglas Daniels, Ronaldo De Juan, Clare and Malcolm Dean, the late Mura Dehn, Michel Fabre, Micheline and Richard Ferrer, Jack Flam, Monique Gonthier, Maurice Girodias, Nan Graham, Adelaide Hall, Geoffrey Holder, Jeannette Hopkins, Jan-Christopher Horak, Nathan Huggins, Joan Jurale, E. J. Kahn, Richard Kaufman, Michelle Lapautre, Steven Lebergott, Alan Lewis, Douglas Liebhafsky, James Lord, Jacqueline Malone, Eleanor Munro, Natalia Murray, Robert J. O'Meally, Marc Pachter, Daniele Scalise, Sally Sloan, Ernie Smith, Anna Sosenko, Jeffrey Stewart, Maya Surduts, Alan Trachtenberg, Denise Tual, Liliane Tuck, Edmund White, Elisabeth Young-Bruehl, Helen Zawisa, Liliane Ziegel.

I am grateful to the many, usually anonymous people who collected newspaper articles about Josephine Baker and to the librarians who put together pressbooks or clipping files. For access to this and other valuable material, thanks to the staffs of the Beinecke Library, Yale University; the Dance Collection, Theater Collection, and Music Collection of the New York Public Library at Lincoln Center; the Historical Sound Recordings Collection, Yale University; the Bibliothèque de l'Arsenal of the Bibliothèque Nationale, Paris; the Schomburg Center for Research in Black Culture of the New York Public Library; Olin Library, Wesleyan University; the archives of *The New York Post* and *Time*; the Film Department of the International Museum of Photography at George Eastman House.

For permission to quote from unpublished material in its possession, I am grateful to the Collection of American Literature, Beinecke Rare Book and Manuscript Library, Yale University, and for permission to quote from unpublished material in its collections, especially the diary of Gwendolyn Bennett, I am grateful to the Schomburg Center for Research in Black Culture, the New York Public Library, Astor, Lenox and Tilden Foundations. For permission to quote from Bennett's diary I am also grateful to Martha O. Tanner, executor of the Estate of Gwendolyn Bennett. For permission to quote from Josephine Baker's letters to Robert Brady, in the possession of John Brady, Jr., I am grateful to Mr. Brady and to Sally Sloan, representing the Estate of Robert Brady. For permission to quote from unpublished material written by Josephine Baker, I am extremely grateful to Maryse Bouillon.

For financial support, and the moral support that goes along with it, I am very grateful to the John Simon Guggenheim Memorial Foundation, the Rockefeller Foundation, and Wesleyan University.

For gifts of friendship and intelligence, especially warm thanks to Annie Dillard, Leslie Garis, Wendy Gimbel, Joseph W. Reed, Jr., David Schorr, Judith Thurman, Nan Talese, and Georges Borchardt.

I am deeply grateful to Teddy Rose, who understands the demands of many callings, from acting to hot dog vending, from politics to writing, and, a 500-yard man, particularly appreciates the difficult rhythms of long-distance efforts.

I will always be indebted to Josephine Baker for leading me to France where I met Laurent de Brunhoff, to whom this book is dedicated.

renewed 1959 Miller Music Corp. Rights assigned to SBK Catalogue Partnership. All rights controlled and administered by SBK Miller Catalog, Inc. All rights reserved. International copyright secured. Used by permission.

Williamson Music: Excerpt from "You've Got to Be Carefully Taught" by Richard Rodgers and Oscar Hammerstein II. Copyright 1949 by Richard Rodgers and Oscar Hammerstein II. Williamson Music Co., owner of publication and allied rights. Used by permission. All rights reserved.

INDEX

Baker, Josephine (*cont.*)
  Shuffle Along, 4, 53, 56–60
  Ziegfeld Follies, 165–70, 174
  on art and love, 155
  automobiles of, 113, 144
  in Berlin, 84–88
  birth and childhood of, 10–17,
    46–47, 118
  as dancer, 25–27, 47–48, 156
  death and state funeral of, 259–61
  as expatriate, 15
  exploitation of, 89–90
  FBI file on, 230
  films with, 119–20, 160–64
  French citizenship of, 176, 177
  French performances of
    banana costume and dance of,
      23, 25, 32, 97, 114, 128, 168
    Casino de Paris, 143–44, 147–48,
      150–52, 156, 158, 184–85, 258
    Folies-Bergère, 23, 28–29, 82,
      88–90, 96, 112–14, 130, 175,
      176, 207–8
    La Créole, 164–65, 189–92
    last dramatic role, 241
    last performance, 257–59, 266
    return performances, 234–35,
      236, 244–45, 247, 249
    Revue Nègre, 4–10, 17–23,
      30–33, 79–83, 86
  as great star, 112–13
  on her lack of talent, 155, 211
  illnesses of, 192, 194, 196, 205, 208,
    246, 249, 253–54
  on importance of rear ends, 24
  Indian ancestry of, 10, 13
  Jewish religion of, 194
  knowledge of French by, 105, 107,
    122, 140, 165, 171
  knowledge of other languages by,
    263–64
  learns to behave like royalty, 143
  leopard of, 143, 144, 147, 151, 158
  at Le Vésinet, 152–54, 158, 176,
    183–84

  marriages of
    to Willie Baker, 50, 174
    to Jo Bouillon, 207–8, 240
    imaginary, to Robert Brady,
      255–57
    to Jean Lion, 176–77
    supposed, to Pepito. *See*
      Abatino, Giuseppe
    to Willie Wells, 47–48
  names of, 138–39
  1928–29 tour of, 121, 123–40
  in 1968 May Days, 247–48, 258
  Parisian craze for, 65, 112–13,
    121–22, 140–41, 143, 150–51
  personal characteristics of
    belief in rabbit's foot, 118, 139
    Cinderella imagery, 14
    clowning ability, 57, 61, 63, 195
    cross-eyed grins, ix, x, 4, 15–16,
      19, 109, 266
    freedom from pretension, 105–6
    improvisation and spontaneity,
      60, 265
    joy in life, 4
    late sleeping, 107
    love of pets, 106, 117, 118, 153,
      185, 190, 192, 204, 205, 264
    making up her life, 114–15, 214,
      265–68
    nudity and modesty, 6–7, 117, 131
    rode in taxis' front seats, 263
    sexual activity, x–xi, 107–10,
      154–55, 159, 175–76, 253
    staging love, 262–65
    transformation of age on stage,
      251–53
  recordings by, 139, 149–50
  religion and, 26–27
  sculpture of, as Francis of Assisi,
    266
  in Stork Club incident, 215–30
  theme song of, 147
  wax museum of, 16–17, 209, 266
  weight of, 113, 138, 141
  works by

BOOK MARK

The book was composed in
the typeface Granjon by
Crane Typesetting Service, Inc.
West Barnstable, Massachusetts.
The display was set in
Alette by Artintype Metro,
New York, New York.

It was printed on 55 lb cream white offset
by R. R. Donnelley and Sons, Harrisonburg,
Virginia.

Designed by Marysarah Quinn